FINDING MY PLATOON BROTHERS

FINDING MY PLATOON BROTHERS

VIETNAM THEN AND NOW

A MEMOIR

GLYN HAYNIE

Copyrighted Material

Finding My Platoon Brothers: Vietnam Then and Now

Copyright © 2019 by Glyn Haynie. All Rights Reserved.

No part of this publication may be reproduced, stored in a retrieval system or transmitted, in any form or by any means—electronic, mechanical, photocopying, recording, or otherwise—without prior written permission from the publisher, except for the inclusion of brief quotations in a review.

For information about this title or to order other books and/or electronic media, contact the publisher:

Glyn Haynie
www.glynhaynie.net
glyn@glynhaynie.com

ISBNs:
Hardback 978-0-9982095-6-2
Paperback 978-0-9982095-7-9
eBook 978-0-9982095-8-6

Printed in the United States of America

Cover Design, Interior Design, and Editing: 1106 Design, Phoenix, AZ
Author Photograph: Shannon Prothro Photography

THE BROTHERHOOD

I now know why men who have been to war yearn to reunite. Not to tell stories or look at old pictures. Not to laugh or weep. Comrades gather because they long to be with the men who once acted at their best; men who suffered and sacrificed, who suffered and were stripped of their humanity.

I did not pick these men. They were all delivered by fate and the war. But I know them in a way I know no other man. I have never given anyone such trust. They were willing to guard something more precious than my life. They would have carried my reputation, the memory of me. It was part of the bargain we all made, the reason we were so willing to die for one another.

As long as I have memory, I will think of them all, every day. I am sure that when I leave this world, my last thought will be of my family and my comrades. "Such good men!"

—Michael Norman

CONTENTS

Acknowledgments . . . . *xi*
Prologue . . . . *xiii*

CHAPTER 1 *Remembering My Platoon Brothers* 17

CHAPTER 2 *Searching for and Finding First Platoon* . . . 23
    Going to the Veterans Administration 28

CHAPTER 3 *Meeting Platoon Members After 46 Years* . . . 31
    Road Trip and Brotherhood 32
    The Search Continues 45

CHAPTER 4 *The Plan for a Reunion* 49

CHAPTER 5 *Meeting Another Platoon Brother* 53

CHAPTER 6 *At Last the Platoon Is Together: The Reunion* . . 57
    Day One—Meet and Greet 57
    Day Two—Dinner and a Movie 58
    Day Three—Together the Last Time 71
    Day Four—Goodbye 78

CHAPTER 7 *Overwhelmed by Reliving My Time in War*	. 81
CHAPTER 8 *Trip Preparation for Vietnam*	. 87
CHAPTER 9 *Planning Our Return*	. 95
CHAPTER 10 *Gathering for the Return to Nam*	. 107
CHAPTER 11 *Our Journey Back to Vietnam Begins*	. 111
Crossing the Pond	. 114
CHAPTER 12 *Landing In-Country the Second Time*	. 117
CHAPTER 13 *With a Sunrise in Vietnam, the Adventure Begins*	. 127
CHAPTER 14 *A Roller Coaster Ride of Emotions*	. 133
CHAPTER 15 *The Field Where I Died*	. 145
CHAPTER 16 *Horseshoe and the River Where We Bathed*	. 151
CHAPTER 17 *Mike and I Will Be Forever Changed*	. 155
Deadly Trench and the Ambush	. 158
CHAPTER 18 *Easy Duty at the Airfield*	. 165
CHAPTER 19 *Hilltop Where Bruce Died*	. 169
CHAPTER 20 *Going Back to Headquarters*	. 173
CHAPTER 21 *Unforgettable Days at the Rice Bowl*	. 177
CHAPTER 22 *The Damn Fire*	. 185
CHAPTER 23 *An Island and a Bridge*	. 189
CHAPTER 24 *Memorial for a Massacre*	. 197

CONTENTS

CHAPTER 25 *So Many Memories* 205

CHAPTER 26 *Last Day in Vietnam for the Second Time* . . . 215

CHAPTER 27 *Going Home for the Last Time* 223

Afterword 231
Remembering the Fallen 247
Postscript: My Best Friend and Oldest Son 249
    Vietnam Trip: Epilogue Written by Mike Dankert . . 250
    Vietnam Trip Written by David Haynie 255
Appendices
    Appendix A: Daily Journal Abbreviations Explained . . 271
    Appendix B: Fire Support Base Hill 4-11 and Surrounding
        Area 277
    Appendix C: The Fire 287
    Appendix D: Fire Support Base Charlie Brown and Bridge . . 289
    Appendix E: Our First Loss, Fire Support Base Debbie,
        and the Rice Bowl 291
    Appendix F: Fire Support Base Bronco 297
    Appendix G: Combat Center 299

About the Author. 301

ACKNOWLEDGMENTS

Thank you, Mike Dankert, for being my brother and traveling with me to the important places that we served together so many years ago in Vietnam and for sharing your thoughts about the trip in the Postscript. And thanks for the Tribute to Peter Zink and the photographs.

Thank you, son, David Haynie, for traveling with me on the trip. It made my time back in Vietnam even more special. Thanks for sharing your thoughts in the Postscript and the photographs. And thank you, Tarie Haynie, for helping make the First Platoon reunion a success.

Thanks to John Baxter, John DeLoach, Dennis Stout, Charlie Deppen, Cliff Sivadge, Barry Suda, Don Ayres, Fred Katz, and Tommy Thompson for the photographs.

Thank you, Chuck Council, for writing the Tribute to Jack Jurgensen and for the photographs.

Thank you, Leslie Hines Americal Division Association Historian, for the documentation you generously provided, including newspaper articles, division logs, casualty listings, maps, and photographs.

Thank you, Alan Brinton, for the maps and guidance on traveling in Quang Ngai Province.

Thank you, Jonas Thorsell, for the guidance on traveling in Vietnam and the recommendations on where to stay.

Thank you, Clark Searle, for the photograph of Fire Support Base Debbie/Thunder.

Thank you, Russell Woodward, for repairing my Peace Sign to wear on the trip back to Vietnam.

Thank you, Lisa Robinson, for the embroidered hats and stenciled travel mugs for the reunion.

Special thanks to John Felchak, David Armstrong, Richard and Leah Kelley, and my wife, Sherrie, for helping me to get the book ready for publication.

Thanks to the First Platoon for being my brothers. You are remembered.

To the Fallen: You are remembered.

PROLOGUE

The first time I repeated the names of the 13 killed was in the early hours of August 16, 1969. A squad member woke me because I was reciting the names out loud in my sleep, and he feared it might attract the enemy. The death of the 13 will follow me for the rest of my life. They do not haunt me, and I don't avoid their presence. I want them with me. I want to honor them and keep their memory alive. It isn't a burden; it is, rather, a duty that I freely accept. With this responsibility, I didn't forget my time in Vietnam, either. Reading my first book, *When I Turned Nineteen: A Vietnam War Memoir*, you will have a better understanding of me, a young 19-year-old who grew up too fast, fought in an unpopular war, and witnessed how war can change a person in one year for a lifetime.

In my second book, *Soldiering After the Vietnam War: Changed Soldiers in a Changed Country*, I shared my struggles and my successes completing a 20-year career in the Army, culminating as an instructor at the United States Army Sergeants Major Academy (USASMA). My story isn't about war, but of service to the country and the consequences of that service for soldiers and their families. There are no claims that I had an extraordinary career, but my career did coincide with extraordinary times within the Army, and I met extraordinary soldiers, NCOs, and officers along the way.

I met and served with many outstanding soldiers, NCOs, and officers during my 20 years of service. They exhibited remarkable leadership traits that molded many young soldiers, including me, into performing beyond their dreams. These young soldiers became better leaders in the Army or in the job they worked outside the military. While serving with the units assigned to after Vietnam, I never had such brotherhood as I did with my platoon in Vietnam.

In the military, it's said that men create a bond from combat, and this bond is understood only inside the military. First Platoon was my family during my year in Vietnam and every day after I returned. We are all brothers and have a bond that cannot be explained. We fought, bled, cried, played, and partied together. After the enemy killed or wounded one of us, the pain we felt was unimaginable. As men, we unapologetically held another platoon member during their grief. I still miss the platoon members who never came back home and regret I didn't get to know them better.

The platoon members helped each other without any questions. Each one of us would give his life to save another. We helped carry each other's load and shared our rations, water, ammunition, and packages from home without hesitation. First Platoon members are my brothers, and the bond we formed in combat will always exist. The men of First Platoon showed up for me every day. We were a family.

Often, I thought of my platoon brothers and wondered what they were doing, and I thought of The Fallen and wondered where they would've been today if they'd lived. It wasn't fair. I knew someday I would search for the rest of my platoon and see them again. I wanted, at least once before I die, for the platoon to be back together and share their successes and failures of the last 47 years and to experience again the brotherhood we had together.

As strange as it may sound, I wanted to return to Vietnam. I needed to visit the sites where The Fallen died: "Bruce Tufts, Juan Ramos, Eldon

Reynolds, Jerry Ofstedahl, Robert Swindle, Richard Wellman, Paul Ponce, Joe Mitchell, James Anderson, Danny Carey, Gary Morris, Roger Kidwell, and Willie Matson." I believed seeing where they walked when they were alive, where they took their last breath, and visiting where my brothers died would bring me peace. I hoped it would in some ways lessen the guilt I felt about their death and my year in the war. As the point man, it was my responsibility to keep the platoon safe, and on those two days in August 1969, seven platoon members were killed, and eight were wounded. I failed them by not giving a warning in time to prevent their death. Their death was my fault. Why did I survive and they didn't?

CHAPTER 1

REMEMBERING MY PLATOON BROTHERS

It was late April 2015, not long after my 65th birthday, and I woke early after another night of not sleeping well—not unusual over the past 46 years. I lay in bed looking at the clock, having a hard time reading the extra-large display, but as my eyes focused, the illuminated digits came into focus: 3:30 AM. Closing my eyes, I repeated the names of everyone in the platoon who'd died while in Vietnam: "Tufts, Ramos, Reynolds, Ofstedahl, Swindle, Wellman, Ponce, Mitchell, Anderson, Carey, Morris, Kidwell and Matson." For most of them, a familiar face appeared when I said the name, but for several of the platoon members, I couldn't remember what they looked like; there was only a shadow instead of a face. I can't forget The Fallen, and I don't want to forget! *They deserve that I remember them.*

I don't know what became of the critically wounded platoon members, except for Dusty Rhoades, who returned to the States for treatment of his injuries. But where are: Dennis Rowe, Nick VanDyke, Frank Brown, Ryan Okino, Tommy Thompson, and Charlie Deppen? I know they lived because their names are not on the Vietnam War Memorial (The Wall). Did they fully recover? Do they have a good life—are they reasonably well after their experiences?

Through the years I thought of my platoon brothers and wondered where they were and how they were doing, but I let life get in the way, and time passed. As I aged, I didn't want to forget them or the brothers who didn't come home.

With the speed of an old man, I rolled out of bed and stood, with joints stiff and aching. I fumbled around the nightstand to find my glasses and slid them on, enabling me to see; then I looked again at the clock to confirm the time. Once I was steady, I walked into the bathroom with light filtering through the bathroom window from the neighbor's floodlights leading the way. With every step, each injury suffered in the past said "Good Morning" to me.

Passing a mirror on the wall, I stopped and looked at the reflection of an older man, medium height and build, with a full head of gray hair with a dash of pepper, wrinkles appearing or deepening on his face, and 15 extra pounds distributed in unwanted locations on a pale, aging body. The young, baby-faced, skinny kid, with dark-brown hair I'd known from long ago was gone. I'm sure my platoon members look as differently as I do now, but I picture only their youthful persona when thinking of them.

Still half asleep, I staggered to the kitchen to start the coffeemaker. After I pushed the button, I listened to the *whirr* of the grinder as it crushed the coffee beans. Once the grinder stopped, the water dripped through the crushed beans, creating an aroma that fully woke me and left me wanting my coffee now. I waited until the last drop of water had dripped into the pot and the buzzer had sounded. While pouring my first cup of coffee, I thought of my days in Vietnam when I drank only hot chocolate in the mornings and how good it tasted. I walked, with coffee cup in hand, to the office at the other end of the house.

REMEMBERING MY PLATOON BROTHERS

Sitting in my office chair and sipping on my morning coffee, I looked out the large window into the cul-de-sac in front of my home and watched tree branches sway with the light wind. Spilling through the blinds was light from the streetlight, and the light created shadows dancing with the breeze along the wall behind my computer desk. In a trance, my mind wandered to December 16, 1988—27 years ago—my retirement ceremony from the Army.

Coming home from the retirement ceremony, I removed and hung my uniform in the bedroom closet just as I wore it that day. In a daze, I stared at the hanging jacket while the years of service flashed by as if a video were playing on fast-forward. Shutting the closet door, I left the uniform hanging in the dark, knowing I would never wear it again. I walked into the living room carrying a Jim Beam and Coke, sat in my recliner, legs elevated, and my thoughts drifted to the assignments I'd had and to those with whom I'd served during and after Vietnam.

I thought of my platoon brothers and wondered what happened to them, and I thought of The Fallen: "Tufts, Ramos, Reynolds, Ofstedahl, Swindle, Wellman, Ponce, Mitchell, Anderson, Carey, Morris, Kidwell, and Matson." As I sat, reclining further back, I pondered my future of not being a soldier. At this point, I realized that I needed to see my platoon brothers, and I made myself the promise that, one day, I would find them.

The shadows gliding on the office wall in an ever-changing pattern stopped moving, and I snapped back to the present day. It was at that moment I did something to remember First Platoon. I started creating a small website, first listing the platoon members I could recall and organizing them by their squad, date to the platoon, and date killed or wounded. Now retired, with nothing but time, I put my programming skills back to work. It was not an elaborate website but a way for the platoon members to reconnect and a place to share our history.

I'd stayed in contact with Mike Dankert, Dusty Rhoades, and Chuck Council through the years, and it was a natural starting point to ask for their help to add names and dates to the platoon website. I hosted the site from my home and became the webmaster, and the platoon website grew from that day.

Figure 1-1 Left to right—Me, Chuck Council, Dusty Rhoades, and Mike Dankert at Hill 4–11 Reunion. July 20, 1990, Nashville, Tennessee. *Photographer Sherrie Haynie.*

We added photographs, letters home, and other memorabilia we had saved over the years. Mike and I wrote short stories of our time with First Platoon and posted them on the website. The website took shape, but we needed more information and participation from others in the platoon. Working on the site made me want to connect to the other platoon members even more.

It's difficult to explain my motivation for finding my platoon brothers. While we were in Vietnam, we formed a bond of friendship, and we depended on each other. We trusted each other with our lives. The men of First Platoon were brothers created by war. I missed that bond, the brotherhood, and the feeling of total trust. We were family;

as an example, John Baxter, the father, Mike, my brother, Chuck the wise uncle, and Dusty and Mississippi, the favorite cousins. The men of First Platoon had various relationships that we recognized as brotherhood.

Chapter 2

SEARCHING FOR AND FINDING FIRST PLATOON

Each morning I started my day by concentrating on finding my platoon brothers. Searching for them and looking for people from almost 50 years past became challenging and tedious work. For the best search criteria, I needed the full name, age, and the city-state where they lived now. When I began searching, I had the first and last name, not always the correct spelling, their estimated age, and sometimes the city or state they'd lived in before going to Vietnam.

Several platoon members had military orders, documentation for the Combat Infantry Badge and Purple Heart, to name a few, and those documents listed the full name and social security number. Finding a middle name proved to be helpful, too. I forwarded a letter to a platoon member, Ray "Alabama" Hamilton, through the Social Security Office, and he received the letter but never responded to the request to contact me. I later found that one platoon member, Dennis

Stout, had an incorrect social security number on the orders I used, so the postal service returned the letter that I sent through the Social Security Office.

For two platoon members, Jack Jurgensen and Leslie Pressley, I found a mailing address through tax records, but no telephone number. I gave Mike the mailing addresses and asked him to write a letter to determine if it was the correct Jurgensen and Pressley, and, if so, would they be interested in reconnecting with the platoon. Within weeks, both called Mike. Leslie showed excitement concerning what we were doing and wanted to take part. Mike said Jack Jurgensen showed interest but wouldn't take part in the platoon website.

Using the Hill 4–11 Association website, I found several platoon members. The association collected names, mailing addresses, email addresses, and sometimes telephone numbers. Mike, Dusty, Chuck and I had attended many of the Hill 4–11 reunions through the years.

Hill 4–11 was the firebase that our Company built in July-August 1969. The Battalion Commander named the firebase to display the joint effort of the 4th Army of the Republic of Vietnam (ARVN) Regiment and the 11th Infantry Brigade; hence, the name "Hill 4–11." The Association included all units—infantry, cavalry, artillery, and engineers—who served on the firebase from 1969 until the Army abandoned it. I believe it was a small group of infantry soldiers who'd served on the firebase in 1971 who started the Association.

Researching for hundreds of hours on the computer, I used: Google, white pages, social media sites, and local tax records, and put in an equal amount of hours making telephone calls. I was thankful that many of the platoon members still had a landline (wired telephone service), because, most times, the phone number displayed when searching for a name. Mobile phone numbers wouldn't show when searching the sites that were free. I used Facebook and LinkedIn to make contact, too. Through these two social media tools, Sherrie, my wife, and I found two platoon members, Ray Hamilton, his ex-wife, and Manny Strauch. Manny showed no interest in participating or reconnecting with the platoon.

During the next 12 months, I found 26 platoon members from a total of 30, and eight who had died since returning from Vietnam: David Abernathy, Allyn Buff, Bill Davenport, Jack Lanzer, Michael Stout, Mike "Doc" Windows, Terry Woolums, and Pete Zink. Several of the eight had succumbed to cancer or other illnesses related to Agent Orange. Jack Jurgensen and Jerry Zwiesler died in 2017; Jerry lost his battle with an Agent Orange-related disease. Leslie Pressley died in 2018 from Agent Orange-related cancer. To date, I know of 11 platoon members who had died since they'd come home.

Most platoon members I called were receptive to being contacted, even though they may not have remembered me. The human memory is a poor long-term storage medium. However, we re-connected in a short time. A few members I found didn't want contact, and I didn't pressure them. Amazingly, I discovered that Ray "Alabama" Hamilton and Charlie Deppen had been living a couple of hours from me for the last 20 years.

So as not to sound similar to a sales call, I had prepared an opening line when calling a platoon member: *"Good evening. I'm Glyn Haynie, and I'm looking for (insert person's name) who served in the Army with me in Vietnam in 1969."* I didn't need them hanging up the phone believing I was looking for a handout, either. I understood that calling someone after 46 years, the platoon member may think my call wasn't a sincere effort to reconnect but, instead, an attempt to get something from them.

When I was making the hundreds of phone calls, I found that, for the most part, the person politely answered the call and my questions. Several individuals I called offered to aid me in finding the veteran I asked about when calling them. I didn't accept their offer, not wanting to duplicate the calls, but thanked them. Only a few of the individuals I called hung up on me.

One elderly lady in the northeast, for example, said I had the wrong number and asked if I'd speak to her husband, an eighty-year-old Korean War veteran because he loved to talk to veterans. I did and spoke with him for 15 minutes. When we finished talking, the wife got back on the phone. She thanked me and said that I'd left him with a big smile and that the call had made his day.

A gentleman in Florida sounded as if he was crying after I told him who I was and the reason I was searching for the veteran. In a broken voice, he volunteered to find the platoon member I was seeking—who had the same name as his. I told him he didn't need to help and thanked him.

On one phone call, a woman answered, and I identified myself and explained why I was calling. She shouted, "He left with a whore 15 years ago, and please don't call me again!" I then heard a click that ended the phone call. I kept dialing numbers to continue my search.

One evening I dialed a number, and an older man answered with a gruff, "Hello."

I started to explain why I called and said, "Hello, I'm—" then I heard the click on the other end of the line ending the call. The older man had hung up on me.

Well, he wasn't the first person to hang up on me. I continued to make calls to other numbers trying to find the same platoon member. Several weeks went by with no luck finding the individual I was searching for. I thought I'd try the first number again, to the same man who'd hung up before I could explain why I was calling.

I dialed the number; the same voice answered as the last time I tried this number, and he said, "Hello," just as before.

I said, "Good evening. I'm Glyn Haynie, and I'm looking for John DeLoach, who served in the Army with me in Vietnam in 1969." I felt relieved that he let me finish talking.

On the other end of the line, the voice replied, "Hello, Glyn. I'm the John who served with you in Vietnam. How are you doing?"

Delighted it was John, we shared a good laugh regarding the first phone call, our first conversation in 46 years. We then talked for more than 45 minutes catching up on the years. It always amazed me how comfortable I felt talking with a platoon brother, even after all these years.

I was astounded by the small, personal details that John remembered about me and some of the other members of the platoon.

Continuing my search, I found relatives of four platoon members killed during my time with First Platoon. Deep in my gut, while dialing the number, I hoped that I had an incorrect number. I had rehearsed what I'd say, but I was not prepared emotionally to talk to a family member who had lost a loved one so many years ago. What can I say after 46 years, and who am I to tell them? But I felt I should call.

The family members located were: Donita (wife of Eldon Reynolds), Deborah (wife of Richard "Rebel" Wellman), Claire (wife of Jerry Ofstedahl), and a niece of Paul Ponce. I also talked to a niece, Susan, of Richard Wellman. Years earlier, Dusty Rhoades and Chuck Council had found Gloria Alejandro, the sister of Juan Ramos. I met Gloria Alejandro and her daughter, Lari Alejandro, when they attended the Hill 4–11 reunion in July 2011 in Tampa, Florida.

The family members were polite, and they even engaged in conversation, but they didn't ask specific questions concerning what had happened to their loved ones. Donita and I communicated only by email—what a relief. One wife said, "I knew this day would come," and she cried. When I realized she'd started crying, uncontrollable tears streamed down my cheeks. Several family members wanted me to include them in the website email update and add them to the contact list.

I emailed each platoon member, including the family members added to the list, with weekly updates to the platoon website. Most engaged with the site and contributed photographs, letters they wrote home, and memorabilia. Everyone's contributions motivated me, and through their donations, we collected pictures of most platoon members. As I found each platoon member, I included him on the contact list with his email address and telephone number.

The website grew larger than my home server could handle, so I purchased a domain name, 1st-platoon.org, and a hosting service to host our site, instead of using a computer from my home. I hoped that the website and emails would help them reconnect with each other. Now I wanted to see them.

GOING TO THE VETERANS ADMINISTRATION

During the time I was searching for my platoon members, I learned that many suffered from Post Traumatic Stress Disorder (PTSD) and other Vietnam-related illness, including Agent Orange exposure. After talking to several of my platoon members and receiving encouragement from my sons, Nathan and Bryan, I decided to go to the Veterans Administration (VA). They told me I needed to get an evaluation, so I could create a record with the VA to document any current or possible future illness.

Within days of calling, I had an appointment with my local VA counselor. Nathan had served in Iraq and Afghanistan (82nd Airborne Division), and Bryan had served in Afghanistan (Ranger Battalion). They told me that the treatment of Vietnam Veterans by the VA was much better than in earlier years.

As I drove to the appointment, I thought of the day I'd gone to the VA 18 years ago. I had to wait hours to see a counselor, and when he called my name, he greeted me with a bored look and condescending attitude; he took my information with even less enthusiasm. He did nothing to help me, and I never returned to seek treatment. I hoped my appointment this day wouldn't have the same outcome.

Entering the building, I went directly to the waiting area. As I walked up to the counter to sign in for my appointment, I noticed the room was half full of veterans of all ages. After waiting for 20 minutes, the counselor called my name, and I stood and walked into his office. The counselor, much younger than me, was prior-service Navy and had served in Iraq.

He had my file and appeared prepared for our meeting. We discussed my medical record, and he asked questions about my current physical and mental health. He scheduled appointments for injuries that had happened during my Army career, including the Traumatic Brain Injury (TBI) I suffered on August 15, 1969, while in Vietnam.

After talking with me, he scheduled an appointment with a psychiatrist for what he referred to as an anxiety-disorder evaluation. His recommended session with a psychiatrist surprised me, because I seldom let my emotions show about my Vietnam days. During my 20 years in the Army, and after, I kept that year hidden and would never admit to having any difficulties from the horrors of the war that I'd experienced in Vietnam.

It was during my session with the psychiatrist that she diagnosed me with PTSD. During the interview, she asked many questions about my year in Vietnam. After my responses, she stopped the discussion and contacted the VA to add PTSD to my record so that we could continue the session. I thought it strange to receive this diagnosis 46 years later, and the VA scheduled no follow-up treatment for PTSD.

However, it may explain the anger, guilt, and other issues I've experienced over the years. At least now, I had my injuries documented with the VA in case the day ever comes that I need help from them. I learned it's never too late to seek help. I was thankful that my platoon brothers and sons encouraged me to go.

CHAPTER 3

MEETING PLATOON MEMBERS AFTER 46 YEARS

Every summer Sherrie and I made a road trip to visit family and friends, and for a couple of years when the Hill 4–11 association didn't hold a reunion, Mike, his wife, Sue, and Sherrie and I would meet somewhere. In June 2015, we decided on Washington, DC. We met and stayed at the Sheraton Hotel in Bethesda. The first day we learned how to use the subway to travel from the hotel to the National Mall and walked nine miles the first day, visiting the different monuments and museums. We spent three full days being tourists, visiting many museums and eating at a variety of restaurants.

At the Vietnam Memorial, Mike and I searched for our platoon brothers who hadn't come home. As we found each name, we made eye contact, one of us would say the name out loud, and together we relived the pain of their loss. With thirteen names of First Platoon on the Wall, I thought, *You won't be forgotten.* We found several more company members from other platoons, two being Kelly and McCoy, killed early July 1969. The company initially named Firebase Hill 4–11 "Firebase Kelly-McCoy," honoring the two NCOs, but the Battalion Commander officially later named it "Firebase Hill 4–11."

Each night, Mike and I stayed up late talking while sipping on our Maker's and soda water. We talked about our families, our children, and how we were enjoying retirement. Mike and I seldom spoke of Vietnam and the hardships we endured. One night I spoke about the many events that occurred in 1969 that we missed or didn't even know happened. Mike told me to read the book *1969: The Year Everything Changed,* by Rob Kirkpatrick, and said it covered most of the events we missed in 1969.

Figure 3–1 Mike and I at the Vietnam Memorial May 2015. *Photograph by Sherrie Haynie.*

After dinner the next evening, we went to Barnes & Noble to buy the book Mike had recommended. I read the book as soon as we got home, and it filled in the gaps I felt existed for the year I was in Vietnam. I found the title fitting because of the changes I went through personally during the year 1969 and how my life changed forever. It was amazing the number of historical events that I'd missed or didn't know about or other incidents that happened in the year 1969.

ROAD TRIP AND BROTHERHOOD

For our August 2015 road trip to visit family and friends, we made plans to include First Platoon members I'd found and hadn't seen in 46 years. It surprised me to learn that many of the platoon members lived near the towns where we'd visited our children, my mother, and my brother or passed on the interstate. I coordinated in advance with five platoon members living near our route and scheduled to meet each member for lunch or dinner near their home. I sent the platoon members I scheduled a meeting with a photograph of the black Kelly-McCoy baseball hat Chuck Council had made up years ago, that I'd wear to help find me in a crowded restaurant.

During our trip, we would meet John "Mississippi" DeLoach and daughter Kelli, John Baxter and his wife Carol, Maurice Harrington, and Charlie Deppen and his wife Melanie and daughter Grace. Only one, Tommy Thompson, couldn't make it because of prior commitments. When we planned our route, we made our first stop Sherman, Texas, to find Ray "Alabama" Hamilton. I had an old address but no telephone number. Going to Sherman would be 80 miles from our planned route but worth the effort if I found him.

We started from our home in Cedar Park, Texas, and drove to Sherman, Texas, to the last-known address I'd found for Ray. We located his home in a well-kept older neighborhood on a tree-lined street shading modest one-story houses. I knocked on the front door, but no one answered. So my wife and I knocked on the door of the homes next to Ray's and talked to the neighbors. We learned that he'd remarried and moved three years ago to McKinney, Texas. His son lived in the family home now, but no one knew when he might be home. I left a note on the door giving my contact information. The search for Ray would continue when we got back home. His son never contacted me.

We left Sherman heading south and then drove east once we'd turned onto Interstate 20. We stopped in Vicksburg, Mississippi, to spend the night. The next morning we departed for Meridian, Mississippi, to meet John "Mississippi" DeLoach for lunch at a Cracker Barrel restaurant right off the Interstate. John had traveled 50 miles to the restaurant from his home.

Thinking back to our time in First Platoon, I remembered John was from Laurel, Mississippi, hence, his nickname. Mississippi was a big man, standing six feet, two inches. In Vietnam, I liked John right away, and we became friends. I am sure we looked like Mutt and Jeff standing

33

next to each other. He took my place as the youngest platoon member upon his arrival to the platoon in early June 1969. He had an easygoing personality; nothing appeared to upset him.

Arriving early, we waited inside the restaurant. Being excited and eager to see John, I went outside to walk around. I saw a tall older man with a young woman standing near the entrance, wearing a black Vietnam Veterans baseball hat with the 11th Brigade insignia on the front. He had gray hair exposed around where the cap fitted his head. I approached the veteran and noticed he stood a head taller than me, his face weathered, as if he worked outside in the harsh weather, and he carried extra weight. We didn't recognize each other.

I looked at him and asked, "John?"

He replied, "Glyn?"

We smiled at each other and extended our hands to shake but embraced instead; the hug is a natural reaction for two old First Platoon members. His longtime girlfriend Jan couldn't make the lunch date—"health problems but recovering well"—but her daughter Kelli came instead. Kelli appeared a pleasant young woman, and I could tell she cared for John. While talking, it was obvious that we knew each other well; John hasn't changed. I had been with First Platoon for a month before John arrived at the platoon.

John and I talked about our time in Vietnam and the different platoon members in First Platoon. One story comes to mind every time I think of John, and I thought this a perfect time to share my version of what happened that day to John. I asked John if he remembered the day he was run over by a track, and he smiled and said, "How could I forget?" I reminded John it was August 13, the day of the ambush.

> I crossed the trench running back toward the platoon. As I got closer to the squad position, the APCs moved in reverse away from the squad while the enemy fired automatic weapons and rocket-propelled grenades. You lay in a prone position 30 meters away from me, not far from the APC positions, in the grass, facing

the enemy. I watched in horror as an APC moving in reverse drove right over you. I thought for sure the track had killed you, but as soon as the APC had cleared your position, you sat up with a look of disbelief on your face.

Once I finished the story, we laughed at the circumstance of a track running over him but also thought of Jerry Ofstedahl, Robert Swindle, and Richard Wellman, whom the enemy killed that day. John asked about Frank Brown, who was critically wounded the same day, and I told John I couldn't find him.

I spoke of the telephone conversations I had with our platoon brothers I'd found and informed him of the Hill 4–11 reunions he could attend to reconnect with people who'd served on the Hill. I mentioned my first telephone call to him, in which he had hung up on me, and John gave a sheepish smile, saying he thought a telemarketer was interrupting his evening, so he hung up the phone. We both agreed that for him to answer the second phone call I made was a good thing.

During our conversation, I discovered that John had followed his father's profession and worked in the oil fields for many years and is now retired. He told us how hard the work was and about the many accidents he had while on the job. Listening to his stories, I concluded that John had a busy life. We had a great time, and the conversation lasted more than two hours.

We moved outside and sat on a bench, and I began using the portable scanner I had with me to scan photographs that John brought to upload to the platoon website. While sitting on the bench, I removed my hat to wipe sweat from my forehead. John and Kelli exclaimed, simultaneously, "Whoa!" They were shocked that I still had my hair. John removed his hat and showed the top of his bald head. We laughed.

When we got ready to leave, I said to John, "I grew two inches since Vietnam, and I'm still much shorter than you."

John smiled and replied, "I grew two inches, too, and I'm six foot four now." We laughed in unison.

While we were still laughing, I looked up at John, and I said, "We still look like Mutt and Jeff standing next to each other."

Figure 3-2 John DeLoach and I outside Cracker Barrel in Meridian, Mississippi, August 2015. *Photograph by Sherrie Haynie.*

Sherrie took several pictures of John and me, and then we said our goodbyes and promised to stay in touch. We left Meridian and drove east on Interstate 20, stopping in Birmingham, Alabama, for the night.

The next morning we left Birmingham, still driving east on Interstate 20. Then we turned onto Interstate 95 heading toward Raleigh, North Carolina, to visit our youngest son, Bryan. We spent two days with Bryan and his family before heading to Charlotte, North Carolina. We scheduled lunch at a Lone Star Steakhouse in Charlotte with Maurice and his wife, Irene, and dinner with John Baxter and his wife, Carol, at a restaurant they selected.

I told Sherrie that Maurice Harrington arrived at the platoon in October 1968, which made him an old-timer when I joined the unit. Maurice was always quick with a smile and a joke. I found him entertaining and friendly and a great distraction to our surroundings. On the serious side, he could take charge and be a

Figure 3-3 John DeLoach in Vietnam in February 1970. *Photograph provided by John DeLoach.*

team leader or squad leader. I recounted the story of Maurice getting shot in the nose by the medic.

> Maurice was eating his C-rations when the medic approached the squad, removed his backpack, and dropped it to the ground. He sat next to his gear, retrieved his cleaning kit, and prepared to clean his M-16. He started to disassemble the weapon to give it a good cleaning. At that point, the rifle discharged a round. The discharged round pierced the end of Maurice's nose and traveled to the soldier sitting next to him, hitting the soldier in the throat. The platoon leader called in for a dustoff, and once on the ground, several platoon members loaded Maurice and the wounded soldier on the helicopter, and the Huey made a rapid takeoff, heading to the Division hospital in Chu Lai. In flight, the crew worked on the wounded soldier, but he died before they could get to the hospital. Later, the hospital sent Maurice to Japan for treatment to repair his nose, and after several months, they sent him back to the platoon.

As I finished the story, we arrived at the restaurant to have lunch with Maurice and Irene at the scheduled time. We entered the restaurant lobby and sat on a bench to wait. The restaurant had several small groups of businesspeople scattered throughout the dining area; it was not very busy. As time ticked away, I became nervous.

Sherrie looked at me and said, "He's not coming."

"He'll be here," I replied. I knew he'd show.

We waited 30 minutes, and no Maurice. I still thought he'd show, but I called him.

I dialed his number and heard the phone ringing. A voice said, "Hello."

I recognized the voice and said, "Maurice, this is Glyn Haynie."

"Hello, Glyn. How are you doing?" he replied.

I laughed and said, "I'm doing great. Are we meeting for lunch?"

"I thought we were meeting Wednesday," Maurice replied.

I said, "No, it's today; we agreed to meet on Tuesday."

Maurice had our meeting on Wednesday, not Tuesday, the wrong day. Hey, stuff happens, especially at our age! We decided to meet at another restaurant closer to his home. He told me that Irene couldn't make it because he'd scheduled our meeting for the wrong day, and she had plans for the afternoon.

We drove 15 miles to the restaurant, O'Charley's Restaurant & Bar, in Monroe, which Maurice selected. I was waiting outside the restaurant when Maurice arrived. He got out of his car, stood, looked around, and then walked toward me with a slow gait. I recognized him at once. He still had dark hair, face free of wrinkles, and a big smile, but he was carrying some extra pounds, the same as most of us. As with John, we extended our hands to shake but embraced instead. Maurice had been with the platoon for six months, an old-timer in the platoon, before I arrived at First Platoon. He had no reason to remember me, the new guy.

Figure 3-4 Maurice Harrington and I outside O'Charley's in Monroe, North Carolina, August 2015. *Photograph by Sherrie Haynie.*

While eating lunch, Maurice told me how he'd worked for the state prison system for more than 20 years and owned an automotive mechanic shop during that time. He talked of his wife, Irene, their adult children, and riding his Harley. He added that he was enjoying retirement. We were comfortable with each other and picked up our brotherhood 46 years later. Maurice and I gradually remembered different things regarding the other while in Vietnam. We had a good time. He still had that easy manner and a big laugh; the scar on his nose was as I remembered, but not as noticeable. After the meal, we went outside, and Sherrie took several pictures; then we embraced and said goodbye, promising to meet again.

Figure 3-5 Left to right—Maurice Harrington on the left with Joe Mitchell (center) and Michael Stout (right) on FSB Debbie. *Photograph provided by Dennis Stout.*

After our meeting with Maurice, we drove back to Charlotte and checked into our hotel, a Holiday Inn. We rested and got ready for our dinner date with the Baxters. I knew this meeting would be different. John, the platoon leader, was an officer, and I didn't have the same bond with him as I had with the enlisted platoon members. There was also a significant age difference—he had seven years on me. Officers and enlisted soldiers didn't become friends, but we had a bond by being together during 1969 and sharing the same experiences in the platoon. I arrived at First Platoon a month after John.

John Baxter, from Gainesville, Florida, had a college degree and had been in the Peace Corps before entering the Army. He arrived in Vietnam in late March 1969 and at the platoon in early April 1969; the

Company Commander assigned him as First Platoon leader. John was aloof personally, but approachable by the platoon members, and he listened to what you had to say. He proved to be an effective leader. He had the respect and trust of the platoon. We would follow him anywhere.

I told Sherrie two specific stories about John Baxter and the leader he was to the soldiers of First Platoon. These aren't stories of combat but about caring and kindness.

> Early in May, on my second day with the platoon, we started walking early, with our gear, ammunition, and weapons, through the hot and humid jungle. I was sweating heavily and drank water until my canteens were empty. My 50-pound rucksack was getting heavier by the hour. After hours of walking, I saw the sky darken and my surroundings spin before I crumbled to the ground, unconscious from the heat. I came to with squad members loosening my clothes and dousing me with water to cool me.
>
> Lieutenant Baxter had the platoon take a break and said to move out in 30 minutes. I appreciated the time to recover. As I sat leaning against a tree, a shadow fell over me, and I looked up to see Lieutenant Baxter standing over me. He asked, "How are you doing, Haynie?" I heard the empathy in his voice, and I knew this Lieutenant cared about the soldiers in his platoon and was not pissed or impatient with me for passing out from the heat. With newfound energy, I replied, "Doing better, Sir." Lieutenant Baxter continued, "Hang in there; we will be back at a firebase in a week."

The second story I recalled:

> It was August 15, 1969, when Owens helped me off the field and placed me in an APC with other wounded platoon members. Deppen sat with a blank stare and a large piece of shrapnel sticking out of his right knee. Okino lay on a stretcher, covered in blood and his legs mangled. He was moaning and in shock. Thompson,

between cries of pain from the large opening blown in his side, looked around the track in shock, too. Blood-soaked bandages, pools of blood, and chunks of flesh covered the floor. I thought I would be sick, so I moved out of the APC and stumbled to the small berm next to the hedgerow. I sat on the ground and cried. As I sobbed like a child, Lieutenant Baxter came over and spoke in a calming voice, telling me the platoon needed me. His reassuring voice and words helped me pull myself somewhat together.

To me, both stories demonstrated the compassion John Baxter showed his soldiers. Baxter wasn't the typical, macho "Get up off your ass and quit whining" but a leader who understood and cared for his soldiers. His methods proved effective for the other platoon members and me. He talked you back into the fight by showing he cared.

Arriving early, we waited inside by the front door of the New South Restaurant. As soon as John and Carol walked through the front door, I recognized him. He hadn't changed; he was older, his hair was gray and thinner, and he was carrying a couple of extra pounds. But, otherwise, he was just as I remembered him.

John and I shook hands, and I said, "It's great to see you, John."

He replied, "You, too, and I bet you never thought you'd be calling me 'John.'"

I said, "I didn't, but I think the time is right." We both laughed.

"You haven't changed; I believe I'd recognize you anywhere," I continued.

We introduced our wives, and then the host seated us at our table. We had an exceptional meal, and Carol entertained us with stories of their family and two sons. I learned that John retired from Bank of America and had a son in Austin, Texas, 15 miles from our home, whom he visits a couple of times a year. We had two sons in North Carolina two to three hours from John.

While at the restaurant, John and I had time to talk about our experience and the effect it had on us. We talked for more than 2 1/2 hours, and I'm sure the waiter wanted us to leave. John, being the platoon leader, may not have had a personal bond with most of us, but the connection of being in First Platoon and sharing the experiences we had together showed.

We went outside to take pictures and say our goodbyes. Carol tried her hardest to get me to smile, but I don't have that automatic camera smile many can turn on when someone points a camera at them. When I extended my right hand to John, he grasped my hand with his right hand, and we embraced. It could have been an awkward moment because he'd been the platoon leader, but it turned out to be a very natural gesture because of the First Platoon bond.

The next morning, we left Charlotte and drove to Columbus, Georgia. We stayed in Columbus for two days with my mother and sister Charlene. I told them of our time with my platoon brothers and Charlie Deppen, the platoon member we would see in Houston. My mom commented that I should've tried to find the platoon members years ago, and I agreed.

On the third morning, we drove toward Katy, Texas, where my brother Wayne resides, and

Figure 3–6 John Baxter and I outside New South Restaurant in Charlotte, North Carolina, August 2015. *Photograph by Sherrie Haynie.*

Figure 3–7 John Baxter, at stand-down in Chu Lai, November 1969, after the awards ceremony. He received a Bronze Star for Valor for his actions on August 13, 1969. *Photograph provided by John Baxter.*

would spend the night. Wayne retired from the Army November 1989 and now lived in Katy, next to his children, Traci and Little Wayne, and grandchildren. The next morning, we would meet with Charlie Deppen and his family for lunch. Charlie chose to get together at the Cracker Barrel in Katy, which was only 15 miles from Charlie's home in Houston.

At Wayne's house, I told him of my excitement at meeting the three platoon members so far on our trip and showed him the pictures we took. During a barbeque dinner, I gave him the details of each visit and how everyone was still the same. Wayne and I talked about our time together in Vietnam before he went to Korea. I retold the story of me getting drunk on beer and how Wayne reacted. This story comes up often when we get together. We also told accounts of the many assignments we had together—in Fort Benning, Germany, and Fort Jackson—during our careers, too.

Getting up later than usual, we had our morning coffee and a small meal. It wasn't long after breakfast that we left for our meeting with Charlie and his family. After saying our goodbyes to Wayne and Dee, we headed to the restaurant for our lunch meeting. We showed up 20 minutes early at the Cracker Barrel and placed our name on the waiting list. The restaurant was busy, and there was not much room inside the store to move or stand, so it was good that we'd arrived early.

Walking away from the crowd of customers, we went outside to wait. I noticed a man with his wife and an adult child approaching the front door, and knew it must be Charlie.

I approached the family and asked, "Charlie?"

He replied, "Yes. Glyn?"

I said, "It's been a long time" as we shook hands and embraced. It was at this point that the hostess announced that our table was ready.

When I first met Charlie, he looked familiar, but I had a difficult time placing him. He said the same of me. I thought it strange, because we were in the same squad for six weeks before he received a wound that sent him home. Charlie arrived at First Platoon one month after me, but we were in different squads initially. I was in the first squad and Charlie the second squad. Squads didn't mingle much, so we didn't know the other members of the unit as well. I thought I got to know him better through the letters he wrote home that he'd contributed to the platoon website.

In Vietnam, Charlie was quiet and kept to himself. It appeared he was reluctant to get to know the squad members or let them know him.

Charlie associated with the other new guys who'd arrived with him in early June, especially Alabama. He'd looked up to Tufts, and his death affected him. The card game Bridge was his favorite topic, which we found odd, thinking it was more of an old person's card game.

Our conversation didn't stop until it was time for us to leave. Melanie and Grace had questions but allowed Charlie and me to talk.

Figure 3-8 Charlie Deppen and I outside the Cracker Barrel in Katy, Texas, August 2015. *Photograph by Sherrie Haynie.*

Charlie did most of the talking, and he told me the stories of his hospital stay, surgeries, and recovery after being wounded on August 15, 1969.

We sat outside for another 30 minutes while I used my portable scanner to scan more letters to home that he'd written from

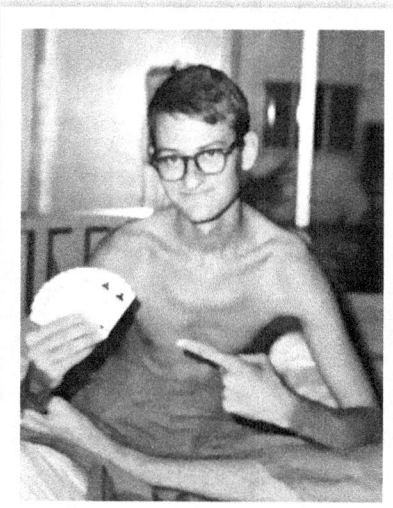

Figure 3-9 Charlie Deppen in Japan after being wounded August 15, 1969. *Photograph provided by Charlie Deppen.*

Vietnam and brought to put on the platoon website. We continued to talk while I scanned the documents. I found that Charlie and his family lived 12 miles from my brother's house. He told me he works for a company that verified software licenses and has had different jobs through the years. By the time I'd finished scanning the letters, Sherrie and I needed to leave for home. Charlie and I embraced and said our goodbyes. We said goodbye to Melanie and Grace and told them we'd had a great meeting and that I was sure this wouldn't be the last time.

After our goodbyes to Charlie and his family, we left the restaurant and headed home. I know Sherrie was tired of me rehashing each meeting because I went on and on about each platoon member, their family, and our conversations. But she acted like a real trouper the entire trip—not one complaint. Well, maybe several on my driving.

THE SEARCH CONTINUES

Once we returned home, I started my search for more platoon members with renewed energy. Finally, after several attempts, I found Ryan Okino and Barry Suda in Hawaii. I was disappointed that I hadn't located them earlier, because in September 2014, Mike and Sue, and Sherrie and I had gone to Honolulu, Hawaii, for my son Nathan's wedding. It would've been an ideal time to see Ryan and Barry. Maybe one day we'll go back to Hawaii.

I talked to both on the telephone several times and thought the conversations went well. I learned that Ryan had remained in Tripler Army Hospital, Honolulu, Hawaii, for two years after being wounded on August 15, 1969; he was listed as 100 percent disabled when he was discharged from the hospital and the Army. Barry, being from Honolulu, visited Ryan several times at the hospital, but they'd lost touch over the years. Ryan is from Hilo, Hawaii, the Big Island.

One week later, I found Ray Hamilton; he lived outside Dallas. Sherrie located his ex-wife, and she gave me his cell phone number. I arranged to meet him and his wife for lunch in Waco, Texas. Waco is the halfway point between our homes, and I had a Veterans Administration appointment in Waco on the day of our meeting for an evaluation of the traumatic brain injury I'd received when I'd been wounded.

While at the VA, Sherrie asked about Ray. I told her that he was from a small town in Alabama, hence, his nickname. He had arrived at the platoon in early June 1969 with many other replacements. Ray was quiet but always engaged in conversation, and he was a welcome addition to the squad. He had a natural, small grin; when he talked, you were comfortable with him. A religious man, Alabama reads his Bible every day. Devoted to his wife, he wrote her most days. I also recounted one story about Ray and me while we were building Hill 4-11.

> One morning Lieutenant Baxter selected Alabama and me to return to Bronco on the battalion supply chopper. We gathered our weapons and ammo, jumped into the Huey, and sat on the floor, with our legs dangling out over the skids. The Huey lifted and banked as it moved away from the Hill. After a short ride, we landed on the helicopter pad at Bronco, jumped out, and walked to the company headquarters. First Sergeant Malpica greeted us as we entered through the screen door. He sent us to supply for clean uniforms and any other clothing we might need.
>
> Next, we went to the bathhouse; there was a line of soldiers waiting their turns. We checked in with the hostess and started our wait. Within minutes, the hostess directed us to our private rooms. I received a steam bath—bathed and massaged by a young Vietnamese woman. After our relaxing morning, Alabama said, "I haven't felt this clean and relaxed for many months," and I agreed. We paid three dollars and left.
>
> We dropped off our old, dirty uniforms at supply and went to the mess hall for lunch. Then we went to the helicopter pad and waited for the Huey ride home. Within 15 minutes, the helicopter landed, supply soldiers loaded ammunition and supplies, and we lifted off and headed back to the Hill. Once we got back to the

squad, Alabama and I talked of the great time we'd had and made sure everyone was sufficiently envious of our trip.

After my VA appointment, we arrived on time and waited for Ray. I looked at the merchandise in the Cracker Barrel country store to pass the time. A cowboy came into the store and stood next to me, browsing a rack of toys. He was wearing a white cowboy hat with short gray hair showing, pressed jeans, a long-sleeved shirt, and fancy, pointed western boots. Not unusual for Texas, but I thought he had to be hot because it was August. We didn't acknowledge each other with a greeting or make eye contact as he looked at the toys. He left shortly to go outside in the heat.

Getting restless, I went outside to walk around while waiting. I noticed the cowboy sitting in a rocker by the front door. When he looked up, I saw his face, with small wrinkles around his eyes and the corners of his mouth and sporting a gray goatee, and I recognized Ray.

Looking into his eyes, I said, "Ray?"

"Yes, I am," he replied as he stood.

I couldn't stop myself and blurted out, "Wow, I wasn't expecting a cowboy. Texas is a long way from Alabama!" I never pictured Ray as a Texan.

Figure 3–10 Ray "Alabama" Hamilton and I outside the Cracker Barrel in Waco, Texas, August 2015. *Photograph by Sherrie Haynie.*

Ray laughed and said, "Yes, I am. How are you doing, Glyn?"

We shook hands and embraced. Ray said his wife, Chris, couldn't make it because she had to watch the grandkids. During our meal, I noticed he still had the same mannerisms and expressions I remembered—in particular, that small smile in the corner of his mouth when he talked. Ray talked of his two favorite retirement hobbies, woodworking and going to casinos to gamble. As with the other platoon members, I felt comfortable with Ray, and we talked for more than two hours before saying goodbye and promising to stay in touch. Sherrie and I started our 90-minute drive home.

Figure 3–11 Ray Hamilton (left), Mike Dankert (center), and Jack Lanzer (right) at Chu Lai during stand-down, August 1969. *Photograph provided by Mike Dankert.*

I found meeting these platoon brothers and their families a remarkable experience. It was as if the past 46 years hadn't happened, and we picked right up from the year 1969. Our faces and bodies had changed but not who we were. We talked about our time in Vietnam and caught up on the missing years.

I continued to support the platoon website, occasionally talked to the platoon members by telephone, and often corresponded by email. I was surprised at the number of platoon members who didn't have computer skills. I guess I shouldn't have been surprised, as the average age of the platoon members was 68 or older. I found that most wives used the computer and knew how to e-mail, text, and use the internet. For many, their technical knowledge helped to keep the communication open between their husbands and me.

When I visited my platoon brothers on the road trip, I asked each one the question: "If we had a platoon reunion next summer, would you attend?" Each one, without hesitation, said, "Yes." Most had had no contact with each other in 46 years! Now, I had another mission.

CHAPTER 4

THE PLAN FOR A REUNION

There were many reasons to hold a reunion. Veterans who served together in the same unit or combat area had a bond, and this bond helped them survive the worst of times. It allows veterans to reconnect and share their experiences, reforge the brotherhood, and rekindle past friendships. A reunion can be therapeutic for some veterans as they renew their relationships of the past. For me, it's not the war stories or photographs but reconnecting with my brothers of First Platoon that was most important.

Mike and I had attended Hill 4–11 reunions over the years, but I wanted a smaller gathering—First Platoon members only—and a more intimate setting for our first meeting as a platoon. I called Mike, and we talked about hosting a reunion. I told him I'd take the lead and even pay part of the cost so it wouldn't be as expensive for the platoon members attending. Many had retired, and I didn't want money to become a reason not to participate. We don't have money lying around, but we had savings I could use. Mike at once volunteered to pay half of the expenses. We both thought to donate money as a way to say "Thank you" for helping us come home. After Mike and I talked, I went to work. Hosting a reunion challenged me; I had no experience organizing or planning an event of this size.

I thought Dallas, Texas, would be an excellent location to hold the reunion. It had several Interstates running through it and two major airports, and it was a central location for most of the families attending. The guys living on the east or west coast would need to travel further, no matter where we would hold the reunion. The hotel was a three-hour drive from my home.

Now that I'd chosen a location, I had to decide on the date and the length of the reunion. After attending many Hill 4–11 reunions, I used them to help model the First Platoon reunion. They had a three-day gathering, generally in July. I checked the calendar and selected July 14 through July 17, 2016. I thought that these dates should work—there were no high school or college graduations to attend, as most were in May and June. During August 2015, I sent out emails to everyone asking who would attend a Platoon Reunion in Dallas, Texas, July 14 through July 17, 2016.

For the next step, I had to find a hotel we would stay at and have our dinner meals and a place to gather. I called and emailed several hotels for pricing and availability. Within several weeks, I'd narrowed the choices to the Holiday Inn and Doubletree, both near the DFW airport. I wanted a hotel near the airport, so the families who flew in could use the hotel shuttle service for transportation from and to the airport. The Holiday Inn wasn't prompt with the information I needed or as flexible as the Doubletree, so I selected the Doubletree as our hotel.

The Doubletree agreed to provide three free breakfast meals per person, one for each day, included with the room rate. They gave us a hospitality room the first day and meeting rooms to use during the day and evening on Friday and Saturday for free. I selected buffet dinner meals for Friday and Saturday night. I scheduled the George Bush Library tour and arranged for tickets and the bus to transport us to and

THE PLAN FOR A REUNION

back from the Library. This coordination took several months, but I got the contracts signed before Thanksgiving 2015.

During the time I worked with the hotel event planner, I put together a video, which was a slideshow with music to play at the reunion. This video took more than 60 hours to create and proved harder than I thought. Mike helped me organize and select the songs for the video. I had a link to the video hidden on the platoon website, and only Mike knew the location. He clicked on the hidden link and viewed the video whenever I made changes and gave me feedback. Mike developed a playlist for our dinner meals, too.

I wanted to keep the itinerary simple and create a relaxing atmosphere. For Friday morning, I scheduled a 10:00 AM meeting with platoon members and family for coffee and a meet-and-greet for two hours. For Friday lunch and afternoon events, I planned free time, with the meeting room open during the day. Friday evening would be a buffet meal, starting with two toasts—one by Mike and one by me—and Charlie Deppen saying grace before dinner.

After the dinner meal, I'd show the video. Mike and I hoped the video would be the highlight of the reunion. For Saturday, I left the morning open, with the meeting room available with coffee, and for the afternoon, I had a trip planned to the George W. Bush Presidential Library and Museum. Mike and I provided the bus and tickets to the Library. Saturday evening would be a buffet meal, starting with Alice Council saying grace. Sunday would be goodbyes and checkout.

Through the rest of 2015 and into early 2016, after many emails and telephone calls, I got 14 platoon members, with family members, and the sister, Gloria, of Juan Ramos (Killed In Action July 14, 1969) to agree to attend. I invited the family members of our Fallen who I'd found, but no one accepted the invitation except Gloria. Tommy Thompson had a conflict with a family reunion scheduled the same weekend and couldn't participate. John Baxter canceled several months later because of a scheduling problem with family plans. We now had 13 platoon members participating. Thirty-one people would attend the reunion, including platoon members, spouses or girlfriends, four adult children, and two grandchildren.

At the start of December, I began authoring my book *When I Turned Nineteen: A Vietnam War Memoir*. I felt the need to write the platoon story, and I started by merging my short stories. My account doesn't differ from those of the tens of thousands of infantrymen who'd served in Vietnam, but it's my story with First Platoon in the year 1969. With the website, reunion, and a book to write, I no longer had to worry about how I used my time in retirement. I now had a full-time job, working eight or more hours a day on the projects.

Platoon members began making reservations for the reunion as early as January 1, 2016, at the Doubletree. I stayed in constant communication with the platoon members who'd committed to coming and made follow-up phone calls and emails to the other platoon members, attempting to change their mind about attending the reunion. I still sent the weekly First Platoon website update each week, including the names of platoon members and family members participating, along with any changes and additions to the website.

I thought we needed mementos to give to each platoon member and family member when they arrived at the hospitality room. I had black-and-navy-blue baseball hats made with the 11th Brigade insignia and other unit information on the front of the cap for the platoon members. On the back of the hat, it read "Vietnam '69.'" Everyone likes a hat. I purchased coffee travel mugs with the same design as the hat on the cup.

A neighbor, Lisa Robinson, donated her time, equipment, and skills to embroider the hats and stencil the travel mugs. I made a DVD, with a cover for the case, of the video I'd show Friday night. David, my oldest son, and Tarie, his wife, would supply black T-shirts for everyone with the same information as the hat on the front and "Welcome Home" on the back. Mike and I hoped these keepsakes would be enough to help everyone remember the reunion.

CHAPTER 5

MEETING ANOTHER PLATOON BROTHER

In early May 2016, we drove to Kansas for two of our grandchildren's high school graduations. On earlier trips to visit the grandchildren, we'd stopped in Wichita, Kansas, for the night and left the next morning for their home. I thought this an excellent opportunity to get together with Tommy Thompson from Tulsa, Oklahoma, and Ronald Owens, who lives in Wichita.

I emailed both with an invitation to meet at the hotel, and Tommy agreed to meet and spend the night in Wichita. Ronald declined, due to health reasons, the second invitation he had refused. Although Ronald never said, it was my impression that he didn't want to meet or get involved in the platoon activities. I found this disappointing because it was Ronald who, on August 15, 1969, gave me cardiopulmonary resuscitation (CPR) and brought me back to life.

When I first telephoned Ronald, he seemed wary of my call, and, after I'd identified myself, I don't believe he remembered me, which I expected, because so many years had passed. I told him about August 15th and how he used CPR to bring me back from the dead and went on to tell him how thankful I was. I told him that I wasn't sure that I'd ever expressed my gratitude to him for saving my life. He didn't seem interested in talking, so I thanked him again and ended the telephone call. I made it a point when contacting a platoon member, never to force my agenda on anyone who was reluctant to reconnect with me or the platoon.

Figure 5–1 Staff Sergeant Ronald Owens at FSB Bronco, September 1969. *Photograph provided by Barry Suda.*

We arrived Friday, May 6, at the Holiday Inn on the south side of Wichita right off Interstate 35 and checked in with no problems. We checked in early and didn't expect Tommy and his wife Connie for another hour, so we waited in our room to rest until they arrived. As usual, the excitement about the meeting took hold of me, and I got tired of sitting in the room. I told Sherrie I'd go to the lobby to wait and text her when the Thompsons checked into their room.

I left the room, walked toward the elevator, and noticed a woman struggling to get a luggage cart through the elevator door. I assisted her in maneuvering the pushcart through the door opening. She looked up and said, "Thank you," and that is when I thought I recognized her from Facebook. I said, "Connie Thompson?" and she replied, "Glyn?" We both laughed and shook hands. After leaving the cart, she said she would tell Tommy to come downstairs. I called Sherrie to inform her that the Thompsons had arrived and asked her to meet me in the lobby.

MEETING ANOTHER PLATOON BROTHER

Tommy Thompson was the newest member of the second squad when he joined the platoon around August 8, 1969. He was from Bristow, Oklahoma. He arrived after we'd built the firebase Hill 4-11. The squad often talked about the Hill, and I'm sure Tommy felt left out of the conversation. I didn't know Tommy well, but in Vietnam, he came across as likable and ready to learn.

When they came into the lobby, Tommy and I shook hands and embraced and then introduced our wives. He wore a hat that concealed his graying hair and that had "FNG" (Fucking New Guy) embroidered on the front. He stood taller than me and walked with a slow gait, as if in pain. I didn't know Tommy well, and he didn't know me well, either.

He'd been with the platoon for less than a week when the explosion of two 250-pound command-detonated bombs wounded him, August 15, 1969, and the doctors sent him back to the States. We didn't have time in that one week to get to know each other. That didn't matter today, though, because we were part of something together that created a bond, especially surviving the ambushes on August 13 and 15. I gave Tommy a First Platoon hat to replace his FNG hat. The four of us talked for 30 minutes.

We noticed it was getting late and nearing dinnertime, and we agreed we should leave the hotel for the restaurant to have dinner. The four of us drove to a local Mexican restaurant that the desk clerk had recommended, several miles from the hotel. There was no wait line, so the hostess seated us at a booth as

Figure 5-2 Tommy Thompson and I at the Holiday Inn, Wichita, Kansas, May 6, 2016. *Photograph by Sherrie Haynie.*

requested. After the waitress served our cocktails, Tommy and I made a toast to First Platoon and our meeting this day. It took no time to order and for the server to deliver our meals.

The food tasted great, and we talked about family and life. Connie, pleasant to listen to, entertained us with family stories. During our conversation, I learned that Tommy finished college and became a teacher and coach at his local high school. Now retired, he was enjoying cooking and being with his grandchildren.

Back at the hotel, Sherrie and Connie said "Goodnight" and left for their rooms. Tommy and I went to a small conference room and visited for several more hours. He read over how I used his recovery story in my first book, When I Turned Nineteen, and I played the video for him, the same one I would play at the reunion. I gave him a DVD of the movie for him to watch at home. I believe the visit went well, and it was a relief to know Tommy recovered from his wounds and was living a fulfilled life. We left early the next morning while the Thompsons slept late.

Figure 5–3 Tommy Thompson Basic Training photograph. No photograph of Tommy in Vietnam found. *Photograph provided by Tommy Thompson.*

CHAPTER 6

AT LAST THE PLATOON IS TOGETHER: THE REUNION

Finally, it was July, and the reunion dates were close. David and Tarie flew into Austin on July 12 to visit for two days and then traveled with us to attend the reunion. Both helped the reunion be successful.

DAY ONE—MEET-AND-GREET

We loaded the two cars Wednesday morning. David was riding with me, and Tarie was riding with Sherrie. We left the house at 7:00 AM, heading to Dallas. We needed two cars for the luggage, projector, screen, scanner, two notebook computers, and the other technology required for the reunion. Tarie and David had a box of 50 black T-shirts they had made to give out at the get-together. We arrived at the Doubletree in Dallas at 10:30 AM.

It was too early to check in, so we unloaded the cars and put everything in the hospitality room, which was on the first floor, near the reception desk. It had two round tables with chairs that sat eight at each table. We had space to stand and move around, too. The hotel had ice water in a large container available in the far corner. Tarie took charge and organized the bags with the giveaway items and explained the itinerary I had in a folder for each platoon member and family as they arrived. She made sure they got the correct size T-shirt and nametags I'd made for each person. Tarie became the reunion photographer, too, which was an immense help, as it reduced the number of tasks for me to accomplish. Her assistance freed me to greet the families as they came in and allowed me to join the conversation.

Mike arrived around the same time as we did. He helped set up and greeted the platoon members and families as they arrived. His wife, Sue, couldn't come because their daughter wasn't well. I could tell her illness distracted him, and he was worried. Mike helped keep everything on track throughout the reunion.

Families arrived throughout the day, and the last two families rolled in around 7:30 PM. During the day and into the evening, the guys and wives sat at the tables talking about jobs, families, hobbies, and other platoon members. I got to spend time with the platoon members I didn't meet on my road trip: Leslie Pressley, Cliff Sivadge, Don Ayres, Fred Katz, Dusty Rhoades, Chuck Council, and Dennis Stout. I stayed up late making sure I talked to everyone.

I watched in awe as my platoon brothers sat together and talked as if the 47 years that had gone by had never happened. I found the spouses remarkable. They met and embraced and spoke as if they had known each other for 47 years, too—incredible! I already thought the reunion successful.

DAY TWO—DINNER AND A MOVIE

For Friday morning, we had nothing scheduled until 10:00 AM, which was a group meeting with coffee and ice water available. I'd planned a free afternoon, so families would have time to visit the Dallas area on their own.

AT LAST THE PLATOON IS TOGETHER: THE REUNION

After waking early, I took my technology bag and went downstairs for breakfast. Noticing Ray "Alabama" Hamilton sitting alone at a table in the restaurant drinking coffee, I pulled out a chair and sat next to him. The hotel provided a buffet breakfast, so I got up and went through the line to get my breakfast—raisin bran cereal, yogurt, and a cinnamon bun—and returned to join Ray. We ate, drank coffee, and talked about our current lives. Then the conversation drifted to the platoon members and who we remembered and who we didn't. After I ate, I told Ray I'd see him at the meeting room and left him sitting alone to finish his coffee.

I found the room open and arranged with four round tables with eight chairs each, as I had coordinated with the hotel. After setting up the projector screen, I positioned it so that everyone could view the slideshow from anywhere in the room. Next, I set up the projector and computer for the slideshow of the photographs the platoon members had contributed to the website. I thought this would give each person the opportunity to view the pictures, particularly the individuals who hadn't visited our site. As I plugged the projector into the computer, the kitchen staff brought in the coffee and ice water.

On one of the round tables, I set up a scanning station. I had the second computer and portable scanner to allow us to scan any documents, letters, or photographs that anyone might have brought with them. In the emails that I'd sent the last couple of months, I requested they carry items that needed scanning for the platoon website. I then hung the 11th Brigade flag that Tommy Thompson had sent me earlier in the year, stretching it out on the side wall of the room. Mike and I thought the flag added a nice touch to our meeting place. I reminded myself to give Tommy another big thank-you for the flag. We were ready!

David worked in technology during his Army career, primarily networking and hardware, so I assigned him as the reunion technologist. He sat at the scanning station all day Friday and Saturday morning to scan the items platoon members had brought. David's technical skills helped and allowed me to take care of other things related to the reunion; I had more time to visit with the platoon and their family members.

Mike showed up not long after I'd set up the projector and computer for the slideshow. He brought his iPad with a playlist of 1960s favorites we played during the day, and his choices made an excellent addition to the slideshow playing at the same time. I had a Bluetooth speaker we synced with his iPad. The quality of sound the little speaker produced surprised me.

Families drifted into the room by 9:00 AM, and I was glad I'd gotten there early to set up the equipment. The conversation picked up where it had ended last night. The slideshow created new discussions as the guys explained the pictures to spouses as they appeared, and the platoon members exchanged short stories, too. Occasionally, I could hear laughter—or an uncomfortable silence—as an image displayed. The silence happened when an image showed a platoon member who hadn't come home or who had died since coming back.

I waited until after 10:10 AM, because we were missing several platoon members and spouses. I had to start without them and gave a short introduction regarding the reunion and what we would be doing. I talked for less than 15 minutes and got choked up during my presentation, being overwhelmed with gratitude for the number of people who'd shown up for the gathering after so many years and seeing some of my brothers for the first time in 46 years.

When I finished speaking, the conversation started, and several members went over to David's table to get items scanned. David worked all day scanning and talking with the platoon members. There was one technical problem with the scanner; it copied the photographs into what appeared to be a negative of the picture. David figured out a workaround and had to re-scan several pictures and documents. Moving around the room, Tarie snapped candid photos of the platoon and family members as they interacted.

Having the time, I visited Leslie Pressley and his friend Brenda Cartee; they were a perfect match. Brenda was a pleasant woman, and I could tell she cared for Leslie and seemed concerned about his health. She confessed to worrying, at one point, that it might keep him from coming to the reunion. She told me of his excitement to be at the gathering and seeing his platoon brothers. Leslie suffered from many illnesses related to Agent Orange, and he was in poor health.

Leslie was Lieutenant John Baxter's Radio Telephone Operator (RTO) when I arrived at the platoon. I didn't have much contact with him or get to know him well while in Vietnam, but I knew he took care of Baxter. When I was around him, he always had a story and could talk the evening away, making you laugh the entire time. It was Leslie who told me about Mike being wounded by the enemy attack the night of June 14, 1969.

Figure 6–1 Leslie Pressley (left) with John Baxter (center) and Terry Daron (right) opening a care package from home on a firebase with the First Platoon in Vietnam, 1969. *Photograph provided by Leslie Pressley.*

Dennis Stout and his wife, Peggy, came to the table, sat with us, and joined in the conversation. Peggy had a great smile and talked about Dennis and their family. Dennis and I talked about his brother Michael. When I joined First Platoon, Lieutenant Baxter assigned me to the first squad, and he introduced the Squad Leader, Sergeant Michael Stout. I found it ironic, because his brother, Dennis, was also in

Figure 6–2 Leslie Pressley at the platoon reunion, July 15, 2016. *Photograph by Tarie Haynie.*

the squad. They were from Iowa, and Dennis was the older brother, several years older than Mike. Mike died in 1986 from cancer, and I could tell that Dennis missed him.

Dennis appeared eager to share stories about Mike, so he asked if I would tell Peggy about the time the platoon assisted a convoy that was under attack. I said, "Sure" and sat next to Peggy and Dennis to share what happened that day.

> Lieutenant Baxter received a radio transmission that a convoy that had come under sniper fire needed help. We reached the convoy in no time and saw 10 vehicles stalled on the highway. The snipers were firing from a steep hill 250 feet high, with large boulders and thick vegetation, located to the west, across the road. Crouched behind a truck, Mike and Lieutenant Baxter talked to the convoy commander, a young lieutenant. Then Mike motioned for me to move up to their location. I ran up and crouched next to Mike, with the truck providing cover and concealment. We continued to receive enemy fire.
>
> Mike told me to fire my M-79 high-explosive rounds behind a group of boulders. As I was shooting, Lieutenant Baxter asked for two volunteers to climb up the hill and check the NVA sniper position. Dennis and Juan Ramos volunteered and moved up on the left flank toward the group of boulders. Lieutenant Baxter told everyone to hold their fire because two platoon members were working their way up to the sniper location. Mike asked, "Who volunteered?" and Lieutenant Baxter replied, "Ramos and your brother."
>
> Mike was pissed that Dennis had volunteered; he'd told him earlier not to volunteer for dangerous assignments. Ramos and Dennis crawled within range of the enemy position and threw several grenades into the same location I'd targeted. They moved to the position and found a blood trail but no enemy soldiers. They scrambled down the hill and re-joined the platoon.
>
> While waiting for the convoy to leave, I saw Mike talking with Dennis. I couldn't hear what either one was saying, but it was

apparent that the conversation was a heated one by the way Mike was waving his arms wildly as he talked. I'm sure it was not good for Dennis.

Peggy looked at Dennis and, without saying a word, smiled, acknowledging the closeness that was shared by two brothers. I'm sure she knew how much Dennis missed Mike. Whenever I think of Dennis and Mike, I can't help thinking of my brother Wayne, the day we traveled together to Vietnam, and the time we spent together at the Combat Center.

Figure 6-3 Dennis Stout with the First Platoon in Vietnam, 1969. *Photograph provided by Dennis Stout.*

Sherrie and I took a lunch break and sat with John DeLoach and his girlfriend, Jan Jacobo. During the meal, John and I talked about his passion, horses. He had many entertaining stories of his riding experiences. He spoke of his work in the oil fields, and his other love, gardening. Jan spoke of family and enjoying living on the property with enough acreage to hold horses. The conversation turned to our days in Vietnam, and John asked, "Do you remember the day we found an RPG sticking out of my rucksack?"

Figure 6-4 Dennis Stout on the right and Dusty Rhoades on the left at the platoon reunion, July 15, 2016. *Photograph by Tarie Haynie.*

I remarked, "John, I could never forget that day. It was August 14, 1969, the day after the ambush where we fought all day." I then told the story as I remembered it.

As the sun appeared on the horizon, we felt relief. We gathered around a berm, exchanging rucksacks to claim our own and to fix breakfast. Someone told Mississippi not to move. An unexploded RPG round was sticking out of the rucksack he'd retrieved the previous night. Everyone unconsciously took a step backward, away from Mississippi. He sat still, waiting for help. Sweat beaded his face and dripped to the ground. Someone approached him and removed the round; it was a dud, and we discarded it.

Figure 6–5 Fred Katz with the First Platoon in Vietnam, 1970. *Photograph provided by Fred Katz.*

Figure 6–6 Fred Katz on the right and his granddaughter, Hannah, on the left and Ray Hamilton in the background, at the platoon reunion, July 15, 2016. *Photograph by Tarie Haynie.*

I told Mississippi, "You had a charmed two days!"

John smiled and replied, "Yes I did!"

When lunch ended, we headed back to the meeting room. I took over for David so he and Tarie could get lunch. Fred Katz came over to the scanning station with a massive photo album. Mike walked over to sit with us, talked to Fred, and looked at the collection of pictures as I scanned. I didn't know Fred, because he'd arrived at the platoon in late January 1970, and this was after I'd left for my rear job. Cliff and Don knew Fred well. It didn't matter to me if we knew each other or not—he was in First Platoon and my brother.

While scanning Fred's pictures, he talked about his enjoyment of living in rural Michigan and retirement. He told me that he had time to work around his property and spend time with his grandchildren. As I neared the completion of scanning the selected photographs, David came back from lunch. He noticed that I hadn't used the workaround, and so the pictures scanned as negatives. David rescanned most of Fred's photos, but he didn't redo every picture I'd incorrectly scanned.

Sean Ayres, the son of Don Ayres, brought a large suitcase into the room. He asked if he could set up a display of Vietnam-era gear. I told him that would be great. Don, Sean, and I pulled an unused table from the wall for him to set up the equipment. He opened the suitcase, and it contained many items: a rucksack, a poncho with a liner, helmet and liner, uniform, boots and other gear we carried in 1969. The collection was impressive, and it surprised me that he'd been able to get that much gear into one suitcase.

While setting up the display, Don and I had time to talk. I learned he'd retired from a defense contract corporation and worked in the aerospace industry. Since retirement, he and Sean had restored a World War II Army jeep, and he was currently rebuilding a World War II airplane, a Stinson L-5 Sentinel. His hobby kept him busy.

As we talked, I had a hard time remembering Don. I knew he'd arrived as a replacement, after we'd lost most of the platoon, in late August, which was about the time I stopped knowing or having friendships with the platoon members. I do remember the day that we were in the mountains, cold and wet, and Don called out "Sergeant Haynie," and I

Figure 6–7 Don Ayres in the mountains located west of Hill 4-11, 1969. *Photograph provided by Don Ayres.*

turned to face the soldier calling my name. At that instant, Don took my picture. That picture, 48 years later, would be on the cover of my first book, *When I Turned Nineteen*.

Figure 6–8 Don Ayres at the platoon reunion, July 15, 2016. *Photograph by Tarie Haynie.*

When the families came for dinner, they checked out Sean's display first, and they found the collection impressive, too. The Vietnam-era collection of gear renewed conversations of our days in First Platoon. I thanked Sean and told him how terrific it was of him to attend the reunion with his dad.

Before I knew it, the room had emptied, and it was after 4:00 PM. The social hour would start at 6:00 PM and dinner at 6:45 PM. I packed the technology gear and headed to the room for a short rest. At 5:30 PM, I headed downstairs to get the projector and screen set up to show the video that Mike and I had made. Sherrie said she would be downstairs before dinner.

Once I got the projector, screen, and computer set up, Mike and I arranged the tables and chairs in such a fashion that viewing the screen would be more of a theater-seating experience. We then went next door, where we would have our dinner meal, and hooked up Mike's iPad and the Bluetooth speaker to play the dinner music. We talked to the food-service manager, and he assured us he'd prepared the meal as requested and that the staff would serve the meal on time.

The kitchen staff assembled the meal in the front of the room, on a long serving table, and on time, right before 6:30 PM. The meal looked and smelled great, and the kitchen had prepared enough food to feed double the number of meals we'd ordered. For a hotel buffet, this impressed Mike and me. The bartender, wearing the standard white shirt with a black vest and black bow tie and black dress trousers, entered the room and went to his bar in the back corner. Mike and I decided we needed a drink, Maker's Mark bourbon, and soda water.

The families showed up in small groups, and the room filled with conversation and laughter. The bartender stayed busy the first 30 minutes, but no one appeared to overindulge with alcohol. Right at 6:30 PM, I asked for their attention. Once the room quieted, I thanked everyone for attending the reunion and offered a toast to First Platoon and *Welcomed Them Home*. I didn't prepare or rehearse the toast. I let it come from my inner self.

After my toast, Mike went to the front of the room and gave an emotional salute to the First Platoon Fallen. Once Mike had finished, Charlie Deppen walked to the front of the room and said grace before dinner. Then, it was time to eat. Table by table, they moved through the line and served themselves a portion from the food-warmer containers. During the meal, the conversation and laughter continued, and it pleased me to hear the platoon having fun.

At 8:00 PM, I looked around and saw that everyone had finished with their meal and dessert, and the servers were removing plates, glasses, and flatware from the tables. I requested that we take a short break and asked everyone to be in the meeting room next door at 8:15 PM to view the video that Mike and I had made. The group moved out of the dining area to stretch their legs or head to the bathroom, and then proceed to the meeting room.

Mike and I went to the meeting room and double-checked the projector and computer. While testing the equipment, I reflected on the last time I'd seen most of my platoon members. We were in the mountains west of Firebase Hill 4-11, looking for NVA and Viet Cong base camps. We were chilled to the bone, wet, and tired from the constant rain of the monsoons and from climbing up and down the mountain terrain while breaking a trail through the jungle growth. But we were young and healthy, and we had complete faith in each other. Today we are older and not as healthy, but we still have the same trust and brotherhood of those days in Vietnam.

Within minutes, families moved into the room and found a seat for watching the video, a slideshow with music that had four parts to it. Mike dimmed the lights, and I started the video.

The first part played the song "Where Have All the Flowers Gone?" by Peter, Paul, and Mary, as photographs of The Fallen and their grave headstones scrolled across the screen; then there were images of the platoon members who'd died since coming home. Photos were displayed chronologically by date of death. The room remained dead silent during this part of the video, and I noticed many of my platoon brothers and spouses wiping tears from their eyes.

For the second part, the video had a brief pause on a slide displaying "First Platoon 1969," and then the song "Born to be Wild" by Steppenwolf boomed with an upbeat tempo that began with a photograph of Lieutenant Baxter standing with his arms crossed. I could sense everyone relaxing, and then a burst of laughter erupted. As the song played, individual photographs of each platoon member from 1969 displayed, chronologically by the date they'd arrived at the platoon. As the photographs flashed across the screen, I thought, *We were so young!*

The third part began with a slide displaying "What We Carried and Where We Went," listing the items we carried and the firebases we served on, while the song "Oh, Susannah" by James Taylor played. Many photographs showed firebases and platoon members during our time together, and halfway through, a new song took over—"North to Alaska" by Johnny Horton. The conversation hummed, and there were bouts of laughter in the room during this portion of the presentation.

The songs "Where Have All the Flowers Gone," "Oh, Susannah," and "North to Alaska" had a special meaning to us. The NVA had played these three songs when we were building the Hill. After the songs, the NVA—in perfect English—told the company to leave, surrender, or get wiped out.

Next, a slide displayed the statement "And Then 47 Years Later," and the song "Fire and Rain" by James Taylor played. The photographs flashed across the screen showing each young platoon member while in

AT LAST THE PLATOON IS TOGETHER: THE REUNION

Vietnam, juxtaposed with his current picture. The laughter and talking continued during this part of the video.

Mike turned on the lights when the video finished, and I saw many huge smiles on the platoon members' faces. I told everyone that I'd uploaded the video to the platoon website, and I passed out a copy of a DVD I'd made to each platoon member; they could play them on a computer or television entertainment system. Many of the reunion attendees approached Mike and me, thanking us for creating and showing the video.

Playing the video was the last scheduled event and ended the planned evening. Most continued to use the cash bar next door and remained in the meeting room talking. Several left in small groups and went to the main bar in the hotel lobby. Mike and I sat at a table with Dusty Rhoades, Leslie Pressley, Dennis Stout, Maurice Harrington, and their spouses. Most conversations were about the current day. A "remember when" story didn't come up often, but if one did, the platoon member who told the story spun a humorous tale, which drew much laughter. At 10:00 PM, I informed everyone that we had to leave the room so that the hotel staff could clean and get the place ready for the next day.

Sherrie tired early and went to bed, and Mike left the room to make a quick call home to check on his daughter. I went to the main bar in the lobby and saw Dusty Rhoades, Ray Hamilton, and John DeLoach sitting at a table near the bar. I walked over and joined them. As I sat down, I noticed Cliff Sivadge, Fred Katz, and Don Ayres sitting on stools at the bar, deep in conversation; they'd been inseparable since they'd arrived. I thought it was fantastic that they had reconnected. They'd come to the unit many months after most of the other platoon members present, so, naturally, they must have felt that they didn't have as much in common with them. I'm sure the old-timers felt the same way. But it didn't matter when anyone had arrived at the platoon; they were brothers.

Ray stood up and asked what I wanted to drink, and I told him a bourbon and soda water in a tall glass. He then asked everyone else what they wanted, took their orders, and headed to the bar. John followed Ray to help carry the drinks.

Dusty and I talked about his projects in the Dominican Republic; he and Joanna lived there six to eight months out of the year, and the rest of the year, they stayed in Florida. He and Joanna scuba dived for salvage and had built a small four-apartment building for rentals. Dusty and Joanna led an exciting life in retirement, and I thought both were adventurous.

Our conversation turned to Vietnam, and I told Dusty the story about receiving his letters after he was wounded July 14, 1969. To my knowledge, no one wrote back to Dusty. I didn't know at the time that, by not getting any responses to his letters, he would carry the guilt of that night, when the enemy killed Eldon Reynolds and Juan Ramos at their bunker, for many years.

> It was after you were sent back stateside to recover from your wounds. One evening as we finished our dinner meal, Lieutenant Baxter called over most of the platoon to his location. He thanked us and told us he'd received two letters from Dusty Rhoades. Lieutenant Baxter opened the first letter and read it out loud to the platoon members gathered around him. Then he opened the second letter and read it to the platoon. Your letters told us you were in the States and doing well. The platoon felt relief that you were healing.
>
> We seldom heard from or knew what happened to our wounded platoon members. At the end of the second letter, you asked about Joe Mitchell, Paul Ponce, and Ryan Okino, and how they were doing, and you asked us to write you back. I could sense the sadness that overcame the platoon members. Lieutenant Baxter asked who wanted to respond to you and said he would give them your address. No one spoke up. I didn't want to tell you what happened on August 13 and 15. Mike didn't, either. I thought that, maybe, if you didn't know, you would heal faster and move on with your life, thinking they were alive.

After telling the story, I told Dusty I was sorry that I didn't write him back. Ray and John came back to the table and joined the conversation. As I finished my drink, Mike returned and joined the group. Dusty and I bought the next round for the table, and Mike helped carry the glasses back. We sat there for another hour talking about our lives—nothing serious.

At 11:30 PM, exhausted, I told everyone "Goodnight," and I headed for the room. Mike said calling it a night sounded okay to him, too, and he left with me. We took the elevator to our floors, and, during the ride, we talked about the evening. The elevator stopped on my floor; I exited and told Mike "Goodnight." I walked a short distance to my room, entering quietly, and found Sherrie sound asleep. I undressed, got ready for bed, and fell asleep right away.

Figure 6–9 Tim "Dusty" Rhoades' basic training picture. *Photograph provided by Dusty Rhoades.*

Figure 6–10 Dusty Rhoades at the platoon reunion, July 15, 2016. *Photograph by Tarie Haynie.*

DAY THREE—TOGETHER THE LAST TIME

Wide awake, I rolled over and saw the clock illuminating the time at 4:55 AM. I closed my eyes and repeated the names: "Tufts, Ramos,

Reynolds, Ofstedahl, Swindle, Wellman, Ponce, Mitchell, Anderson, Carey, Morris, Kidwell and Matson." I rolled out of bed, as quiet as possible, so as not to wake Sherrie, and made my morning coffee. I don't think I could make enough noise to wake her; she slept so soundly.

I took a seat at the computer desk and checked the platoon website. As I drank my hot coffee, I made sure the video link worked. I emailed the group photographs to everyone and texted several pictures of Ray that Chris Hamilton, Ray's wife, requested. After two cups of coffee, I got ready for the day. I packed up the technology bag and quietly slipped out the door, rolling my suitcase behind me, and headed toward the elevator to go downstairs for breakfast.

Entering the restaurant, I saw only two travelers sitting alone at different tables next to each other. I took a table at the opposite end of the restaurant. The waitress approached my table carrying coffee and ice water. After a cup of coffee, I stood and walked to the buffet and got the same breakfast as I had the day before.

Halfway through my meal, Ray showed up and took a seat at the table. We had coffee and talked about the events of last night. Ray thought everything had gone well and said that John, Dusty, and he hadn't stayed up much later after Mike and I left. While drinking coffee, we talked about our failed marriages and how lucky we were with our spouses today. Ray told me stories of his many trips to casinos and how well he'd done at the gaming tables. I don't recall his winnings, but it appeared he did well.

Once I was done with breakfast, I walked along the hall to the meeting room to make sure we had coffee and water. When I arrived, the staff opened the doors to the meeting area. I went into the room and set up the scanning station in case anyone had more pictures or documents that didn't get scanned yesterday. During the morning hours, no one came to the room. Sherrie checked in on me before she got breakfast. Mike came in an hour later and sat with me, and we talked, with our conversation drifting to how it seemed that everyone was enjoying the reunion so far.

Worried that something would go wrong, I interrupted Mike while he was talking about the video and commented that I hoped the bus would arrive on time. I was constantly worried that something would happen and spoil the festive atmosphere. Fortunately, the bus came early, at 12:00 PM. I went out to speak with the driver, and he said we would leave at 12:15 PM for the 45-minute drive to the Library; the hotel was in Irving, and the Library in University Park. I went back into the lobby and asked everyone to board the bus parked near the front doors. As each person got on the bus, Sherrie and Tarie handed them their ticket for the Library, and, within 15 minutes, we were ready to go.

Pulling out onto the interstate frontage road, we headed to our destination, and the chatter on the bus settled to a low hum. The drive to the Library interested me, as the driver took a route through suburbs and parks to give us a flavor of the Dallas area. Forty minutes later, we pulled into a bus unloading zone, and the driver stopped. I told everyone to be back at 3:30 PM to load the bus; we had our transportation until 4:15 PM. The group stood and walked off the bus, heading to the Library.

As we filed inside, security stopped us. We lined up, and when it was our turn to go through the security station, we emptied our pockets and walked through the detectors. Once checked and cleared by security, we picked up our items and walked into the main area. An employee greeted us on the other side of the security stations. Two platoon members, Dennis and Leslie, received wheelchairs so that they could withstand the 2½-hour tour.

A Library employee gave us a brief talk regarding the Library and its contents; he said that donations had built the Library. When he finished his speech, he directed us to move into the large center foyer, around 50 feet across and 200 feet long, with rooms to our left and right, and a courtyard to our front. He had us look up at the domed ceiling as a video displayed, and he explained the video to us.

After the video ended, we separated and visited the different rooms that were available. There were many Bush-era artifacts and interactive displays. I found most to be educational and worthwhile to visit. The 9-11 exhibits became my favorite.

Figure 6–11   The reunion group at the George W. Bush Presidential Library and Museum, second day, July 16, 2016. The group was viewing a video that played on the ceiling. *Photograph by Tarie Haynie.*

Sherrie and I hadn't eaten lunch, so, halfway through the visit, we went to a small cafe on the Library grounds with outdoor seating and bought a sandwich and drink. We joined Dusty and Joanna at their table. Sitting in the shade made it more refreshing, but it was still a hot day. Sherrie hates sitting outside to eat! After we ate, I joined Mike and walked around reading and looking at the various objects. After an hour, Mike and I joined Sherrie, and the three of us walked out front because our departure time was getting close.

There were many platoon members and spouses already outside, sitting and talking; the shade from the front of the building provided some protection from the hot afternoon sun. The bus pulled into the same parking spot it had dropped us off at, and everyone walked toward the bus and boarded right away to get out of the heat and enjoy the air-conditioning our transportation offered. Several people were minutes late.

Leaving at 3:40 PM gave us plenty of time to return to the hotel. The driver took a different route on the return trip and drove through affluent neighborhoods; we saw many gated compounds with large homes behind tree-lined streets. Then we turned onto the interstate. Most were quiet on the ride home, and several squeezed in a nap; I know David did.

Sharing a seat, Mike and I talked during the trip back to the hotel. We arrived on time, and once the bus stopped, everyone stood, strolled down the aisle and the bus steps, and walked back into the hotel.

Fred Katz, sitting in front of Mike and me, stood up and said, "You two sounded like an old married couple of 50 years!"

"Fred, that is a compliment," I replied. We laughed and moved along the aisle toward the open door. We stepped off the bus and headed to our rooms to rest and get ready for the dinner meal.

After I got some rest, I told Sherrie that I was going downstairs to check on the room and meal. She said she would be downstairs before 6:00 PM. I rode the elevator to the first floor and walked to the meeting room where the staff would serve the dinner meal. The catering team had the tables set with napkins, water glasses, and flatware, and started bringing the food in as I was checking the room.

As the bartender entered the room, I saw he had on the same hotel-required uniform as the night before, and he started to set up the cash bar before anyone arrived. I ordered a bourbon and soda water to drink while waiting. Halfway through my drink, families came and sat at the round tables with conversation and laughter flowing through the room. I walked around the room, moving from table to table and talking with platoon brothers and spouses. Everyone seemed in good spirits and said they'd enjoyed the Library visit.

At 6:30 PM, I stood at the front of the room and got everyone's attention. I thanked them for coming and told them they had the floor tonight. After my statement, I sat at the closest table. No one volunteered to speak, and the room fell silent. After a minute or two, several family members, Peggy Stout, Dennis's wife, Grace Deppen, Charlie's daughter, and Gloria Alejandro stood and talked about the reunion and First Platoon.

Irene Harrington, Maurice's wife, pushed her chair back as she rose and stated how thankful that she was that she'd come for the reunion.

She said, "In the months leading up to this gathering, Maurice, my husband, kept getting emails from someone named Leslie, and I wanted to know who Leslie was!" The room burst into thunderous laughter because "Leslie" was not a female but a platoon member—Leslie Pressley.

She continued and said, "Maurice and I are the only African-American people in the room tonight, and we don't feel any different." I believed she understood our brotherhood.

After Irene finished speaking, the group stood and gave a round of applause, thanking Mike and me for setting up the reunion.

Alice Council, Chuck's wife, walked up front and said grace. When she finished, we moved by small groups, table by table, to the buffet to fill our plates. The kitchen staff had overdone it again, with enough food to feed twice the number of people. The chef had prepared a delicious meal. I had to say the two meals served were the best buffet meals I had ever eaten.

As I looked around at my brothers and their families, the room buzzed with conversation and laughter during the meal. Again, my emotions overcame me at the privilege of sitting here this night with my platoon brothers and families, after so many years had passed. After dinner, most families moved to the hotel lobby or main bar to sit and talk. I talked individually with Mike and Dusty, walked around the area near the front desk, and conversed with other platoon members, too.

Noticing Chuck Council sitting in an overstuffed chair facing the window with a view of the front entrance, I sat down and joined him. We hadn't had an opportunity to spend a lot of time together during the reunion. We talked about our families, retirement, and our health. Chuck had some health problems, and he appeared a little depressed about it.

Our conversation changed to our Vietnam days, and we spoke about the fire on May 24, 1969, and the letter Chuck wrote home several days later. Even the stagnant pond we drank from after running from the fire was a topic of discussion. It appeared he still harbored some resentment about our involvement in Vietnam, which I believed he had every right to do so.

When I saw Cliff Sivadge, I stopped and talked briefly with him. We talked about how, after returning home from Vietnam, we had both been assigned at Fort Benning at the same time but had never run into each other. I also shared with him about what I remembered when he first joined the platoon.

As we received replacements in September 1969, Mike and I did a quick evaluation by watching and listening to the new guys. You stood out among the replacements. You didn't act like someone who didn't need training. I was surprised at how many new guys came into the platoon with a swagger, and they couldn't be taught anything. You blended into the platoon well. We thought you might make a team leader or squad leader one

Figure 6–12 Chuck Council with the First Platoon in Vietnam, August 13, 1969. *Photograph by Glyn Haynie.*

Figure 6–13 Chuck Council at his home in Portland, Oregon, 2015. *Photograph provided by Chuck Council.*

day. Mike and I made you our understudy. We concentrated on teaching you the fundamentals of survival in the field and combat. Cliff, you were a fast learner and absorbed the information, wanting more. We felt good about our choice.

Sherrie went upstairs at 10:00 PM. The night had flown by, and at 11:00 PM most retired for the evening. I followed soon after the others left. Once in the room and ready for bed, I turned off the lights. Tomorrow everyone would depart, and I wondered if we would stay in touch with each other after this reunion.

Figure 6-14 Cliff Sivadge with the First Platoon in Vietnam, 1970. *Photograph provided by Cliff Sivadge.*

Figure 6-15 Cliff Sivadge on the right with me on the left and Mike Dankert in the middle at the platoon reunion, July 15, 2016. *Photograph by Tarie Haynie.*

DAY FOUR—GOODBYE

The morning came around fast, and I woke at 5:30 AM, sleeping in this morning. After my morning coffee, Sherrie and I headed to the restaurant. As we walked through the lobby, which bustled with travelers checking out, I saw many platoon members sitting in the restaurant having an early meal. I believe more than half of the families left before 10:00 AM; the platoon members who were driving left the earliest. We had breakfast and talked with Dennis and Peggy Stout and learned that they were heading to San Antonio to visit family, 75 miles from our home. We talked about getting together one year when they were traveling to San Antonio.

AT LAST THE PLATOON IS TOGETHER: THE REUNION

When I finished breakfast, I tried to say "Goodbye" to each platoon member and their spouse before they departed. Around noon, Sherrie took David and Tarie to the airport, saying she would call me when she'd dropped them off and was heading home. I continued saying my goodbyes until Sherrie called and said she'd dropped them off at the airport. Only Chuck and Alice, and Dusty and Joanna remained in the lobby, with late-afternoon flights, so I said "Goodbye" and headed to my car.

I traveled to Interstate 35 heading south for my three-hour drive. As I drove home, my mind raced through the events of the last three days. I thought everything had gone well, and the platoon members reconnected and enjoyed being together. It still amazed me how quick the wives bonded and acted as if they'd known each other before the reunion.

Figure 6–16 The platoon members' first day at the reunion, July 15, 2016. Sitting, left to right: Gloria Alejandro (sister of Juan Ramos [killed July 14, 1969]), Maurice Harrington, Mike Dankert, Fred Katz. Standing, left to right: Glyn Haynie, Don Ayres, Cliff Sivadge, Dusty Rhoades, Leslie Pressley, Charlie Deppen, Chuck Council, Dennis Stout, John "Mississippi" DeLoach, and Ray "Alabama" Hamilton. *Photograph by Tarie Haynie, July 15, 2016.*

Figure 6–17 This photograph shows everyone who attended the reunion. Sitting in the first, row left to right: Grace Deppen, Tarie Haynie, David Haynie, Katz Granddaughter, Hannah, Katz Grandson, Christian. Sitting in the second row left to right: Joanna Rhoades, Irene Harrington, Gloria Ramos, Maurice Harrington, Mike Dankert, Fred Katz, and Dixie Katz. Standing in the last row left to right: Sherrie Haynie, Glyn Haynie, Sean Ayres, Don Ayres, Laura Sivadge, Cliff Sivadge, Dusty Rhoades, Leslie Pressley, Charlie Deppen, Chuck Council, Alice Council, Dennis Stout, Peggy Stout, Jan Jacobo, Chris Hamilton, John "Mississippi" DeLoach, Ray "Alabama" Hamilton, Brenda Cartee, and Melanie Deppen. *Photograph by David Haynie, July 15, 2016.*

The reunion met my expectations of being with my brothers of First Platoon. I enjoyed sitting and watching them interact and witnessing the affection they had for each other. To a man, you would believe they were 20-year-olds again, and the connection they had from their Vietnam days in 1969 held true today. They showed genuine interest in their platoon brothers' accomplishments and failures during the years after the Vietnam War. The wives bonded and became friends and family, too. It was unbelievable how quickly they included each other in their families. Many of the wives are in contact with each other to this day.

CHAPTER 7

OVERWHELMED BY RELIVING MY TIME IN WAR

After we got home, our lives went back to the usual routine. My first book, *When I Turned Nineteen*, was published in December 2016, and, after its publication, I reflected on my time in Vietnam. I wondered if my book would honor the 13 platoon members who hadn't come home. Unconsciously, I repeated the names: Bruce Tufts, Juan Ramos, Eldon Reynolds, Jerry Ofstedahl, Robert Swindle, Richard Wellman, Paul Ponce, Joe Mitchell, James Anderson, Danny Carey, Gary Morris, Roger Kidwell, and Willie Matson. Hopefully, my book honors the platoon members who came home, too.

During the months after publishing my book, I started wearing a Vietnam Veteran hat everywhere I went, to signify that I was a Vietnam War Veteran. Wearing my hat was the first time in 48 years that I announced to everyone, outside of a small circle of family and friends, that I was a Vietnam veteran. Most of my neighbors and friends didn't know I was a Vietnam veteran or that I'd served in the Army for 20 years, and we had lived in our community for 18 years. I felt uncomfortable and embarrassed at first but soon learned I should be proud of my time in the war and my 20 years of military service.

As I went about my daily activities outside my home, I noticed many veterans wearing hats signifying the war they'd fought in or the branch of service they'd served in; they were proud veterans. Many people approached me to say, "Thank you for your service," and a few said "Welcome Home." I preferred "Welcome Home" as a thank-you because I believed the individual who stated this understood the Vietnam veteran. When hearing someone say, "Thank you for your service," after 48 years, the statement sounded hollow or rehearsed, as if the individual didn't understand the meaning of their words. However, the recognition was appreciated.

Most veterans I met talked with me and shared their stories of military service and their time in war. I was surprised how open they were, as if it were their first time talking about their experiences. World War II veterans were exceptionally kind when speaking with me. Most said they were sorry for and how unfair the treatment was that Vietnam veterans received from America after they came home. It amazed me that even children would come up to me and thank me for my service. There were times when people would not make eye contact, and on several occasions, I got that disapproving look, or the individual rolled their eyes as if to say, "You shouldn't have done that."

Not long after my book was published, I had a friend, Kevin, stop by to ask questions after he read my book. He hadn't served in the military and was the same age as my oldest son, David. We sat in my home office, and he asked specific questions from passages in the book. My first reaction was to tell him that I didn't want to talk about it. I was stunned by my own statement, because I'd written about my experiences but still felt uncomfortable talking about them. It was a slow process to talk about the events that I wrote about in my book, but I soon understood I needed to talk about my time in Vietnam when asked questions.

At the beginning of June 2017, Mike Dankert, John DeLoach, Tommy Thompson, and I, with our wives, attended the Hill 4-11 reunion in Cody, Wyoming. I believed more platoon members would participate because of our platoon reunion and my keeping them updated about the Hill 4-11 reunion through emails and the platoon website. It was disappointing that more platoon members didn't attend.

For those of us who attended, we had a great time visiting the historical sites of Cody but, most importantly, seeing and being with each other. The topic of going to Vietnam came up, but Mike and I didn't commit to a trip or talk in depth of any arrangements we would make. The topic went away as quickly as it arose during our casual conversations.

After we got home from the reunion in Cody, I started authoring my second book, *Soldiering After the Vietnam War*. I wanted to tell the story of my experience of coming home from the Vietnam War and the choices I'd made. The paths I took after coming back from the war weren't predetermined but decided by events and people I met along the way. These paths included remaining in the Army for a 20-year career. I don't believe that I had an extraordinary career, but my career did coincide with extraordinary times within the Army, and I met extraordinary soldiers, NCOs, and officers along the way.

During September 2017, the Ken Burns and Lynn Novick documentary, *The Vietnam War*, aired on PBS, of which I watched all 18 hours. I contracted with a public-relations firm to talk on 15 national and regional radio shows to coincide with the airing of the documentary. The expectations were that I would speak about my experiences in the war and as a Vietnam veteran and about my book *When I Turned Nineteen*. I spoke for 5 to 30 minutes on each show and found the preparation and the interviews difficult. All the talk-show hosts were gracious and treated me with respect; it was my apprehension about talking about Vietnam that was the problem. During this time, I also had book signings at bookstores and gave presentations at retirement homes and libraries about my book.

A friend of Mike's, Kathi Dow, heard I was doing radio interviews, and she contacted a radio host, Michael Patrick Shiels, of "Michigan's Big Show," to see if he would interview me about my book. Within days of Kathi contacting Mr. Shiels, I received an invitation to be interviewed live on his show. The show is a regional interview show, and I found him to be a courteous host. He talked with me for 20 minutes, and I received an invitation to come back on the show.

On the radio interviews, the hosts asked the same question, "What was a typical day in Vietnam?" At first, my mind raced through many scenarios, searching for the best answer to describe an average day. I answered, "Each evening when we stopped for the night, I prepared my dinner meal of canned beef with spice sauce, crackers with peanut butter and jelly, pears, and kool-aid. As I ate, I looked around at my platoon brothers and thought, *Who's going to die tonight?* Once I finished my meal, I rolled into my poncho liner, and while lying on the hard ground, I felt the fear rush over me as the darkness approached. I closed my eyes for much-needed rest that seldom came.

"When the sun rose, I got out of my poncho liner, thankful I'd survived another day. I made a breakfast of pound cake, peaches, and hot chocolate. Sipping my hot chocolate, I looked at my platoon brothers and thought, *Who's going to die today?* After breakfast, we slung our 60-pound rucksacks onto our backs and started walking, with slow, deliberate steps, through rice paddies, hedgerows, and fields, and into the jungle. And with each step, I wondered, *Who's going to die today?* all the while knowing the platoon was bait to draw the enemy out into the open. This was a typical day in Vietnam."

It became mentally numbing and physically exhausting to watch the documentary, talk on the radio shows about my time in Vietnam, give presentations about my book, and answer questions. Reliving my experiences daily through this month took its toll. I know this is what I'd signed up for, but I didn't expect that the memories and talking about my experiences would have such an impact on me. It seemed I had to relive the horrors and hardships I experienced in Vietnam every day—and in vivid detail.

I recalled, in my younger years, watching World War II veterans being interviewed by the media so many years after their time in the war and thought, *Why are these old guys crying when they talk about their service and the war they fought?* Now, I understand the emotions that these veterans so freely displayed when being interviewed and talking about their time in the war. I believed they'd kept the horrors they witnessed—and the loss of their brothers—suppressed through the years, and as they'd aged, they couldn't hide from the memories anymore. Now it was my turn—and all Vietnam veterans' turn—to freely display our emotions about our time in war and share the loss of our brothers.

By mid-October, I decided to take a break from my Vietnam days and concentrate on finishing my second book. It was mid-January 2018 that I recalled that Mike had mentioned many times over the years that he wanted to go back to Vietnam. At the time, I wasn't interested in returning to Vietnam, but I said I would go with him. After finishing my second book, my interest in going back to Vietnam grew.

A strange emotion, one that I can't explain, emerged—a desire to revisit the locations where my platoon brothers lost their lives. I felt the need to walk the same path they'd walked and stand where they took their last breath. Somehow, I thought this would bring me peace, maybe even closure, for my time in the war, although, I didn't understand how this would happen and that it would seem so unreal after 48 years. While my mind flashed through my year in Vietnam, I repeated the names of The Fallen: "Tufts, Ramos, Reynolds, Ofstedahl, Swindle, Wellman, Ponce, Mitchell, Anderson, Carey, Morris, Kidwell and Matson."

CHAPTER 8

TRIP PREPARATION FOR VIETNAM

Searching for travel agencies in Vietnam that offered a customized tour seemed like a logical start for planning a trip. We were interested in going only to Quang Ngai Province and didn't have the interest to travel around Vietnam as the typical tourist. I found a travel agency in Hanoi that did custom tours. I checked reviews of the agency; most were positive, and I discovered that they had a current and updated Facebook page along with their website. When you viewed these platforms, they were automatically translated into English. This agency looked promising, but I thought, *How strange—to coordinate a visit back to Vietnam with a company located in Hanoi.*

Over the next seven days, "Sunny," from the travel agency, and I corresponded by email. I found that, when dealing with businesses in Vietnam, the person I coordinated with took on an American name; her Vietnamese surname was Quynh. We emailed back and forth; she answered my many questions and gave me a reasonable quote for a car and driver/translator for a five-day visit. Sunny couldn't understand why we wanted to go to Quang Ngai. She said nothing was there! She finally relented and recommended a hotel in Quang Ngai, the Cam Thanh hotel.

Quang Ngai is a province in the South Central Coast region of Vietnam, on the coast of the South China Sea, located 549 miles south of Hanoi and 521 miles north of Ho Chí Minh City (Saigon). The provincial countryside lies along a vast plain running along the coast, with mountains and hills west of the coastline. Lowlands extend inland along the Tra Khuc River, which is the largest river in the province. The Ly Son islands are part of the Quang Ngai Province. Fishing and farming are the primary employment opportunities. Quang Ngai Province is the second-poorest province in the South Central Coast region.

Quang Ngai Province was one of the first provinces in central Vietnam to organize self-defense units in March 1945 and was the site of the My Lai Massacre, March 16, 1968. Quang Ngai was known to be a Viet Cong stronghold during the war and an area of numerous ambushes and attacks against ARVN and American troops. The province produced popular war literature on both sides of the conflict: The now-famous wartime diary by an NVA doctor, *Last Night I Dreamed of Peace: The Diary of Dang Thuy Tram,* was written here, and from an American perspective, Quang Ngai Province was the primary setting of Tim O'Brien's *The Things They Carried*.[1]

While communicating with the travel agency in Hanoi, I continued to investigate the best way to visit Vietnam. Through several Vietnam veterans organizations online, I contacted veterans who had traveled to Vietnam; they recommended that I make arrangements for the hotel and driver directly and not use a travel agency. Several veterans suggested we stay in Hoi An and not Quang Ngai. They told me that, when they traveled in Vietnam several years ago, they found Quang Ngai

---

[1] "Quảng Ngãi Province." Wikipedia. August 09, 2018. Accessed August 10, 2018. https://en.wikipedia.org/wiki/Quảng_Ngãi_Province.

TRIP PREPARATION FOR VIETNAM

still backward, with accommodations and food not up to standards, compared to other cities.

Talking with veterans who had traveled to Vietnam, I found they thought the local Vietnamese living in Quang Ngai were not very friendly toward Americans and may still hold resentment from the war. However, the same veterans said that, overall, the Vietnamese people welcomed returning veterans and all Americans with open arms and were friendly, polite people.

I received recommendations for hotels and car-rental agencies in Hoi An from the veterans. After taking their advice, I booked a hotel in Hoi An and contracted for a driver and car in Hoi An, too, deciding not to use the travel agency in Hanoi. I became determined to handle all the coordination myself.

Now it was time to check on flights from Austin, Texas, to Da Nang, Vietnam. I wanted to fly into Da Nang because it was 20 miles from Hoi An, and an international airport. Saigon (Ho Chi Minh City) airport was more than 509 miles to Quang Ngai. I didn't want a 16-hour car ride after flying for 24 hours. From the hotel to Quang Ngai, for our daily visits, it would be a two-hour drive along Highway 1. To my amazement, I found many connecting flights from Dallas to Da Nang that would meet our requirements.

In mid-February, loaded with information, I called Mike to discuss my plan for returning to Vietnam. Much to my delight, Mike agreed to return to Vietnam with me. We talked for more than an hour about the trip and the locations we wanted to visit. Mike and I didn't talk about our reason to return to the areas we operated in during the war and suffered the killing or wounding of many platoon brothers. Nor did we discuss how it might heal us from our time in combat or possibly make our memories of war more vivid and harmful. We understood each other's reason without asking.

Mike and I talked about visiting the places we operated as a platoon during our time in Vietnam: Hill 4-11, sites of the August 13 and 15 battles, Duc Pho (Fire Support Base Bronco), Fire Support Base Debbie, the rice bowl, Sa Huynh (Fire Support Base Charlie Brown), the bridge along Highway 1, and Chu Lai. We decided that, while we were visiting the Quang Ngai area, we should go to the Son My Memorial, the site of the My Lai Massacre. I thought five days on the ground was more than enough time to visit and three days of travel time, for a total of eight days. We didn't want to spend several weeks in Vietnam that most tours offered; none of the trips went to Quang Ngai, the primary location for our visit.

After another phone call with Mike, it was agreed that we would leave for Vietnam June 14, 2018, and depart for home June 20, 2018, and that I would take the lead on doing the coordination and scheduling for the trip. For me to take the lead would make it easier on Mike and David; I had the time.

Next, I called my oldest son, David, to tell him of my plan to return to Vietnam. David had mentioned to me earlier that, if I ever decided to return to Vietnam, he would go with me. After telling David some of the travel plans and dates, he quickly agreed to go with Mike and me. He did mention that he thought I would give him a year's notice. All I could say was, "Not this time." I told him I appreciated him going, and it would be a fun father-son time. But I had to ask, "Won't you get tired of being with me for eight days?" He said, "No—let's do it!"

I knew I would need a passport for the trip, so I went through our lockbox that we kept in the closet and found my passport; it had expired five years previous. Damn! I used Google to locate the closest location to get a new passport. I called a post office in Round Rock, a city about 10 miles from my house, and the clerk who answered sounded bored. He acted as if it were beneath him to answer my questions. He told me the office opens at 8:00 AM Monday, Wednesday, and Friday and I should show up early to wait in line. They took the first 25 customers and no appointments.

I asked, "What if I'm customer number 26?"

With a sigh, he said, "Come back the next day they are open."

"That will not work for me," I replied and then disconnected the call.

I called another post office in Austin, and the clerk was cheerful and helpful. What a difference between the two clerks! He told me they worked by appointment only, Monday through Friday. I requested and received an appointment for the following Monday. I asked where to get the passport picture, and he told me the best place was Walgreen's. I repeated, "Walgreen's?" He laughed and said, "Yes." I thanked him and told him how impressed I was with his customer-service skills.

That afternoon I went to the Walgreen's close to my home and walked up to the photography counter. A worker approached me and asked if I needed help, and I requested a passport picture. She replied, "You bet." She took several photographs; I paid and left in 15 minutes.

Monday morning, I arrived at the post office 45 minutes early for my appointment. As I walked into the building, I noticed that it was old and dirty, with two people in line. I didn't see signage giving instructions for passport appointments, so I waited in the queue with two people in front of me. Two clerks worked as slow as they could on the customers in front of their positions. I noticed several people entered the waiting area and formed a line to my left.

I asked, "Are there two lines?" to the woman in front of me.

She smiled and replied, "No—that is the passport line."

I said, "I'm in the wrong line. Thank you." I moved to the passport line.

Once I got to the counter, the clerk helped to handle my passport application. She wasn't friendly or talkative but efficient. Being efficient was more essential. I had my application submitted with the supporting documents, including my expired passport, and paid for within 15 minutes and was walking out the front door of the post office. As I pulled onto the main street, my phone rang.

I clicked on the telephone button on my steering column and said, "Hello."

A voice barely audible said, "I need you to come back and sign your old passport."

"On my way," I replied. *Damn. I'd had the passport for 15 years and never signed it.*

I turned around, pulled into the post office parking lot, and parked my car. I jumped out of the car and hurried to the post office. Once inside, I headed to the counter where the clerk was standing. She stopped helping a customer, gave me a disapproving look, and had me sign my old passport. It's a good thing she caught the signature problem before sending the passport to the Department of State. I was told that I should receive my passport in four to six weeks.

Mike and I worked on and agreed to an in-country five-day itinerary for our visit to Vietnam. We would spend the first three days in Quang Ngai, the fourth day at Duc Pho and Sa Huynh, and the fifth day visiting Chu Lai before our departure time to head home. We wouldn't fly out until 10:30 PM, June 20th. I was getting excited about the trip.

During the first week of March, I completed the itinerary and made the airline, hotel, and car reservations, which took a lot of coordination and several weeks to accomplish. Using email for the coordination appeared, at times, cumbersome.

Eventually, I had to activate my mobile phone international calling to call the hotel and car-rental agency to finalize cost and payment. I talked to "Anna" at the car-rental agency, Hoi An Private Car, and she authorized me to pay by PayPal; this made payment easier. Her English was better than mine. Vo Thi, the sales manager of the Belle Maison Hadana Hoi An Resort and Spa Hotel, required my credit card number for a deposit to hold three rooms. During the call to give her the credit card number, communication was difficult, and I needed to repeat the numbers many times. I hoped she got it right.

Once I secured the hotel and car reservations, I made the airline reservations. We would fly from Austin so Mike and David would arrive at my home on June 13, 2018, to catch our flight to Vietnam on June 14, 2018.

Getting a visa to enter Vietnam was the last requirement to begin our journey to the past. I would request a visa to Vietnam thirty days before the entry date. Mike and David mailed me a color copy of their passport, two passport photographs, and the completed visa form. I included my passport and visa form with theirs and submitted the request for the three of us through a company in Austin. This company would send our visa request by a courier to the embassy in Houston and, once approved, send it back by courier. I thought this was better than trying to use the Postal Service for our request. Mike and David would receive a loose leaf visa, and my passport would have a stamped visa.

While going over the list of items to carry, Mike and I talked about what individual articles we should take with us on our trip back to Vietnam. Mike said he would bring the boonie hat that he bought from a "Coke girl" along Highway 1 and wore in Vietnam and that I should bring my peace-sign necklace that Paul Ponce gave me. I thought this was an excellent idea and told Mike that my peace sign needed a little work, but I could bring it. I was afraid to wear it because where the chain slipped through to hold the peace sign was fragile and needed reinforcing.

David had the peace sign and told me that his uncle, Russell Woodward, a jeweler, could fix it so I could wear it on the trip. I thought it was a superb choice to wear the peace sign because it dangled from my neck every step, every hardship, and every horror that I'd experienced while in Vietnam. I was hoping that it still had some of its good-luck power left.

CHAPTER 9

PLANNING OUR RETURN

The Socialist Republic of Vietnam, known commonly as Vietnam, is a Communist country in Southeast Asia. Its capital city is Hanoi since the reunification in 1976. Saigon, once the capital city of South Vietnam, was renamed Ho Chi Minh City and is the most populous city in Vietnam. When the Communist government unified North and South Vietnam, it remained a poor country and politically isolated from the rest of the world. Vietnam's integration into the global economy began in 1986, when the Communist Party of Vietnam initiated economic and political reforms, and in 2007, Vietnam joined the World Trade Organization. Since the acceptance of Capitalism, Vietnam is becoming more open to the rest of the world, and this includes tourism.

Once we arrived in Vietnam, the driver would meet us at the airport and drive us south 30 miles to the Belle Maison Hadana Hoi An Resort & Spa in Hoi An. Staying in Hoi An would make the stay uncomplicated by offering a city with many of the comforts of home and an abundance of English-speaking residents. I heard that American food was readily available, too. The only drawback of staying in Hoi An and not Quang Ngai was the drive, which was two hours one way.

Travel to and from Quang Ngai would take away valuable time that could be used to spend at the sites we wanted to visit. Mike and I discussed an alternate plan by staying in Quang Ngai one night, probably Sunday, which would give us an earlier start and allow us to visit selected locations later in the day. An 11th Brigade veteran who'd served in Vietnam, Alan Brinton, emailed me after he read my first book, and we began corresponding. He told me that he had traveled to Quang Ngai several times and recommended we stay at the Central Hotel there. Alan also provided images of military maps of our area of operations.

Spending hours on the computer, I researched and retrieved the latitude and longitude of each of the locations we wanted to visit. Not having a lot of extra time in Vietnam, we chose sites that held a special meaning for us. From the Hill 4–11 Association website and others, I downloaded old military maps to my computer and visually guessed the location on Google maps to get the latitude and longitude compared to the grid coordinates on the military map. Although I was guessing, I was sure it would put us within 100 meters of the location we wanted to see.

I also downloaded two months, July and August 1969, of Battalion logs, from the Hill 4-11 website to take on the trip. These logs contained daily and hourly reports of Alpha Company location by grid coordinates, and I thought that using these should help us on the ground. David was tasked to bring current maps of Vietnam and a GPS system.

While searching the internet, weeks later, I stumbled across the Americal Division website, which I found had a trove of information. At first glance, the site appeared not to contain much information, but after drilling down, I located the Division Daily Journals and additional sources of information. After reviewing the Division Daily Journals, it astonished me that they were even more accurate than the Battalion Daily Journals.

I contacted Leslie Hines, the division historian for the site, and he was more than helpful. Les answered my questions and sent me a USB flash drive with copies of the division newspaper, the *Southern Cross News*, which had articles about Hill 4-11, Debbie, and Charlie Brown. He included Brigade newsletters and access to division daily logs, which provided military grid coordinates of locations of interest and maps. The USB drive contained photographs and images of the division area maps, too.

Mike and I pored through the records and found additional sites we wanted to visit. It took weeks to go through the information because I needed to sift through hundreds of files; I found that most of the documents didn't pertain to our unit. But the materials we did find were worth the extra effort.

I didn't know how old the Google Maps images were, and forty-nine years later was a long time, even for Vietnam. Fire Support Bases Charlie Brown, Bronco, and Debbie all looked different, and the areas around the old firebases had many more buildings and roads. I marked on the maps the locations that were important to us. Sites we planned to visit began to take shape, and Mike and I were comfortable that the proximity uncovered in the logs matched what we pinned on Google Maps to get the latitude and longitude. The marked areas on the maps could still be off by hundreds of meters because the Battalion and Division logs, in general, gave company locations, not platoon locations.

Mike and I spent many hours discussing the sites and areas we wanted to visit for the year we were in Vietnam. Many events were of significant meaning to us, and those events, to some extent, shaped the persons we are today. For the trip to be feasible, we narrowed our selection to the engagements and the locations where our platoon brothers were killed or wounded, the sites that held special memories of how our friendship began, and where our friendship bonded us together as brothers.

Military maps provided an excellent visual and analysis of the different terrain: the South China Sea coast, rice paddies, fields, mountains, and jungles that we patrolled and where we lived. The Americal Division Daily Journal entries provided the dates and locations by line item that explained the significance of the places Mike and I wanted to visit.

97

Copying only the entries from the division daily journal that pertained to First Platoon and Alpha Company, I then modified some of the entries by changing the abbreviations to the full wording for readability. I found a listing of the abbreviations used in the journals and an explanation of each, on the Hill 4-11 website. (See Appendix A)

Reading the logs, it amazed me how matter-of-factly they were written, with no emotion, just the facts. I understood why, but it still surprised me. It also made me wonder how the person who'd written the entries must have felt when receiving the reports as the action occurred. I discovered that some entries were missing details that I thought were critical to the recorded event.

Included on the USB drive were articles written in the Division or Brigade newsletters during 1969, reporting some of the events that involved First Platoon and Alpha Company. The newsletters provided a unique firsthand account of several of the engagements, incidents, or tasks that involved First Platoon. I transcribed each article as the author published it.

Using our memories and the documentation we'd assimilated, we narrowed the list to the following areas to visit: FSB 4-11, August 13, August 15, Horseshoe, the Fire, FSB Charlie Brown, the Bridge, Bruce Tufts Hilltop, FSB Debbie, the Rice Bowl, the Track, FSB Bronco, and the Combat Center, and, if we had time, the My Lai Memorial. We knew that going to the mountains, to the sites where the enemy killed Kidwell, Morris, and Matson, would be an impossible task, so we didn't add those locations to our list.

FIRE SUPPORT BASE HILL 4-11 AND SURROUNDING AREA

During our time building and securing Fire Support Base Hill 4-11, we endured many hardships and enemy attacks. The company even had the tail end of Typhoon Tess hit during the first week on the Hill. And the day after Tess moved through our area, the NVA played three songs and then told us to surrender, leave, or get wiped out, and then chided us when our artillery didn't destroy them. We would spend the majority of our time around Hill 4-11 and the Quang Ngai area, where we had operated. Viewing the Google Maps, I found Hill 4-11 first, overgrown with vegetation; the surrounding area appeared the same but much more populated than in 1969.

I searched and found the August 13 and August 15 locations where the enemy had killed and wounded half of the platoon. Overall, the areas looked the same—rice paddies and fields—and the hedgerows looked as I remembered them. However, in several areas, buildings and roads had been built that didn't exist in 1969. I added August 8, to show where the platoon went after leaving Hill 4-11 the first time and received a replacement. August 12 is where the platoon met the other units for the task force before moving out the next morning. August 14 is where we blew many tunnels. The August 19 location is where a tank hit a mine, and the platoon stayed back to secure the area around the tank. On January 14, 1970, the site of the firefight that killed Kidwell and Morris, was added to the map, too. (See Appendix B)

THE FIRE

The First Platoon conducted a Combat Assault on a hot landing zone with enemy soldiers to engage. We had been without food and water for more than 24 hours. After landing in the middle of a forest fire, the platoon spent many hours running from the path of the raging flames. While running from the fire, on May 24, 1969, Mike Dankert and I would start our lifelong friendship. When we got to the bottom of the mountain, we were ordered to climb the hill next to it. After our climb to the top, we received resupplies and set up our night defensive positions. The division journal entry doesn't reflect the forest fire that the battalion dropped the platoon into that day. I added the location to the map. (See Appendix C)

FIRE SUPPORT BASE CHARLIE BROWN AND BRIDGE

Fire Support Base (FSB) Charlie Brown was the first FSB that Mike Dankert and I reported to when joining our infantry platoon. Surrounded by water, we had to take a navy boat to get to Charlie Brown. This was the FSB that I reported to and flew from to join my platoon for the first time, and Bruce Tufts was the first platoon member I met.

During our time operating in this area, we guarded the bridge over the Song Dai River that flowed into the South China Sea, and Mike, with the platoon for only several days, went on his first patrol, where they spotted more than 17 NVA soldiers. There was no journal entry for this day.

While at the bridge and FSB Charlie Brown, I got to know Dusty Rhoades, Dennis Stout, Jack Lanzer, Joe Mitchell, Juan Ramos, and Paul Ponce, and the rest of the first squad. I was hoping that the Buddhist Temple, where the strange music played at night, was still located behind the bridge. I don't recall ever seeing the temple, but I thought I would like to visit it during our trip. The military map has FSB Charlie Brown, the bridge, and where the commander sent the patrol, indicated by grid coordinates. (See Appendix D)

OUR FIRST LOSS, FIRE SUPPORT BASE DEBBIE, AND THE RICE BOWL

After our arrival on FSB Debbie, the platoon went on ambushes and patrolled the Rice Bowl area. We had several significant firefights in this area and frequent contact with the enemy. On June 14, 1969, Bruce Tufts was killed while sitting in his position on a hilltop close to FSB Debbie, off Highway 1. We had a substantial engagement with NVA forces on July 2nd. On July 5, a track from E Troop hit a booby trap that blew the APC apart, and it caught on fire, killing two crew members on the vehicle. Mike Dankert, Doc Windows, and a third soldier were detailed to remove the bodies. I used a military map to identify the locations for FSB Debbie, the Rice Bowl, and where the APC hit a mine. (See Appendix E)

FIRE SUPPORT BASE BRONCO

FSB Bronco was the 11th Light Infantry Brigade Headquarters, the Battalion (3/1) Headquarters, and Alpha Company Headquarters location.

We reported to the company headquarters before going to the platoon and when coming back from the unit. FSB Bronco was the location of the Brigade hospital, and many of our wounded and dead were transported by dustoff helicopters to Bronco. FSB Liz was another firebase in our operating area, but Mike and I never served on Liz. Other veterans requested that we stop at LZ Liz during our trip. (See Appendix F)

The 11th Light Infantry Brigade (11th LIB) was formed as part of the US Army's 6th Division during WWI. Activated November of 1917, its elements at that time were the 51st Infantry Regiment, 52nd Infantry Regiment, 16th Machine-Gun Battalion, and the 11th Field Artillery. The 11th LIB was deployed overseas from June of 1918 and returned to the United States in June of 1919. The 11th was deactivated September 30, 1921, at Camp Grant, IL. The 11th LIB was inactive through WWII after the US Army reorganized its Divisions of 2 brigades of 2 regiments into 3 regiments with no brigades.

The 11th LIB is best known for its service with the 23rd Infantry Division, AMERICAL Division during the Vietnam War from 1967 to 1971. The brigade was organized as a separate Infantry Brigade at Schofield Barracks in Hawaii. It was the first element of the 6th Infantry Division and was scheduled to be activated for deployment to Vietnam. This activation was canceled by McNamara. The 11th Light Infantry in early 1967, trained extensively in jungle operations in preparation for deployment to Vietnam. To stress realism in the Vietnam-oriented tactical training, the brigade conducted "live-fire" operations in the rugged, thickly vegetated terrain of the Koolau Mountains on the island of Oahu.

The 3/1 (Always First), 1/20 (Sykes Regulars), 4/3 (The Old Guard) and 4/21 (The Gimlets) infantry Battalions collectively have more Battle streamers, more campaign ribbons, and more years of continuous service than any comparable collection of units in the United States military. The history of these units reads like the battle history of the United States. The Old Guard and Sykes Regulars fought side by side at Gettysburg. More than 100 years later these same storied maneuver Battalions unite as part of the 11th Brigade under the Southern Cross in beautiful Southeast Asia. However, they were not the only units that made up the 11th LIB. E Troop 1st Cavalry, 6th Battalion 11th Artillery, 6th Support Battalion, 6th Engineer Company, 52nd Military Intelligence detachment, and HHC all were major contributing factors that formed the 11th LIB, not to mention that the various units, while not directly assigned to the 11th LIB, were basically support for the 11th LIB.[2]

COMBAT CENTER

Chu Lai was the Americal Division Headquarters. All replacements received their initial in-country training while at the Combat Center and waited for transportation to their units. Wayne, my brother, and I were held at the Combat Center for six weeks before I went to my infantry unit and Wayne went to Korea. Mike and I first met at the Combat Center. I got my rear job at the Combat Center before I departed for home, and Bill Davenport was my replacement, performing the same duties as the Shipping NCOIC. Behind the Combat Center was the military airfield. (See Appendix G)

The Americal Division was formed from Task Force 6814 in New Caledonia, Southwest Pacific, on 24 May 1942. The Americal name was taken from "Americans in New Caledonia" and was the only U.S. Army Division with a name and not a number. Among its many units were three orphaned infantry regiments split from National Guard divisions: the 132nd Infantry Regiment from the 33rd Infantry Division of Illinois; the 164th Infantry Regiment from the 34th Infantry Division of North Dakota; and the 182nd

---

[2] "Swift—True." Home of the 11th Light Infantry Brigade. Accessed August 10, 2018. http://www.11thlib.com/.

Infantry Regiment from the 26th "Yankee" Infantry Division of Massachusetts.

Part of the Americal Division went into action on Guadalcanal on 13 October 1942, the first Army infantry to engage the enemy in World War II. The entire division soon followed to help defeat the Japanese forces on the island.

The Americal Division fought in extensive operations against Japanese forces on Bougainville and the Philippine Islands (Leyte, Samar, Cebu, Bohol, and Negros Oriental). Division operations included amphibious assaults against fiercely defended jungle islands. The division trained on Cebu for the invasion of Japan when the war ended. The Americal Division landed on Japan on 10 September 1945 to take part in occupation duties. The division was inactivated on 12 December 1945 at Fort Lewis, Washington.

For its service in World War II, the Americal Division was awarded the Presidential Unit Citation (Navy) for its actions on Guadalcanal and the Philippines Presidential Unit Citation. Company E, 182nd Infantry Regiment was awarded the Distinguished Unit Citation for its defense of Hill 260 on Bougainville.

After WWII, the 23rd Infantry Division was activated in the Panama Canal Zone on 2 December 1954. It acquired the lineage, heraldry, honors, and traditions of the Americal Division of World War II. The division occupied a joint headquarters with HQ, U.S. Army Caribbean (USARCARIB) at Fort Amador, Canal Zone. The commander of USARCARIB also commanded the 23rd Infantry Division.

The mission of U.S. Army Caribbean was to "Keep the art of jungle warfare alive in the Army." The 23rd Infantry Division supported USARCARIB in its mission as well as to protect the Panama Canal and the Caribbean Basin during the Cold War.

Principal infantry units of the division were the 33rd Infantry Regiment at Fort Kobbe, Panama Canal Zone; the 65th Infantry Regiment at Camp Losey, Puerto Rico, U.S. Army Forces Antilles, and Military District of Puerto Rico; and the 29th Infantry Regiment at Fort Benning, Georgia. The division did not serve in combat during this period. The division was inactivated 10 April 1956 at Fort Amador, Canal Zone.

During the Vietnam War, the Americal Division (23rd Infantry Division) was formed from elements of Task Force Oregon in Chu Lai, Southern First Corps, the Republic of South Vietnam, on 26 September 1967. The division, although designated as the 23rd Infantry Division, was most often referred to as the Americal Division, in keeping with its jungle-fighting lineage from World War II.[3]

Looking at the military maps, printed 50 years ago, I realized the terrain looked familiar. Viewing Google Maps and current satellite images, I thought several of the areas looked the same as they did when Mike and I were there as young combat soldiers. However, I needed to come to terms with myself. I expected that when I walked around the specific sites during our trip, I probably wouldn't recognize the areas as they were burned into my memory 49 years ago. Finding the exact location where the enemy killed my platoon brothers might prove more difficult than I imagined. How would I react when I saw a site? Would it be harder emotionally, or would it ease the memory of losing so many young and courageous men—men who were my brothers?

My trip back to Vietnam was only days away. Sherrie and I went out for lunch and then shopping for some last-minute items for the trip. Before I knew it, she had me in the sporting goods and hunting section of the store, and she started looking at survival gear. I couldn't hold back the laughter while she picked up different items, asking if I needed it for the trip. It's the thought that counts. Hopefully, I wouldn't need survival gear on an almost-50-years-after-the-fact sightseeing trip to Vietnam!

---

[3] AMERICAL HISTORY. Accessed August 10, 2018. https://americalfoundation.org/cmsalf/americal-history.html.

PLANNING OUR RETURN

I believed that I was ready for the trip. I had all the reservations made, and I had the clothing and gear that I needed for the trip. I knew it would be hot while we were there. The weather forecast was 95° F during the day and 77° F at night, with 80% humidity. I was already sweating just thinking about it.

Mike Dankert would fly into Austin Tuesday, June 12, 2018, and David would arrive Wednesday, June 13, 2018. The three of us would depart from the Austin airport on Thursday morning, June 14, 2018, heading to "Nam."

Chapter 10

GATHERING FOR THE RETURN TO NAM

At 2:45 PM on the afternoon of June 12, 2018, Mike Dankert arrived at the Austin airport. When we pulled into the pickup lane, I saw Mike waiting at the curb for passenger pickups. He looked fit and trimmer than the last time we'd been together, and I immediately thought of our younger days and the first time I met Mike.

While waiting to join my infantry platoon, I was delayed at the Combat Center for six weeks with my brother, Wayne, and worked as a supply clerk. One of my assignments was to accept, log, and store duffle bags and other gear for soldiers leaving the country for leave or other purposes. One day in late March, a young soldier walked into the supply room carrying a duffle bag and other gear. At first glance, I noticed that he looked sad and distracted, so I assumed it was combat related.

We greeted each other, and I asked, "How can I help you?"

He stated he was going back to the States for emergency leave and needed to store his gear. I told him, "No problem. I will handle it."

I asked, "What is your name so I can fill out the log and tag your gear?"

He responded, "Michael Dankert."

I asked, "Where are you from?"

"Wayne, Michigan," he replied.

Once I'd tagged and stored his gear, Dankert left the supply room and got into a jeep. The driver drove along the dirt road toward the airfield. I didn't think of this meeting until much later. Mike Dankert and I would ultimately get assigned to the same platoon. I arrived at the platoon first, and after he returned from leave, Mike received his assignment to the platoon.

Mike smiled as he saw us approaching the pickup lane. I jumped out of the car, giving Mike a big hug and helped put his backpack into the back of the vehicle. It's always a terrific day when I can spend time with Mike. On the ride home, we talked about the upcoming trip.

Once Mike was settled into the guest bedroom, we sat at the kitchen table to review the itinerary and the locations we planned on visiting one last time. I poured our first drink of Maker's Mark and soda water, and we toasted to the 13 platoon brothers who hadn't come home. We talked of family and our expectations for the upcoming trip to Vietnam. During the discussion of our trip, we had several more drinks to ease our apprehension of returning to Vietnam.

We had moved past our younger days of drinking Jim Beam and Coke. If I remember correctly, I introduced Mike to what would become our favorite drink, Jim Beam and Coke, at our first stand-down, June 1969. Our stand-down was in Chu Lai, the Division Firebase, allowing the company three days of rest and recuperation from the constant exposure to the elements and fear—this kind of rest was something we didn't get often.

It was during these three days that Mike and I had more time to connect, and we quickly became good friends. We played one-on-one basketball, drank Jim Beam, and sat around and talked about our home life, high school, and friends. We talked several times about the fire. Mike and I found we had a great deal in common. While eating our steak dinners, the conversation turned to our squads, the different people in each, and how our squad leaders took care of us. It's strange how squads mingled little in the field.

Each night Mike and I got together and listened to a band playing current songs and sipped on our drinks—bourbon and Coke. The last song any band played was "We Gotta Get Out of This Place" by The Animals, a downer song to close the night. I played in the continuous poker game while Mike watched. He filled my glass with bourbon and Coke while I played. Mike made sure I made it back to my bunk after the game.

Figure 10–1 Mike Dankert is holding the last of our bottle of Maker's Mark. *I took the photo on June 12, 2018.*

Mike and I talked and drank for hours. Mike pours a stiff drink! We finished our bottle of Maker's Mark and had a great time talking about life, our families, and our time together in Vietnam. The stories never got old. Stories that included Chuck Council and Dusty Rhoades came up often, and they would be in our thoughts during the trip.

David, my oldest son, arrived in Austin at 2:45 the next afternoon on the same flight Mike had taken out of Atlanta a day earlier. As we stopped in the pickup lane, I got out of the car, hugged David, and helped him with his bags. David has been active the last couple of years and was fit and looking great. Mike and I would have a hard time keeping up with him. On the drive home, the three of us talked about the trip and our expectations.

Once home, I went over the itinerary with David. Of course, the locations we'd marked on the maps made little sense to him, but he knew how important they were to us. He kept telling us he was just along for the ride and wanted to share our experiences as we moved from one location to another. Earlier, David confessed to me that he was a little concerned about Mike and me because we'd been known to get a little rowdy when we were together. It's usually Mike's fault. I promised we would behave. I guess no Jim Beam and Coke on the trip!

CHAPTER 11

OUR JOURNEY BACK TO VIETNAM BEGINS

We were up early and prepared for our trip. I must admit that I was excited but also afraid of what memories the journey may bring back that I had locked away since returning home from Vietnam. Mike confided he felt the same way. With the car loaded with our backpacks and Sherrie behind the steering wheel, we were ready for the drive to the airport for our flight from Austin, Texas, to Dallas (DFW) and then on to Seoul, South Korea, for a 14-hour trip. After a two-hour layover in Seoul, we would board the 5-hour flight to Da Nang, Vietnam. Once we landed in Da Nang at 9:30 PM, June 15, our driver would pick us up at the airport, and drive south for 30 minutes to the hotel in Hoi An. The total flight and travel time would be 24 hours. I was excited about going back to Vietnam but dreaded the 24 hours of traveling.

Sherrie pulled into the lane for American Airlines departures, and the three of us jumped out of the car as Sherrie popped the back door open. I grabbed my backpack and slung it over my shoulder, and David and Mike did the same with their packs. Sherrie gave me a long hug and told me to be careful. I believed she was still worried that something would happen to me on this trip.

Going through the Transportation Security Administration (TSA) security was different from the last time, when I'd flown earlier in the month. I had to take more items out of my bag, any food items, all electronics—not just computers—and I had to stand in a cylinder device for a full body scan. I had about 30 protein bars stuffed into my backpack that I had to locate, pull out of my pack, and put into a bin. For some strange reason, I thought I wouldn't find food that I could eat in Vietnam, even though my research showed Western food was available in Hoi An. But I wanted to be prepared, just in case. The TSA agents appeared grumpier than usual, not answering my questions about the changes.

Once through security, we got everything back into our backpacks, and after we put our shoes on, we walked to the departure gate to find seats. The aircraft would be boarding in a short time. Noticing a couple about my age looking at us and listening to our conversations about going to Vietnam, I thought this an excellent opportunity to ask the wife if she would take a picture of the three of us at the start of our adventure. Women my age are typically more tech-savvy than men.

I walked over and said, "Excuse me, ma'am. Could you take our picture?"

"Sure," she replied. I handed her the camera and explained where the button was to snap the photo.

As the two of us walked over to where David and Mike were sitting, she said, "I overheard you talking about going to Vietnam. Is that where you're going? Are you veterans?"

"Yes, we are. Mike and I served together, and David is my oldest son and a veteran. We are going to Vietnam to revisit the areas that Mike and I operated in 49 years ago."

"Sounds like a trip of a lifetime, but I would think it would be hard on you going back," she replied.

"True, but I believe it will be worth it."

Mike, David, and I stood together and held our airplane tickets up with pride, ready for the photo opportunity. She snapped the photograph several times and then approached, handing me my camera.

I looked through the viewfinder, examining the photographs, and said, "You must be a professional photographer. They came out great!"

She smiled and replied, "Thank you, and thank you for your service," and shook each of our hands.

Her husband approached us and said, "Thank you for your service," and shook our hands. They both smiled, told us to have a safe trip, and walked back to their seats.

We sat on the hard plastic chairs and continued talking about the upcoming flights and returning to Vietnam. While waiting, I thought about the encounter with the couple—it was such a different experience with the public from what soldiers received when leaving for Vietnam

Figure 11–1 Mike Dankert, David Haynie, and I. *An unknown traveler took the photo on June 14, 2018, at the Austin airport.*

and especially the welcome they had when returning. It's the greeting we should've received 49 years ago.

The flight from Austin to Dallas was uneventful. Maneuvering through the Dallas airport wasn't as bad as I'd expected, and we arrived at our gate for the plane to Korea without difficulty. I was concerned about making our connection because we had only an hour before boarding the airplane to Korea after we landed. As we walked by the gate, an employee of Korean Air announced our names over the gate intercom system. We looked at each other, thinking something was wrong. We approached the counter, and a woman asked for our passports and visas and then validated each one. Now that we were checked in, she gave us boarding passes to Seoul and Da Nang. We were good to go!

Mike was hungry, so we discovered an Applebee's for our last American meal for a week. We all ordered hamburgers and fries. By the time we finished our meal and paid, it was boarding time. We walked to the gate and got in a line to walk down the ramp to the open door of the aircraft. The Korean Air employees were friendly and efficient moving the passengers through the boarding process. I was impressed.

CROSSING THE POND

We boarded the flight to Seoul without any difficulty, and our excitement began to show, as the three of us chatted while we found our seats. On our seat, we came across a sealed package that included a blanket, pillow, slippers, sleeping face mask, a toothbrush with toothpaste, and headphones. The flight attendants were young, attractive, and identically dressed in a fitted skirt, blouse, and heels. It looked as if the airlines had a height requirement, because all the flight attendants appeared tall. There must have been more than 10 flight attendants on the flight to take care of the passengers' needs.

Snapping on our seatbelts, Mike and I talked about the last time we'd "crossed the pond," flying to Vietnam so many years ago, and how different this flight would be. "Crossing the pond" was the GI term for flying to Vietnam or back home from Vietnam. The enthusiasm of revisiting my past began to build as the plane backed away from the gate.

It didn't take long for our zeal to turn into boredom. I think David was on his fourth movie, and Mike was watching the news and listening to music. I attempted to watch several films but couldn't concentrate enough to watch them—the same for listening to audio books. The seats on Korean Air were reasonably comfortable and with more legroom than airlines in the States. I guessed our economy seating was comparable to business class with other airlines. I envied the first-class passengers—their seats converted into beds.

After being in the air for seven hours, and with five hours to go, I wanted the plane trip to end. Mike and I got up several times and walked around the rows of seats to keep the blood flowing through our old legs. We were served two meals and a snack during the flight. At last, after 14 hours, we landed in Seoul and had a 2-hour layover before our trip

Figure 11–2 Mike Dankert and I waiting in Seoul, South Korea, anxious for our flight to Da Nang. *David Haynie took the photo on June 15, 2018.*

to Da Nang. I must admit my eagerness to visit the areas we patrolled in 1969 had returned, but I dreaded the 5-hour flight.

Mike and I walked around the large, well-lighted terminal to stretch our legs and talked about what we thought our first impression would be when we stepped outside of the airport terminal into the city streets of Da Nang. Would the heat be overwhelming and the strange smells as strong as they were 49 years ago?

In March 1969, my first impressions of Vietnam were of the heat and the smells. They differed from anything I had ever experienced. The heat was unbearable, as if the sun were closer to the ground in Vietnam than back home. And the stench was a mixture of burning human waste, diesel fuel, jet fuel, strange food, and various human odors. I can still smell that terrible aroma all these years later.

CHAPTER 12

LANDING IN-COUNTRY THE SECOND TIME

Our flight to Da Nang started to board, so David, Mike, and I grabbed our packs and walked to the line of passengers for our designated group. We boarded the airplane in the same order: David first, then me, and then Mike. David had the window seat, I, the middle, and Mike, the aisle seat. As I followed David and the line of passengers to my seat, I felt sensations of anticipation move through my body as I thought of the airplane landing in Da Nang in 5 hours and Mike and I walking into the Vietnam night air for the first time in 49 years. Again, the Korean Air personnel were efficient and had the plane loaded and ready for take-off in a short time.

The flight to Da Nang was full and as dull as the previous flight to South Korea and seemed almost as long. At last, a flight attendant announced for us to prepare for landing at the Da Nang International Airport. Mike and I, with tired, half-opened eyes looked at each other and smiled. We didn't need to say anything—the look and smile said it all. As the plane descended, I peered over David's shoulder to see out the window. It was dark, but I could see Da Nang, a well-lighted city like any other I had observed from the sky.

Within minutes, the airplane wheels touched down on the runway, and the sensation of excitement shook my body; I felt giddy, like a little kid going to the amusement park for the first time, entering the unknown. I don't know if my anticipation was dread, fear, or the hope of finding the real reason why I was coming back.

The plane rolled to the gate and stopped. We clicked open our seat belts and stood. I started getting our packs out of the storage bin and handed them to Mike. With my sore, cramped legs supporting me, I moved toward the exit door, following the crowd of passengers, with Mike and David following me, into a large, bare, poorly lighted, windowless room with many checkpoints. I didn't notice any décor or art on the walls, and there was no seating for passengers waiting to go through security.

Only a handful of checkpoints had what appeared to be a uniformed military employee behind the counter. The line was long and moved slowly—completely different from the efficiency we'd experienced with the Korean Air personnel. For some reason, as I watched the soldier checking passports, I became nervous about entering Vietnam, but the sense of dread soon passed.

When it was my turn to pass through the checkpoint, I stopped and set my backpack on the floor. The soldier didn't look at me or say a word as I handed him my passport with my visa stamped on the inside. He scanned the passport, referenced my visa number on a computer screen, stamped the visa, closed the passport, and handed it back to me without looking at me or saying a word. I said, "Thank you" and walked through the checkpoint as fast as my legs could move.

However, I needed to go through the screening process for my bags. Another worker dressed in what appeared to be a military uniform instructed me to remove my computer from my backpack, take off my shoes, and place everything into a bin that rolled through the x-ray machine. As I did what he instructed, I watched the second worker, dressed the same as the other workers, peer through the x-ray machine as the bags rolled under the viewing mechanism. Once my pack and electronics went through the screening, I grabbed my gear and moved forward to join David.

A sense of relief flooded over me, knowing I was now in Vietnam and free to go where I wanted to travel. As David and I waited, Mike walked through the checkpoint with the same experience and joined us.

Following the stream of passengers to the terminal exit, we found another checkpoint waiting for us just before the sliding glass door that led to the front road of the airport. Another soldier operated the checkpoint, which had an x-ray machine. I placed my pack on the conveyor belt as instructed and followed it as it bumped along the metal rollers. The conveyor stopped, and the soldier peered through a screen looking at the contents of my pack and never once looking at me. Once my backpack cleared the machine, I picked it up and slung it over my shoulders, ready to venture into the streets of Vietnam and find our driver.

Anna at the Hoi An Private Car agency had informed me that the driver would be waiting for us, holding a sign with my name and the agency name on it, and that I should look for that sign. During our coordination, I requested a photo of the driver and vehicle but never received one.

Walking through the open sliding glass door into the front of the terminal, I noted that the strange smell of 49 years ago I was expecting was not present; the odors were different this time, not as unpleasant as my first arrival. The air was warm and humid, and I felt my shirt clinging to my body, already wet with sweat. I was intent on finding the driver and forgot that I'd left David and Mike at the checkpoint as I ventured further into the large group, with hundreds of people waiting for arriving passengers.

Scanning the crowd, I looked at the many signs that were being held high in the air displaying names. I heard a voice behind me yelling,

"Dad, Dad" and then "Glyn!" I turned and saw it was David, and the look on his face showed his impatience with me because I'd broken one of our rules—always stay together.

David said, "Dad, you left us, and Mike is still at the last checkpoint. I had to yell your first name to get you to stop."

I stopped and said, "I'm sorry. I'll wait here." Just as I spoke, Mike walked up behind David with a broad smile that exposed his excitement.

As I started to read the signs, I spotted a Vietnamese man about 40 years old, smoking a cigarette and holding a sign with the name "Haynie" displayed, along with the car-agency name. I yelled to be heard above the noise of the crowd to Mike and David to follow me, and we walked through the throng of people until we met up with the driver. Everyone said "Hello" to the driver and shook hands; he introduced himself as Binh. I noticed right away he didn't speak any English, as he indicated for us to follow him to the parked car.

Figure 12–1 I took a quick photograph of the Da Nang airport entrance as we were leaving. *I took the photo on June 15, 2018.*

LANDING IN-COUNTRY THE SECOND TIME

We walked through a poorly lighted parking lot until Binh stopped at a van that could seat nine passengers, and it had the name of the car agency printed on the side. It was larger than I'd contracted for. I was expecting an SUV, but a van would work. As we climbed into the vehicle, Binh extinguished his cigarette, pulled himself into the driver's seat, started the van, and drove out of the parking lot for the 30-minute drive to the Belle Maison Hadana Hoi An Resort and Spa Hotel in Hoi An.

Through my research, I'd learned that there were hardly any acts of violent crime in Vietnam. However, the theft of personal property was extremely common. One travel site warned the traveler that a trick

Figure 12–2 Loading into the van after our arrival in Da Nang with our driver, Binh. *I took the photo on June 15, 2018.*

criminals used was to impersonate that he was your driver, and once you were in the car, he would drive to an isolated location and rob you. I had told Mike and David about this method before we departed for Vietnam. With this knowledge, I attempted to be aware of what was going on around me as much as I could, which included trying to ensure the driver was who he claimed to be. With Binh carrying the placard with my name, and the vehicle having the company name on it, I felt safe about getting into the van.

As we rolled down the highway, David, Mike and I peered through the van windows, taking in the sights. I immediately noticed that Vietnam had progressed over the decades—the city had tall buildings, lighted roads, and motorcycles, trucks, and cars everywhere. The town was bustling with Friday-night activities, sizeable restaurants, clubs, and small, diner-type restaurants filled with patrons, and some shops were still open for business at this late hour. Most of the residents I observed wore western-style clothing. I didn't see anyone wearing traditional dress, what we referred to 49 years ago as pajamas and the conical straw hat.

I had been to Da Nang only one time during my tour in Vietnam. In September 1969, Bill Davenport and I found a cache of weapons and had received a three-day in-country Rest and Recuperation (R & R) in Da Nang.

> Bill and I exited through the rear ramp of a C-130 and walked to the Da Nang terminal. We checked in at the front desk, and the Marine NCO provided instructions for bus transportation and our quarters. We arrived at the Air Force part of the base and found out what many soldiers had never discovered. The Air Force knew how to live! Air Force quarters (living area) were large, clean, and comfortable, with a hooch girl, a Vietnamese woman, assigned to keep your room clean. The best part was the mess hall; every meal had dozens of entree choices and many desserts. Army mess halls never had as many food choices at any meal. I bet I put on five pounds in those three days. Bill and I spent plenty of time at the mess hall. We went to the movies during the day and the NCO club at night. We didn't even cause any trouble. The three days went by fast, and before we knew it, we were back at Duc Pho, picking up our weapons and gear and waiting to catch a supply

chopper back to the platoon. We never ventured off the base or saw the city of Da Nang from the ground.

After we traveled through the half-lighted busy streets for 25 minutes, Binh turned the van into a dark, narrow alley and crawled at a slower pace. David, Mike, and I looked at each other and quietly acknowledged something might not be right. My fear that a rogue criminal driver had picked us up surfaced. Within several minutes, the driver pulled onto a lighted, busy street and then turned into the front entrance of a hotel. I was relieved but felt guilty of suspecting our driver for any wrongdoing. It was the wrong hotel. The driver talked to a parking attendant, and he told him that our hotel was the next one down the street.

Binh steered the van back onto the busy road and made another left into the correct hotel entrance. The three of us jumped out of the vehicle and grabbed our packs. We'd decided during our trip-planning sessions on how much we would tip the driver and designated David as the "driver tipper" during our travels. David handed Binh a tip while I talked with him about picking us up the next morning at 7:00 AM. It appeared he understood, so we walked into the hotel entrance as he drove away.

Standing in the hotel lobby, I found it decorated with Vietnamese art and furnishings with western-culture touches everywhere. The wood furniture was dark, and the sofa and chairs had red upholstery. Red is a significant color in Asian culture; it symbolizes good luck, prosperity, joy, and long life. The lobby was hotter than the outside, with no air conditioning; many of the ceiling fans stood motionless, instead of moving the hot air around the room.

As sweat trickled down my face and my shirt clung to my damp body, I approached the desk clerk, a young man about 25 years old, wearing black slacks, a white button-up shirt, and black dress shoes. He asked how he could help us in perfect English—what a relief! I gave him my name and told him that I had three rooms reserved. He looked at the computer and searched for and found my reservation.

The desk clerk then gave us our room numbers and asked to see our passports. Scanning our visa numbers into a computer took several minutes, and then he returned our passports and gave each of us a room key with the internet password. The hotel had free Wi-Fi service for their guests.

The desk clerk was eager to talk more, but we were ready for bed because it was 11:30 PM, and we were exhausted from the long travel day and the time change. I requested some bottled waters; he left the desk, returned, and gave each of us two bottles. When he handed me the bottled water, I asked if the rooms had air conditioning, and he smiled and said, "Yes, of course."

After saying "Goodnight" to the desk clerk, we headed to our rooms. Our rooms were on the third floor, on the side facing the pool. I selected these rooms because they faced away from the main road and were advertised as being noise free. Walking through the hallway, I thought it was hotter in the hall than in the lobby, and I hoped the air conditioning in the room worked. We stopped outside our rooms and said "Goodnight"; we agreed to meet for breakfast at 6:30 AM at the hotel restaurant.

Once in the room, I figured out that I needed to put the key card into a card holder on the wall located by the door—this allowed me to run the air conditioner, which I cranked up, and to utilize the lights in the room, too. Removing the keycard from the holder to take with me when I left the room turned off all the lights and, unfortunately, the air conditioner.

The room was clean and well furnished with a queen-sized bed, two nightstands, two chairs with a table between them, a computer desk, and a wardrobe. Opening the mini-bar refrigerator, I found it was full of soda, candy, and other snacks, at a cost to the guest.

The bathroom was well equipped, but the bathtub/shower was high off of the ground. Climbing in and out of the tub was a dangerous activity each morning. I soon learned that, when I took a shower, the water splashing off my body would flow from the top of the bathtub and into a drain on the bathroom floor. This unique design was a topic of discussion for the three of us the next morning at breakfast.

When I opened the patio door, the room filled with the hot, humid night air as I looked at the bright, star-filled sky. Looking downward, I saw a clear-water-filled swimming pool below my balcony. I said out loud, in a quiet voice to no one in particular, "I'm back!" I was exhausted, so I was soon in bed, trying to get some sleep before our first big day tomorrow.

Figure 12–3 The Belle Maison Hadana Hoi An Resort and Spa Hotel. *I took the photo on June 16, 2018.*

CHAPTER 13

WITH A SUNRISE IN VIETNAM, THE ADVENTURE BEGINS

Waking at 4:00 AM, on my first morning in Vietnam after 49 years, June 16, 2018, I was still exhausted because I didn't sleep well. While lying in bed, I watched the sunrise and thought about the beginning of our adventure—and about the reasons that had made me return. I was excited to return to Hill 4-11 this day. When planning the trip, Mike and I agreed that the *Hill*, as we referred to Fire Support Base Hill 4-11, would be our first stop.

As planned, I met Mike and David downstairs at 6:30 for breakfast. The hotel had an incredible free morning meal for guests, and the breakfast bar offered western food, pastries, fresh fruit, and local Vietnamese cuisine for anyone with an enormous appetite. There was an open window at the kitchen to order an omelet just the way you liked it. Located in the far back right corner of the restaurant was a fresh coffee and tea station. As I looked around the breakfast area, I realized that I had no worries about finding food I could eat.

Each morning I had my fair share of coffee, fruit, and pastries. One of my favorites was the fresh pound cake, and it went well with my coffee. The pound cake reminded me of my time here in 1969, drinking hot chocolate and eating C-ration pound cake and canned fruit for my breakfast each day, the best meal of the day. After eating, we went to the lobby to wait for Binh.

Figure 13-1 Mike Dankert and I waiting for the driver on our first morning (note David in the mirror behind us) at The Belle Maison Hadana Hoi An Resort and Spa Hotel lobby. *David Haynie took the photo on June 16, 2018.*

Everyone we'd encountered at the hotel so far had treated us with respect and strived to be a good host. I soon learned that most of the locals, including the hotel staff, had the same four questions: "Where are you from?" "How long will you visit?" "Where will you go today?" and "Are you having a good time?" I suspected they were taught these questions as an attempt to express their interest while you visited

Vietnam. Answering their inquiries, I wasn't sure they understood my response. I regretted that I didn't take time before the trip to learn a little conversational Vietnamese.

At 7:00 AM, the driver, Binh, arrived on time, and we loaded into the van for the 2½ hour ride to Quang Ngai. David sat up front next to the driver, while Mike and I sat on the bench seat directly behind Binh and David, which would become our typical seating arrangement each day while traveling. Once we'd settled into our seats, the driver glided the large van onto the city street and into the fast-moving traffic.

As we drove along the road, we saw hundreds of motorcycles and scooters and a few cars. There were more trucks than cars. Motorcycles were used to transport everything and came in many types. Motorcycles as a dump truck, or carrying a family, or carrying cargo, or carrying livestock—there was a motorized bike to fit any transportation need.

Figure 13-2 A family of four driving to town. *David Haynie took the photo on June 16, 2018.*

In a short time, we were on Highway 1, a paved four-lane highway, unlike the two-lane mostly dirt road that was Highway 1 in 1969. Today a long stretch of Highway 1 to Quang Ngai was a toll road. I'm not sure of the cost, but Binh stopped each morning and paid the toll. The car-rental agency included the tolls, taxes, and fees in the payment I made.

Mike and I watched out the windows and commented on changes to the countryside and the Vietnamese people. We pointed our cameras and snapped pictures as the landscape sped by the moving van. Few young people were working the rice paddies, and the rice fields looked larger than we remembered. It amazed me that they appeared to work the rice fields and use water buffalo—just as they had 49 years ago.

Not once did I see a worker using machinery for planting, tending, or harvesting crops.

After traveling for 30 minutes, the van rolled to a stop in front of a small grocery store. Binh got out, went to the counter to purchase some items, and returned with bottled water and ice. After breaking the ice into smaller pieces, he filled the chest with the ice chunks and water. Stopping at this store became a morning ritual, and Binh would buy, ice, water, fresh fruit, and several boxes of cheese crackers for us to consume while traveling. Each morning after he made his purchases, I reimbursed him for his kindness.

The three of us milled around, talking and taking more photos. I was determined to snap pictures at every opportunity and not miss anything, knowing that I was not coming back to Vietnam. Once the ice, water, and fruit were in the chest, we loaded back into the van and headed south, toward Quang Ngai.

Figure 13-3 Mike Dankert, Binh, and David Haynie at the store we stopped at each morning for ice, water, and snacks. *I took the photo on June 16, 2018.*

Binh asked if we were going to My Lai, and I said, "No. We're going to Quang Ngai." His question surprised me because I gave Anna, at the car-rental agency, our itinerary and asked her to give it to the driver. The itinerary had the latitude and longitude of the areas we were visiting each day. Handing David my mobile phone with the location and directions already displayed on Google Maps, I told him to show Binh. When David showed Binh the site we were traveling to, he seemed confused as to where we wanted him to drive.

It became apparent that Binh and I were not communicating well, so, while driving, he reached for his mobile phone and called his office, and after talking for a couple of minutes, he handed me his phone.

I said, "Hello."

A man speaking excellent English asked, "Are you going to My Lai?"

"No. We're going to Quang Ngai, and I have the locations on my mobile phone with Google maps and GPS displayed," I replied.

The man said, "I understand. Give Binh your phone, and I'll explain to him what he needs to do."

"Thank you," I replied. I then returned the phone to Binh, and he talked for a minute and hung up.

I handed my phone back to David, and, from that point forward, Binh and David coordinated using my mobile phone with the Google Maps GPS without any problems. David was a great navigator. After the first day, David had learned to say "left," "right," "straight," and "bathroom" in Vietnamese. Mike and I thought the word for "bathroom" was the most important to learn.

Traveling south down Highway 1, I looked for landmarks or buildings that would be familiar. Towns that had familiar names—Tam Ky and Chu Lai, to name a couple—blurred by as we sped along the highway heading south. I observed that the countryside seemed the same—rice fields or other crops as far as you could see, without many structures present. But the towns and cities had grown and prospered, with shops that sold different goods or provided a service lining both sides of the highway for miles.

Approaching and crossing the Song Tra Khuc River, Mike and I looked at each other, agreeing that we were now in our area of operations and not far from the Hill. I felt uneasy but eager to see the Hill as we drove through Quang Ngai. I watched the motorcycles, cars, and trucks maneuvering through the heavy traffic, and I peered into shops as we drove by heading west, toward the Hill. David kept the driver on the correct course, giving him instructions on when to turn and what road to take.

CHAPTER 14

A ROLLER COASTER RIDE OF EMOTIONS

As we turned onto a dirt road and drove toward a hill, our anticipation increased, and Mike and I began talking about our time in this area and the meaning that Fire Support Base Hill 4-11 had to us. The dirt road led directly to where the entrance to the firebase was when we built the Hill, and I thought it might be the same road the engineers made in July 1969. Mike and I had traveled on this road many times. While the van bumped along the old dirt road, I thought of the day we arrived on the Hill.

This "Hill" defined our platoon and the area of operation we patrolled. At Fire Support Base Bronco, on the morning of July 8, 1969, in a column of twos, our platoon entered the rear of the Chinook helicopter. It lifted off, taking us to secure the new firebase location on a hill seven miles west of Quang Ngai City. The Chinook landed without receiving enemy fire, and we exited through the rear door as soon as it dropped. We moved up the hill, encountering many mines and booby traps along its crest.

Figure 14–1 Lieutenant Baxter, Alpha Company's First Platoon Leader, taking a break while the platoon and company started building the new firebase Hill-411. *Photo provided by Mike Dankert.*

From the first day our company began building the firebase on this hill, it evolved to support our infantry battalion, artillery, engineers, and other support units. When the platoon left the hill, we patrolled the villages, hedgerows, fields, and mountains that surrounded our new firebase for weeks at a time. And we were happy to return to its safety for a well-earned rest.

Figure 14–2 FSB Hill 4-11 after March 1970. Note fully constructed bunkers and no vegetation. *Louis Bohn took the photo, provided by the Americal Division Association Historian.*

Arriving at Hill 4-11, the driver parked the van, and we stepped out of the open sliding door, anxious to climb the hill. The first thing I noticed was the heat. It was like walking into an oven, and I immediately began to sweat, which was a familiar sensation. I looked around, and nothing appeared the same. The hill was completely overgrown, and there was a construction crew, moving dirt, at the bottom of the hill not far from the original entrance to the fire support base.

Standing below the Hill, I experienced unimaginable awe as I stared at the crest of the Hill. This ground was the same location where Mike and I stood and walked 49 years ago as 19-year-old combat soldiers. I gasped as hundreds of thoughts, stories, and images buzzed through my mind all at once. I was overwhelmed with emotions that I couldn't comprehend and was moved to tears with happiness and sadness at the same time.

Figure 14–3 Hill 4-11 southeast side, near the entrance. *I took the photo on June 16, 2018.*

At first, we roamed at the base of the hill, taking pictures and talking about where the entrance to the firebase was and the location of the platoon bunker positions. Mike and I decided to walk around toward the east side of the Hill to get a view of where our position was when we built the Hill. Walking across some crops and into an overgrown thicket, headed for the front of the Hill, we ran into a fence. Peering through the overgrowth, we saw a large home with a red tile roof sitting against the hill at the location where we thought our bunker would've been, above the roof line.

We couldn't get a good enough view of the east side from our current location, so Mike and I walked back the way we came and approached two women working their crops. Right away, I noticed they wore western-style clothing but also the straw conical hat that I remembered. The younger woman started talking in a rapid cadence, and she sounded angry. Having no idea what she was saying, I tried to talk to her, but she kept on talking. By her tone and body language I sensed she was mocking us but didn't know why. The older woman working with her looked at Mike and me and shook her head as she rolled her eyes. I think she felt sorry for us.

Attempting to ease the situation, I asked if I could take her picture by holding up my camera and pointing at her. She nodded her head "Yes." The older woman nodded "Yes," too. I took several photos of the two women. After snapping their picture, I asked for permission to cross her field, by using my fingers and moving them as if walking and with my other hand pointing in the direction we wanted to travel, to get to the front of the Hill, and she shook her head "No." She was still talking as Mike and I walked away toward the van, disappointed that we couldn't get around to the east side of the hill.

Mike stopped by the van and was talking to David as I continued walking toward the four construction workers loading dirt into a dump truck. As I passed the front loader, I found a trail that was three to four feet wide, well used, accessible, and leading straight up the hill. Stopping, I turned and asked the crew for permission to walk up the path, using the same hand gesture, moving my fingers to indicate walking, and I pointed in the direction I wanted to travel. The driver of the front loader nodded his approval.

Figure 14–4 Two women working their crops on the southeast side of the Hill who declined our request to walk across their field. *I took the photo on June 16, 2018.*

Calling out to Mike and David, I told them I'd found a trail that we could use to walk up the Hill. They joined me, and the three of us followed the well-worn path to the top. Along the route, we found several small public cemeteries among the thick brush and trees. Nothing was familiar. It appeared that part of the Hill had been bulldozed years ago, creating a high mound on the west side.

The Hill was thick with trees and underbrush, unlike the barren, booby-trapped Hill we'd climbed the first time on July 8, 1969. At one point, David stopped walking and said something kept grabbing his ankles. Mike and I laughed and shouted at the same time, *"Wait-a-minute vine!"* These vines had tiny thorns and would latch onto your clothing, causing you to stop for a minute to remove or cut the vine so you could continue walking. Now, *that* was familiar!

Mike and I moved off the trail and maneuvered through the thick stand of tall, thin trees to determine where we thought our bunker position was. Fighting to get through the brush, we looked around and then agreed that where we were standing should be the spot we'd spent a month together while building FSB Hill 4-11. As we looked east through the trees, about 75 feet below us, we could see the red roofline of the house we'd seen at the base of the hill earlier. Standing shoulder-to-shoulder silently for several minutes, Mike and I began sharing some memories of our time on Hill 4-11.

Figure 14–5 David Haynie is checking out one of the small cemeteries on Hill 4-11. *I took the photo on June 16, 2018.*

One of my favorite memories of our time together on the Hill was when we finished sandbagging the bunker.

> Mike laid the last sandbag on the roof of the bunker in the early evening, and we decided to sit back, rest, and enjoy a Coke. As young guys do, we talked smack to each other and used the roof of the bunker as a wrestling ring. We met in the center of the "ring" and grappled to get the best takedown position. I had a good-enough position to bring Mike to the mat and went for the pin and the win (now, if Mike was telling this story, I was the one

getting pinned). At that moment, we heard a loud swoosh sound right over our heads. A 75mm round exploded hitting the west side of the Hill. We crawled to the end of the roof, lowered ourselves to the ground, and got inside the bunker for cover. Once safe, we laughed and claimed the other lucky that the NVA had saved them.

Now here we were, two older men, standing, hopefully, at the exact spot where we were young soldiers and becoming best friends. Who knew at the time that this friendship would continue through the years? Hill 4-11 and our year together in Vietnam secured our bond for life. Tears started to cloud my eyes, so I told Mike that we should try to find the position of Dusty Rhoades, Chuck Council, Eldon Reynolds, Juan Ramos, and Ryan Okino. Without saying a word, we walked back along the trail, heading south to find the location.

As we walked along the trail, I recalled Mike had his twentieth birthday where we'd been standing moments before.

Figure 14–6 Mike Dankert and I standing where our position was on Hill 4-11. *David Haynie took the photo on June 16, 2018.*

On the night of July 19, 1969, Mike and I moved outside the bunker for the first guard shift of the night and took up our positions, sitting next to each other, facing the concertina wire to our front. Visibility was better outside the bunker. I got out two cans of pound cake, opened both, and handed one to Mike. I told him, "Happy Birthday" and that this was his birthday cake. As we ate the pound cake and sipped on unsweetened Kool-Aid, Mike remarked how America had launched Apollo 11 several days previous to go to the moon—but we couldn't end a damn war. Mike's birthday ended with no interruption from the enemy, so he had a happy birthday.

Moving off the trail, we walked through the trees and brush to where we thought their position was likely to be. While surveying the area, Mike and I agreed we were probably standing close to the location of their bunker. It was at or near this spot, July 14, 1969, that the enemy attacked the Hill and their bunker, killing Juan Ramos and Eldon Reynolds and critically wounding Dusty Rhoades. Doc Windows and Ryan Okino provided life-saving medical care to Dusty before carrying him back to the dustoff.

Eldon Reynolds had arrived at the platoon two weeks before being killed on Hill 4–11. He was from Weatherford, Oklahoma, 20 years old, and married to Donita. I didn't know him well because of his short time with the platoon and him being in the first squad. Dusty Rhoades and Chuck Council told me of their trust of Eldon and how well he'd fitted in with the squad.

Juan Ramos was an old-timer, in Vietnam for five months when I arrived at the First Platoon. He was quiet, almost shy, but ready to share his experiences on surviving in Vietnam. Juan took the time to teach me the skills I needed. He was 21 years old, from Uvalde, Texas, and everyone liked him. If things got tough, you wanted him with you.

As I observed the place where their bunker would've been, I spoke to Juan and told him that his younger sister Gloria, an honorary member of First Platoon, and niece Lari give their love and that he would always be in their hearts and never forgotten. Next, I told Eldon that I communicated with his wife, Donita, by email, that she was doing well, and that she'd spoken to your family about the platoon website and reunion. I silently said my goodbyes to Juan and Eldon, and I told them they would never be forgotten.

In silence, we walked through the thicket of brush and trees and joined David on the trail. David commented that he hadn't heard or seen any wildlife or birds. We told him that during our time in Vietnam in 1969, we had the same observation, recalling not seeing wildlife or birds, either. The only birds I remembered where the white birds that landed on the water buffalo for a meal of insects.

While in Vietnam, the days and nights were always surreal to us in their silence. There was one exception: at nights the Tokay Gecko lizard would call out with a distinctive sound "fuckyou" all night long. Hence, the name the soldiers in Vietnam gave the lizard, "fuckyou lizard." During our stay, we never ventured out at night to hear the call of the Tokay Gecko lizard.

Figure 14-7 Mike Dankert and I are standing in the general area where Juan Ramos and Eldon Reynolds died on Hill 4-11. *David Haynie took the photo on June 16, 2018.*

Deciding to head along the trail the same way we'd walked to the top, Mike suggested we drive around the Hill and approach it from the north side to see if we could get a better view. David and I agreed. The three of us walked silently down the trail to meet up with Binh.

When we passed the four construction workers, the bulldozer driver called out to us. We assumed he wanted us to stop. We stopped, and the bulldozer operator with three other workers gathered around us talking in Vietnamese, and we had no idea what they wanted. After a couple of minutes, David and I continued to walk toward the van while Mike stayed and took a picture with the youngest worker. After taking a photograph, he joined us at the vehicle.

Figure 14–8 Mike Dankert talks with the workers before taking a picture on Hill 4-11. *David Haynie took the photo on June 16, 2018.*

We drove around the Hill to the north side and began our trek, with the top of the Hill our objective. We had to trudge past several homes that had barking dogs, but not aggressive, and I saw several of the female residents looking at us as we strolled along the path, without them acknowledging our presence. As we continued up the trail, we had to move around a large cemetery to reach the top of the Hill. The rocky terrain, with not much vegetation, looked familiar on this side of the Hill, which is where 2nd platoon had their positions, and 3rd platoon positions ran along the west side of the hill. It was strange how the south side of the hill was overgrown with trees and brush, but the north side was as familiar to us as when we'd climbed the Hill 49 years ago. After studying the area, we saw signs of a significant fire and deduced that this was why this side was without vegetation.

Talking while climbing to the top of the Hill, Mike and I continued to explain the significance and our memories of Hill-411 and the surrounding area to David. Not only were there no signs that any US military units had ever lived here, but we also noticed that the village of Tu My, what we called *Tin City*, no longer existed, and there were no indicators the resettlement village ever did. At the base of the south side of the Hill, the direction we walked from, was a large cemetery with hundreds of grave markers and monuments.

While I viewed the surrounding area and in particular the mountains to the west, I knew it would be too difficult to travel to the ridges and peaks, where Roger Kidwell and Gary Morris were killed in those mountains January 14, 1970. Looking at the most southern portion of the mountain range, farther than I could see, was the location where the enemy killed Willie Matson on March 15, 1970.

Roger Kidwell received his assignment to First Platoon at the end of December 1969. I left the platoon before he arrived and didn't know him. Although he was with the platoon for only a couple of weeks, the platoon members told me he was a good soldier. He'd married before coming to Vietnam, from Front Royal, Virginia, and was 20 years old.

Garry Morris joined the first squad and platoon around August 11, 1969. I didn't get to know Gary as well as other platoon members because his assignment was the first squad. He came across as likable and appeared to be fitting in with his squad. He was from Lancaster, Ohio, and 21 years old.

As I peered at the high peaks and jungle-covered slopes along the mountains, I spoke to Gary and Roger and told them that I couldn't find a family member but that they were missed, that I'd continue the search, and that they wouldn't be forgotten.

Willie Matson came to the platoon in October 1969, and my memory wasn't as good after August 1969. I remember him as a kind person and that he wanted to serve his country. He fit in well with the First Platoon and was a soldier who could be trusted.

Then I spoke to Willie and told him that his sister Joyce had contacted me and told me that, with a little help from his classmates, she accepted, on November 10, 2017, the High School Diploma from Loomis High School that Willie didn't receive before entering the Army in May 1969. And she went on to tell me how much he was loved and missed by your family. I said goodbye to Willie and then told the three platoon brothers, "You are remembered."

Figure 14–9 Mike and I on the north side of Hill 4-1l. The mountains in the background are where Kidwell, Morris, and Matson died. *David Haynie took the photo on June 16, 2018.*

CHAPTER 15

THE FIELD WHERE I DIED

Leaving the Hill, we headed east, to the ambush site of August 15, 1969. Google Maps was a lifesaver so far. We had to go down many narrow roads, with room enough for only one car, with a thick stand of trees or houses lining the street. It was about a 20-minute drive from the Hill. During the ride, we were quiet, taking in the scenery and looking for any familiar landmarks. My mind raced with thoughts of that horrific Friday afternoon when the enemy ambushed the platoon and detonated two 250-pound bombs, killing four and wounding seven platoon members.

Once Google Maps indicated we were at the location, Mike and I glanced at each other and acknowledged that it didn't look familiar at all. We got out of the car and walked through a thicket of trees and then elephant grass into farmland. David remarked about the tall grass, and we explained how elephant grass could grow as tall as a man and sharp enough to slice through the skin, and if the cuts weren't kept clean and dry, it would eventually cause jungle rot.

Jungle rot was a sore or lesion that developed every time you got a cut anywhere on the body, commonly on the arms and legs, from the elephant grass or thorns in the jungle growth. Not bathing and not changing clothes regularly and exposure to heat, humidity, water, and wet clothing made it worse. The sore appeared in the size of a nickel to a quarter. The sore oozed pus and blood, itched, and hurt. It might be so infected we needed to go to the brigade hospital for treatment. Everyone in the platoon had jungle rot. I still have small scars on my arms and legs.

The area to our front was overgrown with thick elephant grass that was above our waist, and the hedgerows had more trees and brush than I remembered. The overgrown field, between the two hedgerows, was a barren, hard surface in 1969. It was difficult to see the exact location, and we couldn't get close enough to the site because of the elephant grass and crops, and it was private property. We stopped, and Mike and I started pointing out familiar features we remembered from that day; we were pretty sure this was the location. If it wasn't, we were still very close. The two of us stood and talked about what happened that afternoon.

Pointing to the approximate area, in the center of the field, I told David and Mike that this was where I was standing when the NVA detonated two 250-pound bombs and where Sergeant Ronald Owens gave me life-saving CPR. This one booby trap decimated First Platoon, four killed and seven wounded, and almost broke our spirit, as a platoon, to continue. For me, my hatred for the enemy flourished on this ground, and I would never again be young. I continued to stare at the field where the explosion had stripped me of my youth, humanity, and my belief in God, hoping somehow I could get it back, all the while knowing I'd lost it forever.

I then indicated to Mike the locations where I thought Paul Ponce, Joe Mitchell, James Anderson, and Danny Carey were at the time of the explosion. It was hard to look at the overgrown field and imagine what happened on August 15, 1969. It was so quiet I could almost hear the screams of pain and the calls for help from the wounded that day.

The carnage we witnessed was too much to shoulder. Over the past 49 years, I often wondered how I'd survived the explosion, and I continued to carry the guilt that I'd survived when so many others had died.

Trying to see past the large trees in the hedgerow, I thought of the dustoff helicopters approaching to pick up the wounded and dead that day.

> It was behind those trees where Mike and I leaned against the APC and passed a canteen back and forth, not saying a word. Chuck Council stood next to us with a vacant stare. To our front lay four bodies, each covered by a poncho. We were waiting for the dustoff to get the wounded; I saw Chuck dart toward the four bodies and pull the poncho off Paul Ponce, his best friend. Chuck fell to his knees and cried. Mike and I went to Chuck, pulled the poncho back over Paul, and led Chuck away. We heard the dustoff approaching the landing zone and provided covering fire as the Huey landed. We loaded Charlie Deppen, Ryan Okino, and Tommy Thompson onto the dustoff first. Lieutenant Baxter had platoon members put Alabama and Bill Davenport on the dustoff, and I helped Mike onto the dustoff.

Paul Ponce, from Santa Clara, California, had arrived at the platoon in November 1968. He and his wife, Juanita, had no children. Paul was always friendly and talkative, and he would give you the shirt off his back if you needed it. In June, he'd gone to Hawaii on R & R to meet his wife, and it was in Hawaii that she conceived his child.

Joe Mitchell, the first squad leader, was from Chicago, Illinois. Joe had arrived at the platoon in November 1968, which made him an old-timer with experience. He and his wife, Barbara, had no children. Joe was always friendly, talkative, and willing to share his skills and knowledge with the squad members.

James Anderson, 20, was from Smiths Grove, Kentucky, and had a southern drawl. He was one of the newer guys, with the squad for only two weeks, having arrived at the platoon the end of July 1969. James married Janice before coming to Vietnam and had no children. He was adapting to Vietnam and fitting in with the second squad.

Danny Carey, 20, was unmarried and liked to kid around and laugh. He found the good in any circumstance. He'd arrived at the platoon the end of June 1969 and was with us when we built the Hill. Danny was an asset to the squad, and we could count on him during the hard times.

After Mike and I talked about that Friday afternoon, I stood silent and said my goodbyes to Mitchell, Anderson, and Carey. As I stood next to Mike, I began to shed bitter tears, and my body felt numb with grief and guilt. I told my four brothers that I was sorry I hadn't called out to warn them soon enough on that fateful day. *Why didn't I yell, "Hit the ground!" instead of yelling, "Spread out?" What if I'd taken a different route by moving the platoon left or right?* I have run this scenario over and over in my mind every day for the last 49 years, ever since the bombs had exploded.

I made sure I turned away from Mike and David so they wouldn't see my reaction. I spoke to Danny and told him that his hometown, Utica, Illinois, had named a park after him and that Mike had visited the park during the fall of 2015. Next, I told James that I couldn't find his wife, Janice, but the state of Kentucky had built a Vietnam War Memorial with his name proudly displayed, and Mike had visited the memorial in October 2015. Last, I spoke to Joe and told him that I'd found his wife, Barbara, but it was too late; she had died in 1975, and I couldn't uncover any other family members.

I rubbed my Peace Sign, told Paul "Goodbye," and thanked him for my good-luck charm.

> In May of 1969 on the Red Ball (Highway 1), there were plenty of Coke girls around, selling cold Cokes for 50 cents. They had bracelets and peace-sign necklaces, made from our spent brass, for sale. They were young, wearing black or white "pajamas" and a conical straw hat for protection from the sun. I wanted a

peace-sign necklace but didn't have cash with me. Paul Ponce noticed my dilemma, approached the Coke girl, and purchased the peace sign for me.

The peace sign that Paul bought is the same necklace that I'm wearing today. I told Paul the good-luck charm had worked, and I went home and had a good life. Several years ago I talked to a niece of Paul's, and she informed me that his wife conceived a son while he was on R & R in June 1969, so I told Paul, "Congratulations—you are a father and have a son." Before saying goodbye to Paul, I told him that Chuck Council had said, "Hello" and that he missed him. I reminded all four of our fallen that they would be forever remembered.

Figure 15–1 The field and hedgerow, to the right, where Ponce, Mitchell, Anderson, and Carey died August 15, 1969. *I took the photo on June 16, 2018.*

CHAPTER 16

HORSESHOE AND THE RIVER WHERE WE BATHED

We walked back and retraced our steps, heading to the van and the waiting driver. Binh was very helpful and patient with us, and we appreciated it. While walking, we decided the last stop of the day was the Horseshoe. The area known as the Horseshoe was between the river and mountains northwest of Hill 4-11, and it had a shape similar to a horseshoe. It was at the end of our area of operation and was a known Viet Cong stronghold.

We drove along a narrow, winding paved road for 15 minutes and approached the Horseshoe from the north. We passed the area I believed we'd patrolled when leaving the Hill on August 8, 1969, and the same area where we'd received two replacements, Tommy Thompson and Gary Morris. Reaching the designated point near the river, David told Binh to stop, and we unloaded from the van.

Mike and I walked ahead along the narrow paved road talking about our time in this area, the VC, and finding a suspected and abandoned POW camp. We laughed about how we used the river to bathe whenever we had the chance. The platoon would post guards around the bathing area, and the rest of us would strip down and jump into the river. There was always a lot of horseplay and laughter, young combat soldiers showing their actual age for a short period, under such unspeakable circumstances. Bathing was a luxury; we would go weeks at a time without having a bath.

Figure 16–1 Platoon members are bathing at an area in the mountains south of the Song Tra Khuc River, 1970. *Photo provided by Fred Katz.*

We stopped at the bridge that joined our area of operation, the 11th Brigade, to the 198th area of operation and talked about the river, flatlands, paddies, and the mountains that surrounded the horseshoe area, and it was from here that we ascended the mountains for the monsoon season. Mike commented that the river was smaller and not flowing as fast as during the time that we'd patrolled here. We assumed there were dams north of our location slowing the flow of water for crop-irrigation purposes.

Figure 16–2 The Song Tra Khuc river that ended our Area of Operation. *I took the photo in the Horseshoe June 16, 2018.*

While talking, Mike and I heard a sound, a loud whine that pierced the silence coming from behind us, and when we turned at the same time, two motorcycles were almost upon us, and the drivers were wearing military uniforms. Both of us had a flashback to 1969 at that point, and it scared the hell out of us. We thought the NVA were charging our position. Both motorcycles slowed and drove over the bridge, with the drivers giving a glancing solemn stare at Mike and me. We looked at each other and let out a low nervous laugh at the same time.

After the motorcycle incident, we decided to call it a day and head back to the hotel. We'd accomplished more than we thought we would for the first day, and the notion of getting back a little early appealed to us. David had to help the driver to navigate toward Highway 1, and once on the highway, David told him "Hoi An." Smiling, Binh pressed the accelerator, driving north. During the drive back, we were all quiet, and at times our eyes would close, allowing for much-needed rest.

As soon as we arrived back at the hotel, we cleaned up and met downstairs. We moved through the hotel front door and walked along Cua Dai street, which was busy, to find something to eat. Mike wanted to experience local food, so he led the way down the hectic avenue, looking for a restaurant, as David and I followed. I believe David was interested in trying the local food, too. I'm not that adventurous when it comes to food.

Along the sidewalk, there was a steady stream of motorcycles, trucks, and cars zipping up and down the narrow street. There were a few pedestrians. Walking along the sidewalk was difficult because parked motorcycles blocked the walkway. Many times we had to step out into the busy road to maneuver past the parked bikes, while motorcycles and scooters darted around us on the roadway.

After three blocks, Mike stopped at an open-room café, with the front of the restaurant opened to the busy street and the sides and back with walls. The sign in front advertised that they served American food. There were many Australian and French customers eating, drinking, and cheering, watching a soccer match on a big-screen television hanging on the back wall.

Standing at the outskirts of the restaurant, we looked for a table when an Australian woman, dressed in a black t-shirt and tan shorts, about 50 years old, and holding a lit cigarette in one hand and a beer in another, told us to sit at the table in the back corner. The empty table was to our right and in front of her. As we approached the recommended table, she asked me who I was rooting for in the soccer game, and I said, "The USA." Patrons at several tables laughed at that statement. During our stay in Hoi An, I noticed that many Australians and Europeans were visiting the Ancient City and its beaches.

I don't remember what David and Mike ate—it was local—but I had a hamburger and French fries. I can't claim it tasted like an American burger or fries, but it wasn't terrible tasting, either. I looked around at the other customers and envied those who had a fan circulating air at their table. We took our time eating and talked about our first day and the sites we'd visited. The restaurant was loud with the soccer fans cheering for their team, and the night air was hot and humid. After dinner, it was back to the hotel so that we could get to bed early.

CHAPTER 17

MIKE AND I WILL BE FOREVER CHANGED

I rested better that night and was up by 5:00 AM for our second travel day. Our goal today was visiting the August 13 ambush site and the Quang Ngai airport that we'd secured one night in September 1969. The government had closed it many years ago and opened a new airport at a different site.

Using our travel experience from the first day, we learned that visiting a site may take less time than we imagined, so we allotted flexibility in our schedule. After an excellent breakfast, an omelet, fruit, pound cake, and coffee, at the hotel, we walked outside to find the driver waiting for us. While exchanging pleasantries with Binh, we loaded into the van for the long 2½ hour drive south to Quang Ngai.

Using the Google Maps navigation system and my mobile phone, David became a first-rate navigator and worked well with Binh. The roads we mainly traveled were paved, with two to four traffic lanes and at times a divided highway. White or yellow lines marked each lane, with solid white stripes for the shoulders, and there were traffic signs and lights at most intersections, similar to US highways and roads. The traffic lights had an illuminated display hanging below the signal light that counted down the number of seconds that the signal would turn red or green.

All the signage, marked roads, and lights seemed to be for decoration—the drivers rode down the center of the painted lines, weaving, missing oncoming traffic literally by inches; running red lights was a common practice. Motorized bikes of all types and sizes, at times, zoomed all over the roadway but mostly kept to the right, allowing cars and trucks to pass, but some went the wrong way on the road. Riding in the lane of oncoming traffic was common. Beeping the horn was the driver's best friend, or it might be the last sound I heard.

With all the chaos on the road, it appeared the drivers were calm and respected the other drivers. I never saw any driver get angry at another motorist and soon learned that the drivers and the road had their own set of rules that the person behind the wheel or handlebars obeyed. The drivers had complete trust in the others' driving ability, which was scary to me. Watching the scenery out the passenger window and not looking through the windshield at the oncoming traffic was a heart-calming choice for me.

Driving through Quang Ngai, Binh pulled over again at a small grocery store. I'm not sure why he stopped, but I believe he needed cigarettes. We got out of the van and stretched our legs. As I waited near the street, watching the traffic rushing to their destinations and looking at the buildings and other structures, it all seemed familiar for some odd reason, but I'm sure it was my imagination. I know this road would eventually turn into a dirt road that led to Hill 4-11 as it did in 1969. Maybe, this was the road in Quang Ngai that Mike and I drove along when we pulled security for the Armored Personnel Carriers (APCs), during the time we were building the Hill.

MIKE AND I WILL BE FOREVER CHANGED

Mike and I volunteered to pull security for the APCs that were going into the city for a resupply run for fuel, ice, beer, and soda. We met the APCs outside the Hill entrance, did the introductions, and climbed aboard for the ride. We sat to the left and right of the main gunner, watching the road for booby traps and scouring the tree line for possible ambush sites. Mike and I chatted with the crew members, as we tried to pass the time until our arrival in Quang Ngai. The ride into the city was uneventful.

We transitioned from the dirt road to a paved road as we got closer to the city. Within minutes, we entered Quang Ngai, and it was strange to see Vietnamese walking along streets going to work, couples together on a walk, or women shopping for the dinner meal. It appeared so normal. There were many stores open and outside markets selling household and food items. As we passed the pedestrians and shoppers, they looked up and smiled. I knew that smile, and it wasn't real. I didn't sense being welcomed but smiled back. Children ran behind the APC shouting and waving, most asking for chop-chop (food).

Figure 17–1 Young Vietnamese boy with his mother in the background and our driver Binh walking out of the store. *I took the photo in Quang Ngai on June 17, 2018.*

As the traffic continued to speed by, I looked for the NCO club building that Mike and I had gone to that day but couldn't recall what the building looked like or where it was. I started taking photos of the traffic, buildings, and Mike and David. While taking pictures, I noticed a young boy, about eight years old, barefoot, and wearing shorts and a T-shirt, standing outside the grocery store staring at me. As Binh walked out of the store, I asked the boy if I could take his picture, and he nodded "Yes." His mother was behind him in the store and nodded "Yes," too. As I snapped the photograph, he held up both hands raising his index and middle fingers in the "V" sign—the peace sign that US soldiers displayed during the Vietnam War, which meant "peace" and "going home." He must have suspected that we were Americans.

DEADLY TRENCH AND AMBUSH

As the van neared the August 13 location, we remarked that a lot of changes had been made over the years. Again the area, in general, was not familiar, because of the different homes, crops, trees, and terrain features. One thing I observed was that there were no villages as I remembered them. Not once did I see the cluster of straw huts, storage buildings, and animal pens in an area that had 40 or more residents. Today, only single-family homes were clustered together in the hedgerows along the road. I pondered what had happened to all the residents who'd made up the large villages I remembered. Had most of the villagers moved to the cities and were no longer farming? Farms in the US had a similar problem with their young leaving their farming communities, so I was sure it was happening here, too.

Binh pulled off to the side of the road as instructed by David because the only way to get to the site was to walk several hundred meters through the crops, overgrowth, and paddies. We unloaded from the van and stretched. Then we each grabbed bottled water to take on the hike.

We started trekking along a trail until we reached the rice paddy dikes, and then we tottered along them to get to the ambush location where the enemy killed Jerry Ofstedahl, Robert Swindle, and Richard "Rebel" Wellman, and where Frank Brown was wounded. The fields to the left and right of the dike were deep in thick, brown mud and a thin layer of water. Walking along the dikes brought back old memories. With Mike in the lead, I made sure I walked in his footsteps, and I caught myself looking for booby traps or enemy ambushes. I soon brushed those memories away as we walked into the hedgerow near where the trench should be.

Figure 17-2 I was getting ready for what would become the worst three days of my life. I was about two kilometers from the August 13 site. Our company joined Bravo Company, tanks, and APCs to form a task force. *The photograph was taken August 13, 1969.*

Moving through the trees and underbrush, Mike and I found that the large trench that separated us from the enemy was now used to store and transport water for the crops. It appeared the area was a flood zone, too, with markers and foot and car bridges over the water-filled trench. Mike and I were pretty sure we were "close" to the area where the firefight had occurred that day.

Figure 17-3 David Haynie—his first time walking along a rice paddy dike. *I took this photo on June 17, 2018, near the August 13 ambush site.*

We referred to engagements as "firefights" during our time in Vietnam, but I thought of our meeting the enemy at this site on August 13, 1969, as a "battle." The platoon, with Mike and I side by side, fought the NVA from noon to dusk. And that night, Mike and I lay next to each other, waiting for the enemy to attack, afraid to go to sleep. The sunrise that morning would be the best sunrise I'd ever experienced in my lifetime. While Mike told David about the destruction created by the mini-guns and artillery that we found not far from our position, I thought of the patrol that we took out that morning.

Figure 17–4 The trench that divided the NVA and us on August 13, now used to control the water flow. *I took this photo on June 17, 2018, near the August 13 ambush site.*

On the morning of August 14, 1969, after a somber breakfast, Mike and I took a patrol out to search the surrounding area for the enemy. As we walked, we saw more than 10 dead NVA killed the night before and how the mini-guns and artillery had torn the earth up where the fighting had taken place. A search of their pockets and gear yielded letters and maps, possible intelligence. Returning to the platoon position, we turned the materials over to Lieutenant Baxter. I don't know who took the body count, because we kept on moving. Later the Battalion reported that one document recovered, from one NVA company commander to another, stated that there were three NVA companies at the location where the battle had begun on the 13th.

We strolled along the trench and hedgerow and talked for about 30 minutes to make sure this was the spot, and we knew if it wasn't, we were close. Behind us sat a young father and his son fishing in the man-made pond that was once a trench that ran parallel between the two hedgerows. The water that filled the ditch was still and murky with the color of mud. Once they saw us approaching, the father waved, and we waved back.

While standing next to Mike for several minutes, I observed the paddies, hedgerows, and the water-filled trench, thinking of that fateful Wednesday 49 years ago. The thought of Jerry Ofstedahl, Robert Swindle, and Richard "Rebel" Wellman dying here that day brought back memories that had remained hidden for years. They didn't deserve to die so young and not have the opportunity for a full life, as I had. Again, my eyes teared up, and the guilt from that day ran through my body as only a survivor of war would understand.

Looking at the area where the bodies fell that day, I told Jerry Ofstedahl, Robert Swindle, and Richard Wellman that I was sorry for not making sure they'd gotten the warning before I opened fire on the enemy that fateful afternoon. Did I get Jerry, Swindle, and Rebel killed by opening fire on the enemy first? What if I hadn't crossed the trench to engage the enemy but warned the platoon and stayed on our side of the trench? Would the enemy have allowed us to move through without firing on us? If I had, maybe they would still be alive; it was my responsibility to guard their safety.

Jerry Ofstedahl, from Napa, California, was the squad leader for the second squad. Jerry had arrived at the platoon in December 1968, which made him an old-timer with experience. He'd married Claire, his longtime girlfriend, while on R & R to Tokyo, Japan, the month before;

he had no children. I found Jerry to be an outstanding leader, someone I wanted to emulate. He always shared his experiences and knowledge to help us survive our year in Vietnam and treated the squad members without favoritism.

Richard Wellman was from Gastonia, North Carolina, and had a Southern drawl. That's how he got the nickname "Rebel." He was 20 and had married his wife, Deborah, before coming to Vietnam. He'd received his assignment to the platoon March 1969. Lieutenant Baxter assigned him as Staff Sergeant Robert Swindle's Radio Telephone Operator (RTO) in July when Terry Daron left the platoon. Rebel was well-liked and trusted by the men of First Platoon.

Robert Swindle was from Fort Lauderdale, Florida. He was married to Celsa and had a son. Staff Sergeant Swindle, a career soldier, had arrived at the platoon in June 1969 and was assigned as the platoon sergeant. He was a caring leader and always looked out for our welfare and safety. Swindle had my respect because it wasn't often a career noncommissioned officer was assigned to the platoon or Company.

Speaking to Jerry, I told him I had talked to his wife, Claire. I called her one evening, and no one answered the phone, so I left a message explaining who I was and why I was calling, never expecting a return phone call. The next evening, to my surprise, Claire called me back, and we talked awhile, and I found she was living a good, happy life. She told Jerry's sisters about the platoon website.

And then I spoke to Rebel and told him that I had talked with his wife, Deborah, and when I explained to her who I was, and had served with you in Vietnam, she cried and said, "I knew this day would come." I also conveyed to Rebel that I talked to his niece Susan, and she told me he was loved and missed. His sister, Brenda, sent me a photograph of him that he'd sent home from Vietnam in 1969, and she loved and missed him.

Next, I expressed my thanks to Robert, a career NCO, for looking after the young enlisted soldiers of First Platoon, and continued by telling him that I was sorry that I couldn't find any of his family members but maybe someday I would.

I thought of Frank Brown, who Mike and I helped load onto a dustoff that day, never to be seen again. I wondered if he'd survived his wounds. We knew he was from Grand Rapids, Michigan, but I couldn't find him.

I said my goodbyes to Jerry Ofstedahl, Robert Swindle, and Richard Wellman and told them that they were remembered. And Frank—he'd never left my thoughts.

After I said "Goodbye" to our fallen brothers, we headed to the road where the van was parked. Taking a different route, Mike and I climbed a steep bank with little vegetation and then walked across a paddy dike toward the road as David followed. Mike discovered a concrete slab footbridge that had a

Figure 17-5 Mike Dankert and I standing at the August 13 site where Jerry, Swindle, and Rebel died. *David Haynie took the photo on June 17, 2018.*

cable, almost waist high, on each side of the slabs to hold on to about 10 feet above the water-filled trench and road. He walked up the path to the bridge and, while crossing, Mike stopped halfway to the other side to take pictures of the rice fields, mountains in the far background, and Hill 4-11, which was only a couple of kilometers away.

Taking an uncomplicated route, David and I walked along the road and waited for Mike at the other end of the bridge. David decided to join Mike on the bridge, crossing on the opposite side from Mike. After they finished taking pictures, we walked the road to the waiting van and driver.

As I neared the van, I noticed an older woman, maybe 75, wearing typical Vietnamese clothing and a conical hat shading her wrinkled, weathered face, on a bicycle not far from where Binh was standing. Approaching her, I pointed at my camera and asked if I could take her photograph. She immediately shook her head "No" as she moved away from me. I apologized and put the camera away. Some Vietnamese believed having their picture taken would take their spirits away, so it's best to ask for permission before clicking the camera button.

Soaked in sweat and thirsty, we climbed into our seats for our drive to the Quang Ngai airfield. David and Mike commented on how red my face was, but I was alright and ready to keep going. However, I welcomed the cold air blowing from the air conditioner vents.

CHAPTER 18

EASY DUTY AT THE AIRFIELD

The company had the platoon fly from the foothills to the Quang Ngai airfield to pull security for one night. Mike and I thought we would check it out. On the drive to the airport, David gave Binh instructions, and we had to make only one U-turn to get to the road that led to the airstrip. During the drive, we were quiet, deep in our thoughts, while staring out the windows at the city stores, pedestrians, and traffic as they sped by us. Quang Ngai is a large city today.

As we pulled onto the airfield, we found it deserted and parts of the airstrip overgrown with trees and bushes, and I assumed it hadn't seen any use for many years. You could still see concrete from the runway and some asphalt from the roads surrounding the airfield, which the engineers had built more than 50 years ago. There was trash covering the area. Seeing litter was common in Vietnam, even in the remote areas we traveled.

Motorcycles zoomed up and down the old airstrip, sometimes within a foot or two of where we stood. Standing next to Mike, I looked down the forgotten runway, thinking about the Hueys landing near this spot that day years past. It wasn't a bad memory; no one died or was wounded that day, not a memory to hide away. I shared my thoughts with Mike, and we pointed to the area where the helicopters landed and talked about our arrival at Quang Ngai Airport.

Figure 18–1 Mike Dankert and I are standing on the deserted Quang Ngai Airport runway. *David Haynie took the photo on June 16, 2018.*

We recalled when Captain Tyson tasked the platoon with providing security around the Quang Ngai airfield. I don't remember why the airstrip needed protection that night in particular. I can only assume that the command had intelligence that something was likely to happen. We expected the mission to be stress-free and thought of it as a nice change of pace.

We received orders of the mission as the platoon was working the foothills of the mountains west of the Hill. The unit created a landing zone for the helicopters coming to pick us up and fly us to the airfield. A platoon member popped smoke and guided the three helicopters to the landing zone. They landed, and the platoon members climbed aboard their assigned helicopter. Once loaded, the helicopters lifted off and headed to the airfield. The flight took 10 minutes, and the helicopters landed on the airstrip. We jumped off and moved away from the helicopters as they departed.

We established our positions around the airfield and made sure we had excellent fields of fire. The tree line was several hundred meters away, so our visibility was excellent. The enemy needed to travel a distance without concealment to get to us. We settled in before nightfall and had our dinner meal. We established the guard rotation and sat around talking, reading, or relaxing until the sun slid down below the horizon.

The night passed without incident. We woke the next morning and had breakfast. After breakfast, we packed our gear and waited for our transportation back to the mountains. At mid-day, we boarded the Hueys and flew back to the foothills west of the Hill.

Nothing exciting happened on this airstrip in Quang Ngai. But it was a piece of real estate in Vietnam where Mike and I had stood, laughed, and talked like two teenagers 49 years ago, and shared a moment of peace during the war. It wasn't often we could let our guard down and be a 19-year-old again, even for a short period. It was a good memory.

CHAPTER 19

HILLTOP WHERE BRUCE DIED

Mike and I decided we would head south to the hill where Bruce Tufts was killed and where Mike, Dennis Rowe, and Nick VanDyke were wounded. Looking at Google Maps, I thought we could climb this hill. Clambering back into the van, we grabbed bottled water and settled in for the 30-minute drive south. With eyes closed, I dozed off while listening to the hum of the wind passing and the roar of the engine as we glided along the highway. I knew we were in safe hands with David navigating.

Once we arrived at our destination, we decided that it would be an impossible task to ascend the hill. There were homes at the base of the mound, and any trail leading up was overgrown and no longer existed. Even if we tried, we would need to cross private property, which was not a good idea. Binh steered the van into a large service station parking area facing the hill. As soon as he parked, the three of us jumped out of the vehicle and walked to the edge of the parking area to view the hill.

Figure 19-1 The hill along Highway 1 where Bruce Tufts died. *I took the photo on June 17, 2018.*

Our first observation was that there wasn't a village below the hill—just smaller homes that appeared to surround the high mound. What I saw as a trail on Google Maps didn't exist, and we were disappointed that we couldn't climb the hill to find the positions we'd been at that night. Mike and I talked about this hill, where the first member of the platoon died, and it was Bruce Tufts. He was the first platoon member I'd met when reporting to the unit, and I could still recall that afternoon in early May 1969.

> As the helicopter descended after 20 minutes in flight, I looked down on the rugged terrain and jungle growth. I spotted a small field covered with tall elephant grass and watched the grass flatten from rotor wash as the helicopter descended and landed. As I jumped off, with no idea what to expect, a dirty, menacing-looking soldier with red hair and beard darted out of the jungle growth,

ran toward me, and yelled, "Follow me," which was my introduction to Bruce Tufts.

Mike and I spoke about our time here in June 1969. First Platoon was working around Highway 1, which continued to have a VC and NVA presence.

We were moving in the low areas, checking villages for weapons and food caches. In the late afternoon, we moved to the high ground overlooking the valley below, and we stopped at the top of the highest point to set up our perimeter for the night. The hilltop was flat and broad, too broad for one platoon to cover adequately. The command group manned a position on the perimeter; they were usually in the center of the perimeter.

Lieutenant Baxter assigned the positions for the best use of the terrain. My location had a 40-foot clearing to the front, with rocks jutting up from the ground, scattered across the clearing that ran downhill into the dense overgrowth, which was so thick that there was no way we could see anyone approaching. After eating, I heated a cup of hot chocolate and then walked over to Mike's position to visit.

There had been many times since the fire, during breaks or before nightfall, that Mike and I would talk about "the world" and our families or our squads and what we had been doing. As we spoke, the sun faded, and the dreaded nighttime approached.

Figure 19–2 Mike Dankert and I sometime in June 1969 at the vicinity of the hill where Tufts died. *Photo provided by Chuck Council.*

How I hated the night. I told Mike I would see him later and moved back to my position. It was midnight when the NVA attacked.

Bruce Tufts taught high school before joining the Army; he was from Mendham, New Jersey, and was 26 years old. Charlie Deppen and I referred to Bruce as a Viking because of his solid build, red hair, and beard. He was a kind man with a big heart and would give you his last drink of water. Everyone in the platoon liked and respected him.

As I gazed at the hilltop, I spoke to Bruce and told him I couldn't find any of his family members, but I remembered his enormous heart and helping hand to a young kid when he reported to First Platoon. Thanks, Bruce. I silently said my last goodbye to Bruce Tufts and told him he was remembered.

After we looked at the hill from a distance and talked about that fateful night, Mike and I decided to visit Duc Pho (Fire Support Base Bronco), the 11th Brigade, Battalion, and Alpha Company Headquarters.

CHAPTER 20

GOING BACK TO HEADQUARTERS

Once we were in the van, Binh drove north on Highway 1 toward Duc Pho. Mike and I talked about some of the disappointments at several of the sites because we weren't confident that it was the exact location, or the place was in an area that the terrain prohibited us from reaching. Within a short time, Mike spotted the hill, Montezuma, a recognizable landmark, that stood behind the company and battalion headquarters. The Marines before us had named the mountain "Montezuma," and the name continued even when the Army took over the area in 1967.

We found the company location based on the contour lines of the hill to our front. It appeared that nothing remained of FSB Bronco, and they had removed part of the mountain. It looked as if the Vietnamese had built public and Martyr (NVA or VC) cemeteries where military unit firebases once existed. However, it was still easy to visualize the location, in 1969, of the company headquarters, helicopter pads, and the airfield. Staring at Montezuma, I recalled my first time arriving at FSB Bronco on May 1, 1969.

At the Chu Lai airfield, I walked along the tarmac with other soldiers and approached the C-130, using the open rear door as a ramp. I found a seat near the front. Once everyone was on board, the door closed. There was equipment, supplies, and 10 soldiers on board the airplane. The C-130 taxied along the runway, gathering speed until it lifted into the air. It was early morning, and I was flying to a Fire Support Base (FSB) named Bronco at Duc Pho, located 90 miles south of Da Nang.

Figure 20-1 Paul Ponce on the left, standing with Leslie Pressley at FSB Bronco, 1969, the company headquarters. Note the hill behind them, the same one we visited. *Leslie Pressley provided the photo.*

Figure 20-2 Mike Dankert and I standing in front of Montezuma. *David Haynie took the photo on June 17, 2018.*

GOING BACK TO HEADQUARTERS

After the plane landed, I got a ride by jeep from the landing strip to the Alpha Company headquarters. The company First Sergeant, First Sergeant Malpica, smoking a large, smelly cigar, greeted and briefed me on the company and its current location and mission. The First Sergeant was a career soldier in his mid-thirties, with dark hair and medium build. He sent me to supply to store my luggage and receive my combat issue of equipment, including a helmet with liner (worn under the helmet for fit and comfort), rucksack, poncho, poncho liner, three canteens, first-aid pouches with bandages, three days of rations, and M-16 rifle with ammunition. Within several hours, I was traveling to join First Platoon.

While talking about the different times we were at Bronco, David took several pictures of us with the hill in the background, the public cemetery at the base of the mountain, and the Martyr cemetery behind him. When Mike received his "rear job" in late December 1969, he worked in supply at Bronco. Being here for 3½ months, Mike had more memories to share about Bronco and Duc Pho.

We agreed that it was time to depart for the hotel. Binh responded to the words "Hoi An" as he wheeled the van out onto Highway 1, heading north. The drive was long and tiring, and we were the passengers.

Figure 20-3 Mike Dankert at Duc Pho—FSB Bronco, February 1970.

Once we returned to the hotel, we cleaned up, changed, and met downstairs for dinner. David and Mike wanted to go downtown to find a restaurant, but a rainstorm made the decision easy—eat at the hotel restaurant. When we entered the restaurant, I tried (I think, unsuccessfully) to hide my happiness from Mike and David that a rainstorm had appeared at dinnertime. I ordered a margarita pizza, while David had the outdoor (by the pool) prepared Vietnamese style barbeque, and Mike ordered a different-looking beef and potato stew. While waiting for our meals, I asked our server to take a photograph, and she happily agreed.

Figure 20–4 Mike Dankert, David Haynie, and I in the hotel restaurant waiting for our meals. *Our server took the photo on June 17, 2018.*

The food was splendid, and we had an opportunity to relax and talk before an early bedtime. After dinner, we sat at a table by the pool and had ice cream for dessert. Having ice cream became a nightly ritual. Once we'd consumed our ice cream, it was time to head to our rooms for a good night's rest. Tomorrow would be another long day.

CHAPTER 21

UNFORGETTABLE DAYS AT THE RICE BOWL

Waking early, I posted to my Facebook page and website blog about yesterday's adventures. I promised everyone at home that I would try to write about our excursions each day. Within no time, I needed to get ready for breakfast and the long day and drive. We planned to travel to Debbie, Charlie Brown, the Bridge, and the Fire today. Therefore, we would be going to the southernmost point of our trip, the southern end of the First Platoon's area of operations during my assignment to the 11th Brigade while in Vietnam.

Once downstairs, I met Mike and David. We sat at the same table each morning and had our breakfast meal. Surprisingly, this meal would hold us until supper, except for a small snack as we traveled. This was how we ate when we were here during the war. After breakfast, I went to the lobby to wait for David and Mike to come back downstairs.

As usual, one of the female desk clerks approached me, as one of them did each morning, and asked where we were going today. I noticed her name tag had the name "Mai" printed on it. She had her long black hair layered into a bun and was wearing a traditional white *Ao Dai*, which is a long dress with slits almost to the waist on both sides, worn over black silk pants, and she wore low-heeled black dress shoes. All of the female employees at the desk wore this uniform. She appeared as one would imagine a Vietnamese woman would look like to a westerner.

I tried to explain where we were going, but she didn't comprehend why we wanted to go to Quang Ngai, so I told her that Mike and I were here during the "American War" and visiting areas we were at during the year 1969. In Vietnam, the Vietnamese referred to the conflict as "the American War," not "the Vietnam War," which was understandable to me. Her eyes widened, and she said, "You're not that old." How kind of her.

Mai became my favorite person to converse with each morning. When returning in the afternoons, we moved directly to the elevator or stairs to avoid being stopped and asked the same questions; we were tired when returning from trekking across the countryside all day and the long drive.

Arriving on time, and as he did every morning, Binh asked if we were going to My Lai. I responded "No, not today," with a smile, and then I handed David my mobile phone with the location and directions to Debbie displayed. We stepped into the van, buckled our seat belts, and the driver drove south. While stopped at the same grocery store south of Hoi An, Binh purchased fruit, ice, cheese crackers, and bottled water. Our next stop was Debbie. Driving along Highway 1, we passed the hill Bruce Tufts died on, and I silently said my goodbye one more time.

Fire Support Base Debbie was a large firebase north of the brigade headquarters located at Bronco. Its original name was Thunder, but when LTC Ellis became the battalion commander, he renamed the FSB to Debbie. The rumor was that LTC Ellis daughter's name was Debbie. The firebase was on top of one of the highest hills in the area. Looking east, you could see the South China Sea. If you looked south or west, you could see what we called the Rice Bowl area. First Platoon spent a week protecting Debbie and patrolling the surrounding area in the Rice Bowl.

Arriving at Debbie, Binh pulled off to the side of the road when instructed by David. We walked up to the base of the mountain and knew there was no need to go any higher because of the rugged terrain and thick forest. David passed us and scrambled up the path until he reached the tree line and soon returned, following the same trail. While waiting for David, Mike and I discussed where we thought we were, and it took 15 minutes or more to get ourselves oriented.

Figure 21–1 Mike and I at the base of the west side of FSB Thunder/Debbie getting our orientation. *David Haynie took the photo on June 18, 2018.*

When David joined us, we decided to go on to the Rice Bowl, where the action occurred on July 2, and the track hit a booby trap several days later. I had us going in the wrong direction, so we needed to turn around. It was at this point I realized we were at the northwest side of Debbie, as Mike had said we were, earlier. For some reason, I thought we were on the southeast side. We stopped at the southwest side and took more pictures, and the terrain started to seem more familiar.

Figure 21–2 The photo was taken from the southeast side of FSB Thunder/Debbie on Highway 1. *Photo by Clark Searle, 1967.*

Figure 21–3 Fire Support Base Debbie/Thunder from the southwest side. *I took the photo on June 18, 2018.*

As we gazed at Debbie, Mike and I shared several memories of the days we were on the firebase and patrolled the Rice Bowl area. One memory that came to mind happened in early July 1969.

On July 1, we received word that Second Platoon had hit a booby trap that killed Sergeant Joseph Kelley and wounded another soldier. That night, First Platoon departed the FSB about 2130 hours for an all-night ambush. We set up our ambush position on the side of the mountain in an ant bed off Debbie; there was no enemy contact that night but plenty of ant bites. I got little sleep because I kept sliding downward on the steep incline and had to keep crawling back to my position.

Returning the next morning about 0600 hours, we settled in for sleep while the rest of Alpha Company, with the Cavalry unit, E Troop, worked the vicinity below us, the Rice Bowl. The company ran into a U-shaped ambush and engaged an undetermined-size enemy force. An APC hit a booby trap, and the company and E Troop had casualties within minutes—five Americans killed and seven wounded in action. One of the five killed was Sergeant Bobbie McCoy.

Lieutenant Colonel Ellis alerted Alpha Company's First Platoon, at 1520 hours, to reinforce its other two platoons. It was a terrifying, long day. It was after these two men that Hill 4-11 was first named Kelley-McCoy.

We climbed back into the van and started driving to the July 2nd site. Once there, we found the Rice Bowl had changed entirely. There was a massive dam in the middle of the bowl, and the area where we'd fought that day was under water. And the location where the track exploded was on the backside of the dam in a heavily overgrown area. I still felt sorry for Mike because he was one of three who were assigned to remove the bodies from the burned-out track that day.

Standing on the dam, we observed a group of teenagers hanging out, and they shouted and waved at us, just like teenagers in the US.

When I approached the edge of the dam railing, I stepped into a pile of water-buffalo dung, and the group of teenagers started laughing and pointing at me. Heck, I had to laugh with them because it was funny. Fortunately, the dung didn't stick to my shoes—these were the only pair of shoes I'd brought with me.

Figure 21-4 Mike Dankert and I standing at the end of the dam. Below the water was the area where we'd fought the NVA on July 2, 1969. *David Haynie took the photo on June 18, 2018.*

Looking at the Rice Bowl, now a lake, I thought of the day when we were called to reinforce the company.

> It wasn't long after the helicopters dropped us into the fight that Dusty and Lanzer, following me, broke through the hedgerow at a different place from me and stopped. Dusty turned and faced the hedgerow, and I heard him yell something but didn't understand what. As I moved toward Dusty, he pointed his M-60

and fired one round and then yelled that his gun had jammed, and he saw an enemy soldier in the hedgerow.

Lanzer pulled a grenade from his rucksack strap and pulled the pin. He took several steps backward like a quarterback, released the handle, and threw the grenade into the hedgerow. Dusty and Lanzer hit the ground. Seeing Lanzer throw the grenade, I hit the ground and covered my head with my arms. The blast vibrated the ground. Dusty got up and checked that the explosion had killed the enemy soldier hiding in the hedgerow. We then moved toward the fight.

Mike and I talked about the events that surrounded Debbie and the Rice Bowl as we took in the view of the hills that surrounded the area. During our time here, those same hills had hidden the NVA and VC. We were disappointed that the dam was here but still happy we'd come to the Rice Bowl.

CHAPTER 22

THE DAMN FIRE

At this point, we decided to drive to the site of the forest fire and then on to FSB Charlie Brown and the bridge. We called for Binh to come down from talking with the kids and told him we were ready to drive to the next site. Pulling up the GPS for the forest fire, I then gave David my phone. Binh started the van, and we drove off, excited about our next stop.

After we left Debbie, we headed south toward the fire we'd outrun on May 24, 1969. At this site, the platoon landed on the hilltop in the early afternoon, and Mike and I didn't know each other very well. But this is where our relationship began. Being so close to death created an unbreakable bond between us. On that day, both of us had been in the platoon less than a month.

As I remembered that day, the helicopter circled the landing zone, and we saw large plumes of smoke and fire started by the artillery and Huey gunship helicopters that had prepped the hilltop before we landed. The helicopters made a rapid descent to the landing zone, and those who hadn't already loaded a round in the chamber locked and loaded their weapons. We jumped off before the skids touched the ground, hitting the ground hard, fanning out to secure the landing zone.

As the platoon gathered, the fire in the distance burned everything in its path behind and to both sides of our location. The flames climbed the trees and tall brush, and we heard the loud crackling of the burning wood. The thick, toxic smoke choked us. The wind shifted, and there was plenty of fuel for the fire at our current location. The roar of the approaching fire grew louder as the flames seemed to reach to the sky.

Flames singed our clothing, rucksacks, and hair as we ran, and the heat became unbearable. The squads were no longer in a formation; we followed the person in front of us, running. Mike and I found ourselves together. We ran along a trail and moved out of the fire's path. Mike and I were afraid, and our fear seemed to produce some kind of silent communication and understanding between us. Without talking directly about what we would do if the fire caught us, we nevertheless managed to agree to a plan of action. Without words, we knew what the other meant. Mike and I would not be burnt to death. We immediately and completely trusted each other.

Binh pulled the van over in a parking area on the other side of the highway when David instructed him to stop. The hill loomed over us, but it didn't appear as high as the day we ran down it from the fire. After Mike and I surveyed the area, we deduced that the highway was moved about 300 feet up the hillside, and, therefore, by the pictures, it does not look as tall. We walked down a trail on the other side of the road, and you could easily add another 300 or more feet to the elevation. I later told Chuck Council that we couldn't find the stagnant pond we drank from that day, as he requested I try to locate.

Figure 22–1 The hill where we outran the fire. *I took the photo on June 18, 2018.*

Mike and I stood staring at the hill as if in a trance. I assumed his thoughts mirrored mine, outrunning the firestorm so as not to burn to death. Neither one of us wanted to die, and especially by fire. We knew what we communicated during the firestorm but never talked about it. But I made a friend for life that day and knew he would do anything for me, as I would for him.

It was at this location that Chuck Council wrote a letter to his father. His letter, written several days later on those same hilltops, told about what had happened on May 24, 1969, and his thoughts about the political and military leadership, Vietnam, and the war. His Dad sent the letter to their U.S. Congressional Representative, Edith Green. She read the letter aloud on the floor of the U.S. Congress and entered it into the Congressional Record under the heading of "Troop Morale."

CHAPTER 23

AN ISLAND AND A BRIDGE

Next, we headed north toward Charlie Brown and the bridge. We had to make some corrections with my navigation instructions, but we made it to Charlie Brown without a problem. After stopping alongside the road, Mike, David, and I got out and started taking pictures. We didn't try to go to the island; seeing it from a distance was good with us. Charlie Brown was the first firebase that Mike and I served on, and the same firebase that I flew from earlier when reporting to First Platoon. My memory of Charlie Brown was mostly pulling KP, picking up trash and "shit burning" detail for the week I was on the firebase. We did get to swim in the South China Sea. Getting to know the platoon members during my stay was my best time at Charlie Brown.

After taking many pictures, we loaded back into the van and started driving on the divided highway to the bridge, which was only 10 minutes away. At first, we couldn't find it, but after several minutes, Mike and I saw the terrain we recognized and yelled for Binh to stop. Our call for him to pull over was too late, and Binh passed the location where he could get off the road. Stopping in the middle of the northbound divided two-lane highway, he allowed several cars and trucks to go around him, and then he put the van in reverse gear and slowly drove backward, in the middle of the road, about 200 feet to an area where he could park. He then pulled off the highway onto the right shoulder.

Figure 23–1 FSB Charlie Brown location, which is the island in the distance. *I took the photo on June 18, 2018.*

When Binh parked, we climbed out of the van to walk to the other side of the highway, anxious to see the bridge. We crossed the road, hiked through a small neighborhood, and then walked through a passageway under a train bridge toward the southbound lanes of the highway. Walking out the other side of the train bridge, we saw the road, and further along the highway was the location of the bridge we'd guarded.

To our amazement, we found the area to our front was identical to the last time we were here, in 1969; there were no changes that we could visualize. The valley with rice fields, the palm trees at the base of the

AN ISLAND AND A BRIDGE

hills, and the foothills that ran parallel to the highway hadn't changed in 49 years.

As Mike and I studied the hills in the distance, I recalled guarding the bridge. An FNG joined the platoon by the name of Mike Dankert.

> I didn't recognize him as the soldier I'd met in the supply room at the Combat Center. Lieutenant Baxter assigned Mike to the second squad, and the squads interacted little. I remember the bridge was close to a small Buddhist temple near the South China Sea. You could hear sounds of chanting and bells ringing during the day and night, which sounded strange. We tried to concentrate and protect the bridge from the enemy, but the sounds were a distraction.
>
> One evening Lieutenant Baxter briefed the platoon of a possible attack and told us we needed to stay vigilant. It was surreal as we lay there waiting for the enemy, with odd sounds and foreign music playing. I commented that it felt like something in the movies. Juan Ramos, from Uvalde, Texas, reminded me that this was "not the movies but real life."
>
> While standing in amazement of our view, we talked about the patrol that Mike went on into the foothills to our front. The patrol ran into approximately 17 NVA soldiers, but the platoon sergeant told the patrol members to remain hidden, and the small group of soldiers returned without anyone getting injured. I talked about the Buddhist temple that played strange music and the monks chanting at night, making the darkness even scarier.

Figure 23–2 The bridge during our tour in May 1969.
Photo provided by Leslie Pressley.

Figure 23-3 Mike and I are walking on Highway 1, discussing the bridge location when we were here in 1969. *David Haynie took the photo on June 18, 2018.*

David overheard me talking about the temple and saw part of an ornate building through the trees to our rear and yelled, "Dad, I think I found the temple."

Turning to face David, I looked in the direction he pointed, and I, too, saw the outline of an ornate building. Retracing our steps, we walked up a path that led to the front entrance of the temple. I couldn't believe it. Listening to the strange music and chants years ago, I always wondered where this temple was and thought it might not exist. Before we reached the entrance, there was a small graveyard with five or six graves. These graves were as we remembered from 1969, mounds of earth with a modest marker. Mike and I pointed them out and told David that these are the graves we recalled, unlike the concrete tombs and grave markers we had seen so far.

The hot sun had been relentless, with the humidity at 80 percent and our energy depleted from the constant exposure. We decided to call it a day and head back to the hotel. Mike, David, and I retraced our steps along the

AN ISLAND AND A BRIDGE

Figure 23–4 Mike Dankert is standing at the entrance of the Buddhist temple. *I took the photo on June 18, 2018.*

same path, passing homes, and we crossed the highway to where Binh was waiting. David climbed into the front passenger seat and told Binh, "Hoi An" as Mike and I boarded the van and slid onto the bench seat. The driver smiled, nodded his approval, and drove the van onto the divided highway, heading north along the familiar route back to the hotel.

Back at the hotel, we later met downstairs in the lobby and strolled outside into the busy street, looking for a

Figure 23–5 Mike Dankert on the beach, not far from the bridge. Note the two Vietnamese graves behind him, May 1969. *Photo provided by Mike Dankert.*

restaurant to have dinner at. When stepping out onto the front steps of the hotel, the heat and humidity attacked my body, leaving wet marks of sweat that covered my shirt. Mike and David felt adventurous about where they would eat and wanted local food to consume.

As we walked along the sidewalk, with Mike in the lead, we avoided the parked motorcycles as we had on our last walk along the roadway. Following Mike, I noticed the shop owners smiling and inviting us into their stores, children helping their parents in the stores, and an elderly couple sitting side by side on their walkers, nodding a welcome as we strolled by. With a grin, I nodded back, and a toothless smile appeared on the wrinkled, weathered face of the man and woman. Toddlers ran into the sidewalk from their home or a storefront and then ran back into the safety of their shelter, never attempting to step into the busy street.

Mike stopped walking, peered into a restaurant, and asked David and me if this was a good choice for dinner; for my benefit, they mentioned they served hamburger and fries. Agreeing that this was as good as any other open-air restaurant, we entered and were seated by the owner at a table in the center of the room. He moved a fan that was blowing air on his three daughters playing with Barbie dolls at a table in the corner to face us. The circulating air did help, but I felt sorry for the three little girls.

After we ordered, I sat quietly watching the patrons of the restaurant and observed the chaos of traffic on the main street that was still in our viewing area. Mike and David ordered a local dish, and I, playing it safe, ordered a hamburger with fries. I ate about half of my meal while David and Mike enjoyed the Vietnamese cuisine they'd ordered.

There were about 12 wooden tables with four chairs each, and several were occupied by tourists; two middle-aged Vietnamese couples occupied two of the other tables. One of the tables of tourists was a family of four—the dad, mom, and a teenage girl looking bored, with her younger brother keeping the dinner conversation alive. I believe the language they were speaking was German. The other table, which had three tables pushed together, held a group of eight young men and women who sounded Australian, and they were loud, but not obnoxious, while they ate and drank beer.

Once we paid $5.00 each for the meal, the three of us headed back to the hotel for our typical evening treat of ice cream. Sitting by the pool and enjoying our ice cream, the three of us talked about our plan for the next day. We decided that going to My Lai first was a good choice. While heading back north to Hoi An, we would stop in Chu Lai and visit the Combat Center. When the last of the ice cream was gone, it was off to bed to get some much-needed rest for the next day.

CHAPTER 24

MEMORIAL FOR A MASSACRE

After breakfast, we walked through the lobby and out the front doors to find the driver waiting by the van. Once I approached Binh, I said, "My Lai." He gave a broad smile and repeated, "My Lai." My suspicious nature took hold, and I assumed going to the My Lai Memorial was a trip that he wanted to make during our stay because he got a fee for taking tourists there. But I didn't care, because Mike and I had decided that, if we had the time, we would go and pay our respects, and I thought Binh deserved any extra cash he could get; he'd earned it.

As I slid onto the bench seat behind the driver, I thought of the first time that I heard of My Lai.

When I returned stateside from Vietnam in March of 1970, I watched television reports that stated that on March 16, 1968, Lieutenant William Calley's platoon had killed as many as 500 villagers near the village of Son My, at a hamlet called My Lai. The Army charged Lieutenant Calley, at Fort Benning, Georgia, on September

5, 1969, and the Army court-martial convened on November 17, 1970, eventually convicting him on March 29, 1971, of murdering 22 unarmed South Vietnamese civilians. He received life in prison. After President Richard Nixon reduced Calley's sentence, he ended up serving three years under house arrest.

Mike and I were in the same division and brigade, different battalion than Calley, arriving one year after the massacre. My Lai was in the same province, Quang Ngai, across the Song Tra Khuc River, from the area that our platoon patrolled and where 13 of our platoon brothers died. When this story broke, the division, still in Vietnam, changed all signage from Americal Infantry Division to read "23rd Infantry Division." This was how damagingly the name "Americal" reflected on the soldiers and the Army. Throughout my Army career, fellow officers, NCOs, and soldiers kidded me about being a "baby killer" when they recognized the Americal Division insignia that I wore on the right shoulder of my uniform. "Baby Killer" became a popular chant among war protesters.

Three years after the war, the government of Vietnam built a memorial in 1978 to the victims of the My Lai Massacre in Son My. The Vietnamese media referred to the incident as the Son My massacre because My Lai was not the only hamlet involved. Mike and I thought it a good idea to stop at the My Lai Memorial while visiting the Quang Ngai Province.

As the van rolled along the highway heading south toward Quang Ngai, I settled in for the more-than-two-hour drive and watched the now-familiar scenes pass rapidly by the passenger window. I no longer looked out the windshield to observe what the driver saw; it was more relaxing to look out the passenger window. The unceasing blare of car, truck, and motorcycle horns prevented me from sleeping.

When nearing Quang Ngai, I saw several large, new factories with workers' parking lots mostly full of motorcycles and some cars. We passed car dealerships with showrooms and lots displaying their latest models, as they do in the States. The names of the cars and trucks were not familiar. Motorcycle dealerships displayed what appeared to be thousands of motorized bikes, with many different types that one would need in Vietnam. The progress that Quang Ngai Province exhibited along the highway was amazing compared to our time here in 1969.

Turning off Highway 1, we drove through small towns that looked like the rest of the small towns we had driven through on this trip. Many shops of all types, selling or repairing different products, and small, outside-seating restaurants; some of the restaurants had a pig roasting on a spit near the tables where customers sat. One of the most popular types of repair shop was for motorcycles, and I would estimate every third shop fixed bikes. Small, modest, one-story buildings lined the roadway on both sides. People stared or waved at the three Americans sitting in the van as the driver wheeled the van along the narrow roads. Smiling, I waved back, and Mike and David did the same.

When nearing the village of Tinh Khe and the My Lai Memorial, I began to feel uneasy about being a soldier who'd served here during the war, and it even triggered a reaction of guilt. I didn't understand why these sensations surfaced, because, after all, it had happened before I even arrived in Vietnam, and there was no reason for me to have these emotions. Maybe the reactions I sensed were embarrassment and shame that American GIs would commit such an act.

After what seemed like many miles of driving on narrow roads through small towns, I saw a sign ahead with what I understood was the Son My Memorial, glaring at me. Binh turned left into the entrance and then right to park the van under a large, aging tree that shaded a portion of the red-cobblestone courtyard. After we climbed out of the vehicle, Binh and I walked over to the ticket counter to pay the admission fee for the three of us.

The ticket agent, a slender young Vietnamese woman wearing a white polo shirt and black slacks smiled and told me the price for three tickets. I was unclear about the amount she cited. I pulled out a roll of Dong, the Vietnamese currency, confused about what denominations to use and the ticket price. Binh reached across and took a 100,000 Dong bill from my hand and gave it to the clerk. I received change, but I wasn't sure how much. The price of admission for the three of us was about $4.50.

When I turned to walk along the courtyard toward the Memorial area, I observed to my front and in the center of the courtyard, an ornate building of dark wood; beside it was an enormous monument representing the indomitable will of the Vietnamese people. There was another building behind the first, and to my left was a field made to look like a rice field with a life-like figure of a farmer with a water buffalo plowing. Past the field was a reconstructed village on the site where the massacre occurred.

Figure 24–1 The monument represented the will of the people. *I took the photo on June 19, 2018.*

We went into the second building, saving the museum for last, and walked through the sizeable open-air room. On display in the center was a brass panel with the names of the victims that American soldiers had killed that day. The writing on the heading of the plaque was in Vietnamese, and some English stated the 504 named victims killed by American GIs on March 16, 1968.

MEMORIAL FOR A MASSACRE

Once we left the room, we separated and walked along the concrete trail, embedded with bare footprints, representing the Vietnamese killed that day, and the boot prints of the American soldiers that invaded the village. This trail led to the replicas of the villagers' torched homes in My Lai.

One path led to a reconstructed house of a villager that was left standing after the massacre. I saw three Vietnamese, two young women and a young man, all in their mid-to-late twenties, looking at the home. The two women wore jeans, a button-up shirt, and sandals, and the man had on blue jeans, t-shirt, and tennis shoes. I wandered around, looking at other artifacts, waiting for them to leave. The last thing I wanted to do was talk to a Vietnamese about My Lai.

As they turned away from where I was standing and walked along the trail in the opposite direction, I strolled over to the building to see the artifacts that were inside. When I'd almost reached the front entrance of the dwelling, the three young Vietnamese turned around and approached me. They stopped about 20 feet from me; one of the young women walked up to me, and she was crying—which was exactly my nightmare about coming here: having to face a Vietnamese, as an American, about what happened at My Lai.

With tears streaming down her cheeks, she said in perfect English, "Hello. I'm here with my sister and boyfriend," as she pointed at them. Each nodded "Hello" with a smile. The woman she'd introduced as her sister was crying, too.

I responded, "Good morning," as I flashed a weak smile.

"Where are you from," she asked?

"I'm from the United States," I said. I saw her eyes widen and flash with recognition and thought, *Oh, shit—just what I wanted to avoid.*

"How do you feel about being here and what happened that day?" she asked while she placed her hand over her heart and moved it as if her heart was fluttering with emotion.

I said, "What happened this day shouldn't have happened. It was a criminal act by a few, and it was horrific for anyone to kill unarmed women, children, and men. I feel sorry for the villagers who died that day." What else could I say to her?

She gave a weak smile, wiped at her tears, nodded, and the three of them turned and walked away in the same direction from which they came. I knew coming here that this might happen, but I still wanted to come. As we walked around looking at the displays, Mike and I received many stares. To the Vietnamese, I'm sure it was apparent that we were American and, by our age, that we'd probably served here during the "American War."

Figure 24-2 The replica of a village home where I talked to the Vietnamese woman about what happened that day in March 1968. *I took the photo on June 19, 2018.*

The three of us met near the My Lai water well, displayed at the end of the trail, and then walked over to the museum together. Upon entering, I took in the quiet, somber atmosphere of the museum. We went in different directions and read the place cards near each artifact. There were photographs of Lieutenant Calley, Captain Medina, and other soldiers who were there that fateful day. Only one display showed an American soldier positively, and that was Hugh Thompson, a helicopter pilot, who stopped the killing that day. There was a book written about Thompson and the massacre, *The Forgotten Hero of My Lai: The Hugh Thompson Story,* by Trent Angers.

After paying our respects, we departed Quang Ngai for the last time and headed north toward Chu Lai. I admit that I was eager and happy to leave My Lai. The Americal Division Headquarters was in Chu Lai, which was also the location of the Combat Center. Division replacements waited at the Combat Center to get transportation to their unit. It was also the location of my "rear job," after I left my infantry platoon, where I was responsible for shipping these soldiers to their units.

CHAPTER 25

SO MANY MEMORIES

While driving on a narrow one-way road, just big enough for the van, we reached a point where a bar was about six feet above the street. We deduced that this meant a vehicle that wasn't low enough to drive under the bar couldn't proceed past this point. Binh started driving in reverse, retracing our route, slowly passing homes and small businesses. He reached a point where he thought he could turn around, but it took five or six attempts to maneuver the van to face the direction we needed to travel.

After an hour's drive, we reached the Combat Center. We passed resorts that were open and some new resorts under construction along the coast. The view of the South China Sea as we drove along the beachfront road was familiar, but the coastline seemed altered and the sand not as white as I remembered.

David asked Binh to stop at the location Google Maps indicated was our destination, and he did as requested. Stopping alongside the road, we got out of the van and headed to an opening in the concrete wall that ran parallel to the street to the entrance to what we thought was the Combat Center.

Of course, nothing was there from the days of the military base, just barren land covered in white sand and sparse vegetation. As we walked to the point where I thought was the entrance to the Combat Center, it wasn't too hard to visualize the location of the Shipping Shed and where my hooch was on the right side of the entrance.

Figure 25-1 Americal Division Combat Center, from where we received training and departed for our units. The shipping shed is the first building on the right. *Photo provided by Clint Whitmer.*

I pointed out to David and Mike where Wayne and my hooch would've been when we arrived at the

Figure 25-2 Mike and I standing close to the entrance of the Combat Center at Chu Lai. *David Haynie took the photo on June 19, 2018.*

Combat Center. Then I showed them the area where we watched movies at the outdoor theater, and where the shower was that Wayne used to get me cleaned up from one night of me drinking too much beer. Assuming the road that paralleled the beach hadn't been moved over the years, the locations I pointed at were correct.

Being at the Combat Center held special memories for me because it was the location where I felt safe from war and shared time with my brother, Wayne. We flew to Vietnam together. Later, the Combat Center became my sanctuary after my time with First Platoon. I recalled the time Wayne and I spent at the Combat Center together.

Figure 25-3 Wayne and I standing in front of our hooch, March 1969, at the Combat Center, waiting for orders.

After the first roll call, the Company Commander opted to keep us at the Combat Center, until he decided what to do with us. Two brothers in-country presented a problem. I was disappointed. For me, going to an infantry unit is why I'd enlisted in the Army and *wanted* to go to Vietnam and serve my country. It was my duty. I wasn't trained as an infantry soldier to come to Vietnam to work as a supply clerk.

Having Wayne with me at the Combat Center was great because we were best friends, and I never became lonely living away from home in a foreign land. However, the need and obligation to be with an infantry unit never subsided. After six weeks, Wayne went to South Korea, and I joined First Platoon Alpha Company 3rd Battalion/1st Infantry Regiment 11th Brigade. We departed for our new assignments two weeks after my nineteenth birthday.

When I left the Combat Center to join my infantry platoon, I was young and naive about war. It was eight months later that I came back to this same spot looking for any job that would be safer than being with an infantry platoon. While serving with First Platoon, it took no time to discover that war wasn't about service to my country, or duty, or fighting Communism, but daily survival for my platoon brothers and me. Nothing else mattered but watching over each other and going home.

Little did I know how the hardships, the horrors, the killing, and the dying would affect me during my time in Vietnam and long after the war ended. The *fear* and *guilt* that war and combat produced have since followed me every day of my life.

It was at my hooch that Mike came to visit after he got a rear job, working in supply, in Duc Pho. We sat on the front porch watching the South China Sea, sipping on our Jim Beam and Coke, while talking about our time together and our platoon brothers. As we walked to the area where we thought my hooch would've been, Mike and I spoke of those days. We had many good times at the Combat Center.

I recalled early one morning my NCOIC notified me I was to transport a prisoner to Long Binh Jail (LBJ) near Saigon by C-130 and turn him over to the military police there. It wasn't an unusual order—just an extra duty assignment. The military police would meet us at the airfield. I asked my NCOIC for and received permission for Mike to go with me, which coincided with one of Mike's visits.

I told Mike I'd gotten permission for him to go with me. Mike said, "Let's go." We went to the arms room, and each of us checked out a .45 caliber pistol and two clips of ammunition. After strapping on the .45s, we got a jeep and driver and drove to the Division military police stockade to pick up the prisoner.

After we signed for him and got the handcuff key, we put him in the back seat of the jeep with Mike, and I sat in the passenger seat up front. The driver headed to the airfield for our flight. When we landed, two MPs met us and signed for the prisoner. Mike and I got on the next plane back to Chu Lai. The driver met us and drove us back to the Combat Center. We turned in our weapons to the arms room. And once we returned to my hooch, we opened the Jim Beam and sat on the front porch talking, drinking, and enjoying the sunset.

While watching the water and waves moving along the coast, I commented that the beach and sea seemed a lot closer in 1969 than it was today. The three of us decided to walk toward the beach, and we stopped on a dune looking down at the small waves as they broke for shore. Where we stood seemed about how far my hooch was from the beach when I was here. We could see the peninsula jutting out and the location of the Division Headquarters and hospital.

My thoughts wandered to the day that Mike and I went to the 91st Evacuation Hospital that was near the Division Headquarters.

> Mike called me and told me what had happened. Alpha Company and the First Platoon engaged in a firefight with the enemy and suffered casualties. Killed were Gary Morris and Roger Kidwell. Wounded were Bill Davenport and Pete Zink; they were medevacked to the Chu Lai hospital. He said he was flying to Chu Lai that afternoon and asked if I would pick him up at the airfield to check on Bill and Pete at the hospital.
>
> I had the company jeep and was waiting for Mike at the airfield. Mike arrived by C-130. We hugged, said "Hello," and headed to the hospital. We checked on Bill first; he had a wound in the leg. His wound would heal fast, and he didn't need to go to Japan. I told him once the hospital released him, I would do what I could to get him a rear job with me. We visited Pete next. The first thing I noticed was how swollen and cut-up his face was. Not long after our visit, the hospital transferred Pete to Japan or the States—I'm not sure which one.

Figure 25-4 Mike and I are standing close to where my hooch was when I was the Shipping NCOIC. *David Haynie took the photo on June 19, 2018.*

Looking along the shoreline, we noticed the litter that had washed into piles or was partially buried by the tide. There were shoes, clothing, food boxes, and drink containers of all shapes and sizes everywhere. Mike commented, "If Vietnam wanted tourism, they would need to clean up the countryside and beaches from the litter."

Figure 25-5 Mike and I on stand-down at Chu Lai, June 1969. *Photograph provided by Mike Dankert.*

It was time to head back to the hotel, but Mike wanted to go south on the road for about 500 meters to a monument that we'd passed driving to the Combat Center. The statue appeared to be a Sickle with a Hammer, so we thought maybe there was a Russian connection. We drove back and pulled into a parking

SO MANY MEMORIES

area. It seemed to be ominous, built alongside the beach without any other structures. We saw two women sitting with their motorcycles in the shade of the monument. I asked if I could take their picture and both said "No" as they touched up their hair and straightened their clothing.

Figure 25–6 Mike and me standing in front of the monument. *David Haynie took the photo on June 19, 2018.*

When we returned home from our trip, I had the sign at the monument "loosely" translated and learned it had nothing to do with Russia. The sign read:

HISTORIC SITE

Here, on August 15, 1933, Phu Tam Ky reputation was established (This includes Nui Thanh District Commissioner, Tam Ky City Commissioner Phu Ninh District Commissioner). This establishes Phu prestigious and vital milestone in the development process of the movement of the local revolutionary.

Chairman Quang Nam Di ranked as a historical site under Decision No. 1116 / QD -UBND Immediately on April 1, 2015.

Binh offered each of us a beer, but I declined and thought how ironic it would be to drink a beer here after I got so drunk on beer at the Combat Center 49 years ago. Wayne had to take me to the shower to get me cleaned up and sober. However, how cool for David and Mike to be sharing a beer here in Vietnam. I thought *What a fitting ending to an emotional trip back in time.* After they finished the beer, we climbed into the van, and Binh pulled the vehicle onto the road, heading toward Hoi An.

As we drove along the road that paralleled the beach, I recalled the day Mike and I said "Goodbye" and embraced for what we thought would be the last time, when I left Vietnam to go back to the States.

> The Army scheduled me to leave Vietnam on March 10, 1970, but I received a three-day drop and was rescheduled to go home March 7, 1970. I called Mike to let him know that I was going home early and asked if he could come up to Chu Lai before I left. Mike received permission and arrived on March 6.
>
> We had dinner together at the mess hall and then went back to my hooch and sat on the front porch and drank Jim Beam, reflecting on our time together. We never talked about the combat actions—only the fun times like stand-down, R & R, the platoon members, and the funny or strange circumstances we had together.
>
> It wasn't awkward to say goodbye to Mike, but it felt like I was deserting him. The next morning, my ride pulled up to the hooch. We hugged, and I jumped into the jeep, heading to the Chu Lai airfield to start my journey home. You'd think I would be thrilled, but I felt sad that Mike and I might not see each other again.

I looked over to where Mike sat, gazing out the passenger window, watching the small waves come ashore. Who knew at the time, March 7, 1970, that we would stay in contact and remain friends over the past 49 years? We had been through so much as young combat soldiers and shared many memories. If it wasn't for Mike, I might not be sitting here today. How fitting for us to be sitting next to each other while leaving the Combat Center, heading to Hoi An, and the next day flying back to "The World," *together*.

With Chu Lai behind us, Mike said he needed to stop—and soon. David said, "Phong tam," giving him the opportunity to use one of the Vietnamese words he'd memorized. Binh looked at David and indicated that he didn't understand what David was saying. David tried again and repeated, "Phong tam," with the same response from Binh.

Believing he sensed the urgency in David's voice he picked up his mobile phone and pushed a button for a quick dial number. Within seconds, he spoke rapidly into the phone and then handed the phone to David. As he explained what we needed, I believe the person he talked to spoke English. After David gave the phone back, Binh had a brief conversation with the person on the other end of the phone, and then he ended the call.

Pointing at a tree line, David told the driver to pull off to the side of the road next to a heavily wooded area. Mike jumped out of the van and walked as fast as he could to the tree line. Waiting only a minute, I, too, climbed out of the van and headed to the tree line. Once we returned to the vehicle, Binh said, "toilet." We learned "toilet" was a universal word!

The rest of the drive back to the hotel was like the last four days on Highway 1. As we drove, I watched the fields, villages, and towns speed by because I knew this would be the last time I would be on Highway 1. When we pulled into the front of the hotel, David tipped Binh, and I instructed him to pick us up at 6:30 PM tomorrow evening to take us to the airport. I had the instructions, time, and airport name written on a piece of paper that I showed him. He nodded that he understood.

We decided to eat at the hotel this evening. David and Mike had the margarita pizza, and I tried the beef-and-potatoes stew that Mike had several evenings earlier. It wasn't bad but tasted different. After dinner, we sat at a poolside table and consumed our ice cream and talked about the day's events. Then the three of us strolled up the two flights of stairs to our rooms for a good night's rest. Tomorrow night, we would leave Vietnam.

CHAPTER 26

LAST DAY IN VIETNAM FOR THE SECOND TIME

After I woke, I wrote my Facebook and website blog entries about our travels from yesterday. We had no plans for today, only to have a day of leisure. I was afraid to venture back to Quang Ngai, worried that we wouldn't get back in time to check out of the hotel and catch our flight out of Da Nang. And the last six days had been lengthy and tiring, with the many hours of travel time, the walking in the heat, and standing at the different sites we'd come to Vietnam to visit.

At 7:30 AM, we met downstairs for breakfast, just like the previous mornings. I felt more relaxed as we ate and talked about our travels and our families. We still had a full day in Hoi An, so I asked Mike and David what they wanted to do for the rest of the day. After a discussion, we decided to take a walk along the main street outside the hotel and relax around the hotel. Mike wanted to go swimming in the hotel pool. We had to check out by 11:00 AM, so I kept my room for an extra night. After our walk, Mike and David would put their backpacks in my room and check out before the required time.

Figure 26–1 Mike Dankert and David Haynie waiting for their omelets. Our last breakfast in Vietnam. *I took the photo on June 20, 2018.*

When we left the restaurant, Mike and David went to their rooms to get some items for the walk, and I went to the lobby. As soon as I sat down on the sofa, my favorite desk clerk, Mai, approached and said that Binh had waited for us for more than an hour and then left when we didn't show. I was surprised that he arrived at 6:30 AM because I wrote on a piece of paper and told him that we needed to be picked up at 6:30 PM to go to Da Nang, and he'd agreed that he'd understood. Mai went on to tell me he left a phone number for me to call.

Knowing that Binh didn't speak English and I didn't speak Vietnamese, it would be useless for me to call. I asked Mai if she would call Binh and explain he needed to arrive at 6:30 PM to drive us to the airport and apologize for missing him this morning. She agreed and dialed the number. After a short pause, she spoke for a few minutes, paused for a moment, and then spoke again. Then she placed the phone into the cradle to end the call. She looked at me and said, "Binh will be here at 6:30 PM to take you to the airport." I let out a long sigh and thanked her. Mai was still my favorite desk clerk.

When Mike and David came downstairs to the lobby, I explained what had happened, and they were as surprised as I was that Binh had misunderstood the time for picking us up and where we were going today. The three of us left the hotel and turned left, heading down the sidewalk, trying to stay in the shade of the trees along the busy road.

As every day we'd been in Hoi An, the traffic was a steady stream of motorcycles, with a few cars and trucks clogging the streets. Only a handful of pedestrians strolled on the sidewalks. The aromas coming from the shops were still strange to me but not as nauseating as the

Figure 26–2 Mike Dankert and I are strolling down Cua Dai street in Hoi An. *David Haynie took the photo on June 20, 2018.*

first day I landed in Vietnam as an 18-year-old in 1969. But the heat and humidity were the same, and I was soaked in sweat after a short time strolling along the street.

Both sides of the street were lined with shops and homes as far as you could see. Shop owners were opening the store doors as we strolled by in the early morning; they beckoned us into their small stores to purchase their wares. Many of the owners and patrons of the stores waved and smiled at us as we strolled along the sidewalk. One shop owner, while rolling a portable fueling station onto the sidewalk, beamed and asked if I needed fuel as she held the fuel pump handle. I held out my right arm as if this was the location of my fuel tank, and we both laughed at her offer. I must have looked tired, but I enjoyed her sense of humor.

I thought it was unique that a motorcycle could stop along the busy street and get gas from a portable station from a convenience store while parked on the sidewalk. Several women along the way stopped me and asked the same four questions about my stay; I answered them

Figure 26–3 A portable gas pump on wheels. *David Haynie took the photo on June 20, 2018.*

the same as I had many times during the trip. I smiled and continued along the sidewalk.

Walking almost two miles along the road, Mike and I spotted a floating bamboo basket boat, which we incorrectly called a *sampan* during our tour, tied to a tree in the Thu Bon River, and a second one upside down on the ground. These were the first *sampans* that we'd seen during our visit. We stopped and talked briefly about the boats we'd encountered years earlier, especially around Charlie Brown. The three of us snapped some pictures and then continued our stroll.

Figure 26-4 Mike and I with a bamboo basket boat (*sampan*) between us on the Thu Bon River. David Haynie took the photo on June 20, 2018.

It wasn't much farther along the road that we turned around and headed back to the hotel. There were many gardens and even small rice paddies behind and between the homes and stores. Old women and men, some wearing traditional clothing and the conical hat, tended the gardens and fields, seldom looking up when we walked by as they took care of their crops. There was a constant stream of tourists out on the roadway riding bicycles and motorcycles zipping among the local citizens along the crowded street. The Hoi An beach was not far from where we stood.

Trekking back seemed longer, and it was hotter than when we started. The only people who paid any attention to us were the shopkeepers beckoning us with a smile to enter their store. We would wave and smile back and continue our stroll along Cua Dai street. At last, the hotel was in view, but we passed it by to see what was along the opposite direction we just traveled.

Mike and David wanted to get some snacks and a soda, so we stopped at a convenience store. The female clerk smiled as we walked through the open front of the store and waited to see if we needed any help. It took a couple of minutes for them to decide on what to purchase and then a couple more minutes selecting and counting out the Dong for the merchandise.

Figure 26–5 David Haynie and Mike Dankert shopping in a convenience store. *I took the photo on June 20, 2018.*

LAST DAY IN VIETNAM FOR THE SECOND TIME

We decided to go back to the hotel and rest up before dinner. When we got to the room, Mike said he was going to the pool for a swim. David and I stayed in the room and dozed off as we talked. At one point, David opened a cloth bag that held two rocks and said he'd picked them up at Hill 4-11. I hadn't even thought about getting something from the Hill. David offered me one of the small stones, and I gladly accepted.

When Mike returned to the room, we sat around talking until it was dinnertime. We decided to have a large meal at the hotel restaurant before departing for Da Nang. During dinner, I often had thoughts that Binh may not arrive on time because of some confusion about our scheduled departure time, but I quickly pushed these thoughts away. He'd proven himself a patient, friendly, and safe driver, and reliable during our stay. There was no reason for me to worry or doubt him.

After dinner, we gathered our backpacks and double-checked the room to make sure we had everything. As we entered the lobby, David and Mike sat on the sofa while I went to the front desk to check out of the hotel. The desk clerk sent someone to my room to make sure I hadn't forgotten anything. (I believe it was to check the minibar and make sure I hadn't taken anything that was hotel property.) The checkout process went smoothly, and after running my credit card for payment, we were ready for the drive to the airport.

CHAPTER 27

GOING HOME FOR THE LAST TIME

Walking through the front entrance doors into the courtyard, I saw Binh standing next to the van; he smiled and waved. I grinned and raised my right hand to acknowledge him; I felt relieved that he was on time. The three of us loaded our backpacks into the vehicle and then slid onto our seats just as we had every day this past week. David sat in the front passenger seat while Mike and I sat on the bench seat behind him and the driver. Binh started the van, cranked up the air conditioning, and then pulled into the fast-moving traffic driving north to Da Nang. He didn't need David to navigate for this trip.

Driving along the traffic-congested streets, I took in the scenery as we sped along the road. The new Vietnam had progressed and appeared to be a thriving economy; most of the citizens were doing well, compared to my first time here. As we passed shops and restaurants, I found them full of customers purchasing products or consuming a meal.

The bright lights of Da Nang soon appeared, and I observed the high-rise buildings, casinos, and upscale restaurants. The streets and sidewalks were well lighted, and motorcycles, cars, and trucks streamed along the roadway while pedestrians moved with purpose along the walkway. Da Nang could have been any city in the US.

As I watched a traffic cop direct the vehicles at a traffic circle, I thought of how seldom we'd observed police during our visit. We'd seen police officers along Highway 1 several days ago at two different accident scenes; they looked like police at any accident, measuring, placing chalk marks, and talking with the drivers involved while taking notes.

Mike pointed out what appeared to be a War Monument, or a park that displayed machines of war—a tank, an airplane, and helicopter with other weapons left behind—most likely the Army of the Republic of Vietnam (ARVN), the government of South Vietnam. We saw soldiers only a couple of times during our travels, and it appeared to be platoon-sized units taking a break in the shade near military installations, or traveling to and from work on a motorcycle.

Binh eased the van to a stop at the entrance to the departure terminal. We climbed out of our seats and grabbed our backpacks from the back of the vehicle. Each of us shook hands with Binh and thanked him for being such a good driver and guide. As we'd agreed on earlier, David handed him a generous tip. He smiled and stuffed the Dong bills into his front pocket without looking at the value of the currency. We turned and headed into the terminal without looking back at the city lights of Da Nang or the heavy traffic that buzzed by the entrance.

In the large terminal, it was mass confusion, with the sound of hundreds of people talking, milling around the doorway, and hundreds more in several lines at five of the open ticket counters at the far corner of the terminal. There were 30 or more ticket counters lined up against the far wall, most without any signage. To our right was a long line of passengers for Vietnam Air, and that was the only airline sign I saw. We stood behind the crowd, looking for Korean Air, but didn't see any signs.

The terminal was a large, windowless room, about 300 feet in length, 60 feet wide with a 20-foot ceiling, and "No Photography" signs posted everywhere. I could see no boarding gates or waiting areas that provided seats for the passengers. Mike asked a police officer what gate was for Korean Air. He pointed out ticket counters 23 through 28 to Mike. The police officer continued to give commands in a loud, authoritative voice, telling the waiting passengers to move out of the doorway, as he herded them deeper into the terminal.

Walking through the roped path, we found that we were the first passengers for our flight. We lined up just like we had when we'd departed Austin: David first because he had the window seat, then me with the middle seat, and Mike last because he had the aisle seat. David stretched out on the floor with his backpack as a pillow because we had an hour before the ticket agents opened the counters. While we waited, I was unsure if we were at the correct line but stood there waiting, anyway.

After an hour's wait, Korean Air employees entered the terminal from a doorway behind the ticket counters. Most were female and dressed in uniforms similar to the flight attendants on the plane we'd boarded when flying to Vietnam. They moved to their assigned positions, turned the computers on at each station, and began organizing their paperwork. Within minutes, we heard music playing from our front, and all the Korean Air employees walked forward of the counter, stood in a line facing the passengers, bowed, said something that I didn't understand, and then returned to their stations.

We went to the first counter and had our passports and visas examined, and we were issued boarding passes. A Korean Air gate associate guided us through a doorway that led to an area where Vietnamese officials, wearing what appeared to be a military uniform, checked our baggage. The Korean Air employees were as efficient in Da Nang as they were in Dallas or Seoul. I had to complete a form stating that I didn't have any soil, rocks, plants, or vegetation, and checked "no" to all the questions. I did have the rock David gave me from Hill 4-11.

Once through customs, we followed the crowd to a waiting area to board our aircraft for the five-hour flight to Seoul, South Korea. Our connecting flight from Seoul to Detroit, Michigan, was a 12-hour Delta flight with a five-hour layover in Detroit. Mike's wife, Sue, would pick him up there, and David and I would continue to Austin.

Within a short period, we boarded our plane and followed the other passengers along the aisle to our seats. After stowing our bags and getting comfortable, we talked about the Da Nang airport, finding the gate, and going through security and customs. In no time, we heard the exit doors closing and locking, and the plane began to back away from the terminal. The pilot maneuvered the aircraft onto the runway; the plane accelerated and lifted off the ground. While the plane gained altitude, I heard the wheels retract into its housing.

When the tone sounded alerting us that we could remove our seatbelts, I thought of the last time I'd flown out of Vietnam. It was March 7, 1970, and I was at the Cam Ranh Bay airfield, waiting for my flight home.

> A sergeant instructed the hundred or more servicemen to follow him to the tarmac to board the waiting airliner. We walked up the steps to enter the cabin of the plane and moved along the aisle to find a seat. Mike Smith, a friend, and I found two empty seats next to each other and sat for the long flight home. Once the plane had taxied along the runway and left the ground, everyone was quiet, but, after the pilot announced that we were at a safe altitude and that we could remove our seat belts, the plane erupted with shouts of joy. Vietnam was behind us!

I believed David and Mike nodded out not long after we took to the skies. As the airplane engine hummed and the chatter of the passengers subsided, I started thinking about the past week.

After reading about traveling in Vietnam, I was amazed that we'd encountered absolutely no restrictions on our movements. I had never gone to a Communist country before this trip. Not once did government officials approach us and ask questions about our purpose for being where we were. No citizens asked why we were walking through the fields, climbing a hill, or observing a dam. No one ever attempted to stop us. Not one landowner stopped us from crossing through his crops or walking across his overgrown fields as we searched for the significant sites we needed to visit. Binh drove us to every location we wanted to travel to without question and never suggested that we not drive or walk in the areas we did. As far as restrictions go, being in Vietnam was no different from being in the US.

I was stunned at all that we'd accomplished visiting Vietnam for the last six days. I traveled to all the sites I wanted to visit. Finding my platoon brothers and telling them about their families and how I'd lived my life because of their sacrifice was the purpose of me returning to Vietnam. And I did this while standing at, or close to, the location where they last walked, talked, laughed, and died.

I assumed that a few sites, mainly the Combat Center and the August 13th and August 15th battle areas weren't the "exact" location, but I'm sure we were within hundreds of meters of those sites, and that was close enough for me. For all the other places, Mike and I were confident we were at the exact location.

As I relived the trip, I thought of those hills, rice paddies, fields, and mountains where soldiers from all walks of life became brothers; this brotherhood became a family, and we fought the enemy as family. The encounters with the NVA and Viet Cong lasted for seconds to hours to days. Battles were total pandemonium, without any plan of action; it was all reaction and instinct. During a battle, I didn't think of the American flag, defending the United States, patriotism, or even holding the ground we stood on. My thoughts were of my brothers to my left and right. Life-and-death situations brought men, my platoon brothers, closer, and we protected each other without regard to our safety. That is brotherhood.

The plane lurched, snapping me back from my thoughts, and I looked over at Mike and David, sleeping. I thought, *What a fitting ending to an exciting, unforgettable, and emotional trip back in time—a trip I could do only with Mike. And what a joy to have my oldest son, David, to share this experience with me.*

Once home and after all the time spent researching and searching for my platoon brothers, writing and talking about my experiences, and the trip to Vietnam, some friends had asked if I had become obsessed with Vietnam. I had to pause to ponder the question for a moment; initially I thought they might be right. But after careful reflection, I responded, "If I don't remember the men of First Platoon, who will?"

Remember The Fallen of First Platoon: "Corporal Bruce Tufts, Private First Class Juan Ramos, Private First Class Eldon Reynolds, Sergeant Jerry Ofstedahl, Staff Sergeant Robert Swindle, Corporal Richard Wellman, Specialist 4th Class Paul Ponce, Specialist 4th Class Joe Mitchell, Private First Class James Anderson, Private First Class Danny Carey, Specialist 4th Class Gary Morris, Private First Class Roger Kidwell, and Corporal Willie Matson."

Remember the First Platoon members who'd lost their last battle after returning home from war: "David Abernathy, Michael Stout, Peter Zink, Bill Davenport, Jack Lanzer, Terry Woolums, Allyn Buff, Michael Windows, Jerry Zwiesler, Jack Jurgensen, and Leslie Pressley."

Remember the First Platoon members that continue to fight the war today: "Mike Dankert, Chuck Council, Dusty Rhoades, John Deloach, John Baxter, Charlie Deppen, Tommy Thompson, Ryan Okino, Barry Suda, Don Ayres, Cliff Sivadge, Maurice Harrington, Dennis Stout, Ray Hamilton, Ronald Owens, and Fred Katz." I apologize if I missed anyone.

These 40 soldiers, my brothers, are why I continue to remind anyone I can about the sacrifices they made for our country while serving with the First Platoon Company A 3rd Battalion/1st Infantry Regiment 11th Brigade Americal (23rd) Infantry Division.

For me, going back to Vietnam had nothing to do with seeing how the country had grown or progressed, or what the Vietnamese think of Americans today, or seeing tourist destinations in places like Hanoi, Hue, Da Nang, or Ho Chi Minh City (Saigon). I had no desire to meet and greet with ex-NVA or Viet Cong soldiers and exchange stories. I understood the NVA and Viet Cong soldiers were protecting their country and their way of life, and I don't harbor any unkind sentiments against them. My hatred of the enemy had long ago faded. Their patriotism was no different from the American soldier's patriotism, going to war because he was called to service by his country.

My goal and desires were to find my platoon brothers. And for those who died during the war, going to the battle sites that took their lives was the only way for me to reconcile their death and be with them one last time. Having no idea how returning to the mountains, hilltops, rice paddies, fields, and jungles of Vietnam would affect me, it was still the only way to stand close to or on the same ground where they'd lost their lives.

I had a need to talk to them one last time. I understood that I couldn't speak to the dead and that they wouldn't respond, but I do know, while standing at a battle site and talking to each platoon member, I felt a connection with my platoon brother, and a sense of peace and calm surrounded me. While in Vietnam, I learned that I wasn't looking for closure but seeking forgiveness.

THE END

AFTERWORD

The war didn't end for First Platoon when we came home from Vietnam. Most of the platoon members carried memories that plagued them for the rest of their lives. Some turned to drugs and alcohol to fight the demons that surrounded them or appeared out of nowhere to torment them. And eventually, the fears of war won and took their lives.

Many had an illness or had cancer eating away at their bodies, caused by Agent Orange, which was sprayed by aircraft covering the vegetation we walked through and seeping into the water we drank. It got the name "Agent Orange" because the 55-gallon drums containing the chemical had an orange stripe.

When searching for my platoon members, I determined eight had died since returning home; two more platoon members passed in 2017, and one more left us while I was writing this book, for a total of 11 platoon brothers. I'm sure Agent Orange killed more brothers over the years whom I didn't find during my search. With no certainty can I confirm how many died from drugs, alcohol, or Agent Orange, but I do know that most of the platoon members died an early death.

There were many studies conducted through the years on Agent Orange, but it wasn't until 1991, 16 years after the war ended, that the Agent Orange Act established a presumption of service connection for diseases associated with herbicide exposure. Some of the diseases that are caused by Agent Orange are Hodgkin's disease, multiple myeloma, non-Hodgkin's lymphoma, early-onset peripheral neuropathy, porphyria cutanea tarda, prostate cancer, respiratory cancers, soft-tissue sarcoma, chloracne, type-2 diabetes mellitus, light chain amyloidosis, ischemic heart disease, chronic B-cell leukemias, and Parkinson's disease.[4]

At the time of writing this book, I had four surviving platoon members confide in me that they had cancer or were cancer survivors. Three of the four men confirmed that Agent Orange exposure caused their disease. Another three surviving platoon members admitted to a diagnosis of diabetes caused by contact with Agent Orange. Several platoon members had a diagnosis of heart disease related to Agent Orange. Many of the platoon members confessed that, at some time after returning home from Vietnam and for most, many years later, they received a diagnosis of Post-Traumatic Stress Disorder (PTSD). They left Vietnam to come home, and the war came back with them.

Figure 28–1 David Abernathy riding on jeep next to the dog. *Photograph provided by Don Ayres.*

---

[4] US Department of Veterans Affairs, Veterans Health Administration. "Public Health." PTSD and Vietnam Veterans: A Lasting Issue 40 Years Later - Public Health. December 10, 2013. Accessed September 16, 2018. https://www.publichealth.va.gov/exposures/agentorange/conditions/.

AFTERWORD

I included the 11 members of First Platoon who had died since returning from the war in Vietnam. I understand that 11 platoon members might not appear to be a large number, but it amounted to 27 percent of the platoon who had died since returning home. They deserve to be remembered the same as The Fallen and the surviving platoon members.

David Darrell Abernathy was born on February 8, 1949, in California and died on June 10, 1978, at the age of 29. He was buried at Rose Hills Memorial Park, Whittier, Los Angeles County, California. David last resided in California. He served in the First Platoon August 1969 to August 1970. I couldn't find any information about David or locate a family member.

OBITUARY FOR MICHAEL STOUT PUBLISHED BY THE HAWK EYE

Michael L. Stout, 37, of rural West Burlington, died from complications of cancer Thursday, December 18, 1986.

He was born January 25, 1949, in Burlington, the son of LeRoy and Lois Brockway Stout. On October 18, 1975, in Hamilton, Illinois, he married Lori Humphry.

Mr. Stout was a fireman paramedic at the Iowa Army Ammunition Plant. He was a veteran of the Vietnam War, receiving the Purple Heart and Bronze Star. He was a member of the Pastores Class, a member of the board of directors of Beacon House, a volunteer fireman in West Burlington, a member of the West Burlington Lions and belonged to Grace United Methodist Church.

Figure 28–2 Michael Stout on a break. *Photograph provided by Dennis Stout.*

Surviving is his wife; two sons, Wesley and Travis; one brother, Dennis Stout of New London; his father and stepmother, Mr. and Mrs. LeRoy Stout of Bettendorf; and his mother and stepfather, Mr. and Mrs. Robert Bratton of New London. Visitation will be between 7 and 8 PM Friday at the Sheagren Funeral Home.

Funeral services will be at the Grace United Methodist Church at 2 PM Saturday, with the Reverend David Streyfeller officiating. Burial will be in Aspen Grove Cemetery, with military rites at the grave. A memorial has been established at Sheagren Funeral Home.

Peter Zink was born May 3, 1949, and died on October 31, 1991, at the age of 42, and was buried at Saint John's Cemetery at Lansingburgh, New York. I couldn't find a relative of Pete's, so I asked Mike Dankert to write a tribute.

TRIBUTE TO PETER ZINK WRITTEN BY MICHAEL DANKERT

Peter (Pete) Zink was one of our post-August 15 replacements. Pete was from Troy, New York. He had an eastern accent and, like all guys I've met from New York, liked to talk. I liked Pete immediately. He never went through that "FNG-Why Vietnam?" phase. Pete adjusted to Vietnam quickly. When the monsoons hit, while others stood around and grumbled, Pete stuck an entrenching tool in the ground, centered his poncho over it, staked out the ends, crawled underneath and went to sleep. He did whatever he was asked to do. Pete said he had seen us receive commendations and decided that "Sgt. Glyn" and "Sgt. Mike," as he called us, knew what they were doing, and he was going to follow along. He never complained. Once when we were on LZ 4-11, I felt bad because I had to assign him to a garbage detail. I checked on him later, and Pete was all smiles. They let him drive a 3/4 ton truck to pick up the garbage, and he was ramrodding all over 4-11 picking up garbage and hauling it to the 4-11 dump. Another time I had to "tell" Pete and Manny Strauch to go to the 4-11 mess hall so that the

AFTERWORD

Donut Dollies, who were visiting, had an audience of GIs to cheer up. Pete and Manny did their duty and learned how to fold paper to make paper whales.

My favorite memory of Pete is a time on 4-11. We were on the hill for Thanksgiving 1969. I wasn't feeling well enough to go the mess hall for Thanksgiving dinner, so I stayed behind in the bunker. Pete brought me back a plate with turkey, potatoes, dressing, and pie—the works. I ate while Pete opened a package he had gotten from home, from his family or his drinking buddy Tommy, I can't remember which. It was the only time I heard him complain. He started carrying on about a loaf of bread in the package. It was dried up and hard. He couldn't figure why someone had sent him that. Why did they think he'd want a loaf of bread? And they should have known it wouldn't be any good by the time it got to him. Disgusted, Pete took the box and put it in a trash barrel near our bunker. I finished my plate and went to throw it in the barrel and noticed something shiny. I pulled out the bread and found a bottle. Uncle Louie had carved out the bread so a small bottle of whiskey fit inside it. Apparently, the bread had cushioned the bottle and kept it from breaking. I asked Pete if he was sure he didn't want the loaf of bread as I opened it and held up the bottle. He got a big smile on his face. Pete opened the bottle, and we raised a glass, actually canteen cups, and drank a toast.

The last time I saw Pete was in January 1970. He and Bill Davenport were wounded on January 14, the same date Gary Morris and Roger Kidwell were killed. Pete and Bill were medevacked to Chu Lai. I visited them in the hospital. An RPG had exploded near Pete. His face was a contorted mess. His face was bruised, swollen and cut. He could see out of only one eye. He drank using a straw through the corner of his mouth. He never complained or felt sorry for himself. He said not to worry about him; he was going home.

The last time I spoke to Pete was 1985. Terry Woolums had contacted us separately and told us about the Hill 4-11 reunion in St. Louis, Missouri. Pete called me. I recognized his voice immediately—that New York accent. He told me he had recovered from the wounds and had only a small scar on his face. We talked about what we had done after Vietnam. Pete was working in a small bar. Not a surprise—Pete was known to drink a few beers. He had gotten married and was divorced but still friendly with his ex. At one point in the conversation, he said, "So are we going to do this thing?" meaning attend the 4-11 reunion. I said, "I will if you will." We agreed to meet in St. Louis. I went to the reunion, but Pete never showed. Later I tried to call him, without success. I never heard from him again.

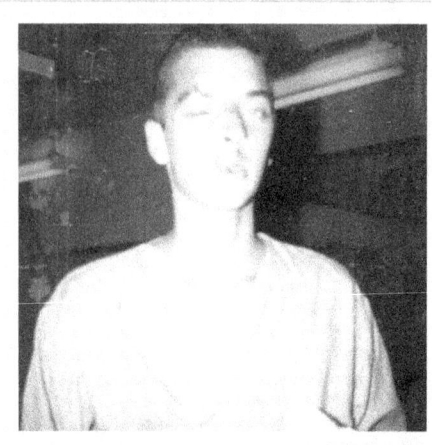

Figure 28–3 Peter Zink at the Chu Lai hospital after being wounded on January 14, 1970. *Photograph provided by Bill Davenport.*

A few years later, I got a call and heard what I thought was a familiar voice. It was Ed Zink, Pete's brother. He had opened Pete's safe deposit box and found my name and phone number. Ed told me that Pete had died from cancer attributed to Agent Orange. As Pete was dying, he asked his brother to contact me, but Ed was unable to find my number. I missed the funeral, but Ed gave me his address, and I sent him money, telling him to buy a round for the guys at the bar in memory of Pete.

OBITUARY FOR BILL DAVENPORT PUBLISHED BY THE DAILY NEWS ONLINE

Longtime resident **William Davenport**, 62, of Longview passed away July 30, 2011, at the Veterans Administration Rehabilitation Center in Vancouver. He was born Dec. 13, 1948, in Yakima, and moved to the local area 51 years ago.

Bill served in the Army during the Vietnam War from 1969 to 1970. He was awarded the Bronze Star with an oak leaf, a Purple Heart with two oak leaves, and a Combat Infantry Badge. Bill was an emergency medical technician with American Medical before retiring in 2006. He enjoyed fishing with his buddies at the county line.

He is survived by a sister, Linda Davenport, of Long Beach; a brother and sister-in-law, Ben and Nancy Davenport, of Castle Rock; two nephews, Benjamin Davenport of Chehalis and Ryan Davenport of Castle Rock; a niece, Lindsey Lonner, of Kelso; two great-nephews, Chase and Nathan; and two great-nieces, Kehna and Maddison. Bill was preceded in death by a brother, Bob Davenport.

Inurnment with full military honors was at the Willamette National Cemetery in Portland. Cremation has taken place under the direction of Davies Cremation & Burial Service, Vancouver.

Jack F. Lanzer was born on October 6, 1948 and died on August 22, 2012 at the age of 63. Jack is buried at Calverton National Cemetery in Calverton, New York. I could not find any information about Jack or locate a family member.

Figure 28–4 Bill Davenport at the Chu Lai hospital after being wounded on January 14, 1970. *Photograph provided by Bill Davenport.*

Figure 28–5 Bill Davenport at the mini-reunion in Portland with Mike, Chuck, and me. July 1986. *Photograph provided by me.*

TRIBUTE TO JACK LANZER WRITTEN BY GLYN HAYNIE

Jack Lanzer was from New York and proud of it. Lanzer had arrived at the unit October 1968, which made him the individual who had been in the platoon the longest. Jack was respected and liked by his platoon brothers. He was always willing to share his stories of life in New York and left the unconfirmed impression he had two choices before coming to Vietnam: Going to jail or enlisting in the US Army. We never knew if it was true. He didn't appear to be the criminal type.

Jack was a great storyteller, and his favorite story was about a bone. He wore a bone around his neck and told every FNG who came into the platoon how he got it, where he got it, and why he wore it. Jack called it his good-luck charm. We knew what story he'd told by the look in the FNG's eyes. Knowing Jack, we didn't believe his grim tale but always pretended we did while talking with him. We were sure it was an animal bone.

Figure 28–6 Jack Lanzer is getting ready to go back to Duc Pho. *Photograph provided by Mike Dankert.*

He wore a huge Bowie knife that fits in a sheath on his right hip. He claimed that the knife had come to Vietnam with an original platoon member from Hawaii. Jack was getting short (tour almost over), so he called me over and said, "Haynie, I have something for you," and handed me the knife. He said the knife was unique and passed on to special soldiers. I felt honored to receive the knife and told him I would take care of it and pass it to an exceptional soldier. The next day he got on the supply chopper and flew back to Duc Pho for a rear job. I passed the Bowie knife on to Bill Davenport in December 1969. Bill was a special soldier, and I hoped Jack approved. Jack, you are missed.

OBITUARY FOR TERRY WOOLUMS PUBLISHED BY GRACELAND / FAIRLAWN FUNERAL HOME

Terry L. Woolums, 63, formerly of Decatur, passed away on Sunday, January 20, 2013, in Danville. Terry was born March 30, 1949, in Decatur,

IL, the son of Arthur and Mollie (Seay) Woolums. He graduated from Mt. Zion high school and proudly served his country in Viet Nam as a member of 3rd Battalion, 1st Infantry Regiment.

Terry is survived by his daughter, Mollie Woolums, of Indianapolis, grandchildren, Tianna, Morkell, and Mareco; sisters, Cathy Rittenhouse of Forrest, IL. Nancy (George) Wallis of Boody, many cousins, nieces, nephews, family members, and friends. Terry was preceded in death by his parents.

Figure 28-7 Terry Woolums (on your left) in a position with Cliff Sivadge. *Photograph provided by Cliff Sivadge.*

Services to celebrate Terry's life will be 1 PM Thursday, January 24, 2013, at Graceland/Fairlawn Funeral Home. Burial will be at Graceland Cemetery with Military Rites by the Macon County Honor Guard and conclude with the "Flight Home Ceremony." Instead of flowers, please direct contributions to the Disabled Veterans of America.

The family of Terry L. Woolums is being served by Graceland/Fairlawn Funeral Home. Online condolences and memories may be shared with the family at www.gracelandfairlawn.com.

OBITUARY FOR ALLYN BUFF PUBLISHED BY THE WESTERN NEWS

Allyn Paul Buff, 64, of Libby, died Wednesday, July 24, 2013, at his home. He was born Dec. 13, 1948, in Pomona, Calif. He attended school and lived most of his young life in Cucamonga, Calif.

Allyn was drafted into the U.S. Army in 1969 and served his country in Vietnam, earning two Bronze Service Stars as a combat infantryman. He was honorably discharged from service in 1971.

Upon returning home, Allyn married his sweetheart, Darrylyn Stockrahm, in 1972. They had three children. Their family moved to

Libby in 1979. The couple divorced in 1984 but remained friends until Darrylyn's death.

Allyn spent his early years in Libby working as a mechanic at Libby Dam until 1990. He then purchased a well-drilling rig and started his little company, Clearwater Drilling, with the help of his dear friend, Marlene Raitt.

Figure 28-8 Allyn Buff on FSB Hill 4–11. *Photograph provided by Don Ayres.*

When he wasn't drilling holes in the ground all over Lincoln County, the avid fisherman could be found somewhere on his beloved Kootenai River trying to best his record catch of a 19-pound, 34-inch rainbow trout. Many people also knew him as a classic-car and hot-rod enthusiast, and he spent much of his time tinkering with his old Chevys.

Allyn was preceded in death by his mother, Alice Rantos. He is survived by his daughters, Cyndi (Joe) Miller of Libby, Paula Buff of Seattle, and Lynda Buff of Libby; his sister, Lynn (D.J.) Martin of Arizona; brothers, Rick (Gloria) Tham of Prescott, Ariz., Chris (Sherri) Tham of Petaluma, Calif.; an uncle, Paul Buff of Mobile, Ala.; four granddaughters,

Figure 28-9 A more-recent photograph of Allyn Buff. *Photographer unknown.*

AFTERWORD

Natesha, Tiahna, Shalen and Dustina; and numerous nieces, nephews, good friends, and neighbors.

A funeral service will be held at the Libby Cemetery at 3 PM Saturday, Aug. 10, with military honors. Arrangements are by Schnackenberg & Nelson Funeral Home & Crematory in Libby.

OBITUARY FOR MICHAEL WINDOWS PUBLISHED BY AKERS FUNERAL HOME

Michael H. Windows, 65, of Adelphia Road, Everett, passed away on Sunday, October 5, 2014, at home. He was born on February 22, 1949, in Pittsburgh, PA; a son of the late Hubert and Mildred (Brady) Windows. On February 30, 1997, in Cumberland, Maryland, he married Connie L. (Strait) Windows. She preceded him in death on March 6, 2013.

He is survived by a stepson, David L. Strait, and wife Tammy (Price), Everett, PA; Step-Grandchildren: Megan, Tyler, Trevor and Madison Strait; Sister-in-law: Linda Windows; Three Nieces and Two Nephews.

He was preceded in death by two brothers and a sister-in-law: Kenneth Windows and Jack Windows and wife Mary Ann.

Mike attended Seven Dolors of the B.V.M. Catholic Church, Beans Cove. He attended Bedford High School. He served in the United States Army during the Vietnam War.

Mike was a jack of all trades working various places throughout the years, but mainly working in the metal

Figure 28–10 Michael "Doc" Windows and his wife, Connie. *Photographer unknown.*

industry. He was a member of the Everett Redman Social Club and the Everett American Legion Post No. 08. He enjoyed hunting.

Family and Friends may call at the Akers Funeral Home, 299 Raystown Road, Everett on Thursday, October 9, 2014, from 1:00 PM until the hour of service.

Memorial Service will be held in the Chapel at Akers Funeral Home on Thursday, October 9, 2014, at 2:00 PM with Father Derek Fairman officiating. Everett Area Honor Guard will be conducting military rites. Burial will be held privately at Seven Dolors of the B.V.M. Catholic Church Cemetery, Beans Cove.

OBITUARY FOR JERRY ZWIESLER PUBLISHED IN DAYTON DAILY NEWS

Zwiesler, Jerome M. "Jerry," age 69 of Vandalia, passed away Monday, January 30, 2017, at Christ Hospital in Cincinnati, where he had been treated for congestive heart failure. He is preceded in death by his parents Leo M. and Angela Zwiesler. Survived by his wife of 45 years Ann (Ziehler), daughter Jennifer (James) Duckro of Columbus, son Matt Zwiesler of Chicago, 2 grandchildren Walter and Ella Duckro, sister Sue (Lou) Schulker of Dayton, brother Marty (Lynn) of MI, sisters and brothers-in-law Carolyn (Chick) Klohe of Dayton, Paul (Carol) Ziehler of WI, Tony (Marg) Ziehler of Akron.

He was a 1966 graduate of Chaminade High School and the University of Dayton from 1974 to 1978.

Jerry was a US Army Vietnam Veteran and a member of St. Christopher's Catholic Church. Mass of

Figure 28–11 Sergeant Jerry Zwiesler is sitting front. *Photograph provided by Don Ayres.*

AFTERWORD

Christian Burial 11 AM Friday, February 10th at St. Christopher Catholic Church 435 E. National Rd. Vandalia, OH 45377 by Father John Tonkin. Interment Dayton National Cemetery.

The family will receive friends Thursday, February 9th from 4 to 8 PM at Baker-Hazel & Snider Funeral Home 5555 Philadelphia Dr. at N. Main St. Memorial Contributions may be made to The Christ Hospital-Heart and Vascular LVAD team, St. Christopher Church or Chaminade Julienne High School, in Jerry's memory. Online condolences for the family may be sent to www.bakerhazelsnider.com

Figure 28-12 Jerry Zwiesler before his death. *Photographer unknown.*

Jack Jurgensen was born August 10, 1949, and died peacefully in his sleep on September 9, 2017, at the age of 68, at his home in Redding, California. He is buried at the Northern California Veterans Cemetery, Igo, Shasta County, California. I couldn't find an obituary, so I asked Chuck Council to write a Tribute.

TRIBUTE TO JACK JURGENSEN WRITTEN BY CHUCK COUNCIL

I met Jack Jurgensen in April of 1969, and when assigned to 1st Platoon, Alpha Company, 2nd Squad, Jack was one of my squad members. At the time, Alpha Company was on Landing Zone (LZ) Cork. The squad leader assigned me to KP duty along with Jack. He was from Redding, California, and I was from Portland, Oregon, and because of the proximity of our hometowns, we had an immediate connection.

Over the next two months, Alpha Company had Combat Assaults (CA) along the coastal sugar cane fields, Bridge Guard off of LZ Charlie Brown, and we swam in the South China Sea as therapy for our jungle rot. We all had jungle rot, but Jack had it worse than any of us.

At a stand-down at Chu Lai at the end of May, all of us in 2nd Squad relieved our stress by drinking lots of beer. We all wanted to get out of the bush, and one way to do that was to re-enlist in the Army. Sometime about the middle of June, Jack did just that. He reenlisted and received an assignment to a communications company in Da Nang. That was the last I saw of Jack until June of 2015.

Figure 28–13 Jack Jurgensen eating dinner, June 1969. *Photograph provided by Terri Holt.*

Through the 1st Platoon website, I obtained Jack's phone number. He was still living in Redding, California. On a trip to Redding with my wife that June, we visited with Jack on two different occasions, sharing stories, experiences, and photos.

Figure 28–14 Left to right—Chuck Council and Jack Jurgensen when they met in California, 2015. *Photograph provided by Chuck Council.*

In the accompanying photo, my tank top reads "Army" and Jack's T-shirt reads "Loyalty." Putting those two words together "Army-Loyalty" speaks volumes of the brotherhood among Vietnam veterans.

AFTERWORD

Rest In Peace, My Friend. You are loved by all who served in 1st Platoon, Alpha Company.

OBITUARY FOR LESLIE CURTIS "L.C." PRESSLEY
PUBLISHED BY LIBERTY MORTUARY

Leslie Curtis "L.C." Pressley, 69, of 133 Crimson Leaf Lane, passed away peacefully on Saturday, July 21, 2018, at St. Francis Hospital. Born in Greenville, he was a son of the late William Curtis and Katherine Lesley Pressley.

He graduated from Liberty High School and later received two Associate Degrees from Tri-County Technical College. He later retired from Delta Woodside Mills, where he was an industrial engineer and manager.

L.C. was a United States Army veteran of the Vietnam War, where he served with the 1st Platoon Company A 3rd Battalion/1st Infantry Regiment 11th Brigade Americal Division, January 1969–January 1970. He was Lieutenant John Baxter's Radio Telephone Operator (RTO) until July 1969 and then served in the battalion communications section.

Surviving are a daughter, Rhonda Segars of Pickens; two sons, Blake Pressley of Seneca, and Mitch Pressley of Liberty; a sister, Darlene Fowler

Figure 28–15 Left, Leslie Pressley with Maurice Harrington, center, and James Shelton at FSB Bronco. *Photographer unknown.*

Figure 28–16 Leslie Pressley at the First Platoon Reunion at Dallas, Texas, July 2016. *Photograph by Tarie Haynie.*

of Liberty; a special friend and companion, Brenda Cartee of Liberty; also surviving are 7 grandchildren, Cy Rampey, Colby Pressley, Cal Rampey, Haleigh Pressley, Dillon Pressley, Brent Segars, and Carlie Pressley. In addition to his parents, he was preceded in death by a brother, Billy Pressley.

 The family will celebrate and honor his life by hosting a visitation Friday evening, July 27, 2018, from 6:00 until 8:00 PM at the Liberty Mortuary.

REMEMBERING THE FALLEN

Bruce Tufts   22 Dec 1942–14 Jun 1969
                                     Mendham, New Jersey

Juan Ramos   2 Jan 1948–14 Jul 1969
                                     Uvalde, Texas

Eldon Reynolds   15 Jan 1949–14 Jul 1969
                                     Eakly, Oklahoma

Robert Swindle   28 Nov 1938–13 Aug 1969
                                     Fort Lauderdale, Florida

Jerry Ofstedahl   27 Jun 1949–13 Aug 1969
                                     Napa, California

Richard "Rebel" Wellman   3 Aug 1949–13 Aug 1969
                                     Gastonia, North Carolina

Joseph Mitchell	11 Oct 1948–15 Aug 1969 Chicago, Illinois
Paul Ponce	22 May 1948–15 Aug 1969 Santa Clara, California
Daniel Carey	30 Apr 1948–15 Aug 1969 Utica, Illinois
James Anderson	25 Oct 1948–15 Aug 1969 Smiths Grove, Kentucky
Roger Kidwell	20 Oct 1949–14 Jan 1970 Front Royal, Virginia
Gary Morris	7 Dec 1948–14 Jan 1970 Lancaster, Ohio
Willmer Matson	23 Jul 1949–15 Mar 1970 Loomis, Nebraska

POSTSCRIPT: MY BEST FRIEND AND MY OLDEST SON

During our first time in Vietnam, Mike Dankert and I formed a special bond of brotherhood. We shared the same wet ground, the shallow foxhole, our rations, the unsweetened Kool-Aid, the same fears and horrors of combat. The two of us fought the enemy side by side, and we had complete trust in the other, even with our lives at stake. It was as if Mike and I had come together to protect each other from harm. The names "Dankert" and "Haynie" became one. Through the years, after Vietnam, our friendship and brotherhood flourished. Mike joining me on this trip made it complete.

David took time away from his job, wife, children, and grandchildren—not to mention paying the cost, to be with Mike and me as we made this journey. He was our navigator with my mobile phone and Google Maps, and he learned phrases in Vietnamese—"left," "right," "straight," and "bathroom" so he could communicate with the driver. He was more than just a helper on the trip. I noticed his concern as Mike and I, two old guys, climbed Hill 4-11, teetered across dikes, walked through elephant grass, along trails, through heavily forested areas, and climbing up Debbie. Not only did he help make our trip a success, but he left me with a remarkable memory of our time together, as father and son.

After we returned from our trip to Vietnam, Mike and David said they were going to write about their thoughts and what the trip meant to them. I asked if they would share their writings in this book, and both agreed. I cannot think of a better way to end than disclosing what they wrote about our trip to Vietnam.

VIETNAM TRIP:
Epilogue Written by Mike Dankert

I went back to Vietnam (2018) because Glyn asked me. I didn't need any more reason than that. That's not to say that I didn't have a personal interest in going. I did. I wanted to see the places the First Platoon had been to, how those places that had been so important to me once were today. I wanted to see what Vietnam was like today; to talk to the people of Vietnam and learn what they thought about the "American War" then, and what they think of us today.

I wasn't going to Vietnam to reclaim the sites where we fought the Vietnamese and where our friends were wounded and died. I don't think like that. I wasn't looking for "closure," if that means "to forget what happened there." I want to remember Vietnam. I want to think of it often to remember the men I served with, especially those who died there then and the men who brought their war home and have died here. I have suffered survivor guilt since August 15, 1969. It has taken me a long time to learn to live with it, to develop an uneasy peace with my time in Vietnam. Most nights now I can sleep, but there are times that I go over and over again in my head what happened there, wishing I had done more—something different that might have saved a life. I tell myself remembering is okay—it keeps alive the memories of those I served with in Vietnam. As long as I remember, some part of them is alive. I want to remember how hard it was just to survive, how it felt to lose friends—even those I wasn't close to. I want to remember the

POSTSCRIPT: MY BEST FRIEND AND MY OLDEST SON

cost of war so that it doesn't become too easy to accept the deaths of different generations in America's military actions around the world. I sometimes question if my life has been meaningful enough. Have I taken advantage of the opportunities that Tufts, Jerry, James, Danny, and the others never had? Those are thoughts I struggle with today.

Vietnam taught me many lessons; among them was the meaning of friendship. It's more than just accumulating acquaintances, people you socialize with, or those with shared interests. A true friend is one who supports and forgives you when you are at your worst, champions you when you are at your best, and someone who will risk his life for you. I have that kind of friend in Glyn. I also learned to choose my battles, literally and figuratively. There are things worth fighting for: family (that includes a best friend who is like a brother), a way of life, ideals, and freedom. Things that endure. Girlfriends, possessions, ideology, and opinions—not so much.

To say Vietnam had changed is an understatement. Forty-nine years allows for a lot of change. We found all the places we remembered with the help of military action reports, military maps, and Google Maps. The places didn't look the same, but they were still familiar, especially "the bridge," where I first joined the platoon and where Glyn got to know Lt. Baxter and the First Platoon soldiers.

There were no monuments to the North Vietnamese or the VC, or propaganda against us that we saw. No signs of the bitter fighting that took place 49 years earlier other than stark and untended "martyr" cemeteries near LZ Bronco and LZ 411. Nature and the villagers have reclaimed the land. The rocky hilltops where we fled the fire and where the enemy killed Tufts is now lush and green with trees. LZ Charlie Brown is a resort area because of its beautiful beaches. LZ Debbie's barren, rocky surface, was reforested at some time, and it, too, is green. The "Rice Bowl" that was the site of heavy fighting, casualties, and deaths was now a man-made lake with clear, blue-green water. People were boating and fishing at the lake. Kids hang out at the dam built to create the lake. Even the site of what Glyn and I call the "Rice Bowl" incident has changed. It is part of the irrigation pathway for the valley below a dam. The August 13 and August 15 areas were flat and dry. The farmers excavated the land, created irrigation channels, and widened the ditch that was so prominent on August 13th. The flat, dry, and barren area where we left Vietnamese bodies is now fertile—a part of acres of rice paddies, watermelon patches, and cornfields. LZ 4-11 is the site of a public cemetery. The "hill" is slowly "eroding" as construction workers dig away the soil and rocks on its south side to use for construction projects elsewhere.

The contrasts between 1969 and 2018 were surreal. In 1969, we slept in the field on ponchos on the ground. In the heat and humidity, we sweated just trying to sleep. We had to spray insect repellent around the edges of our ponchos to keep ants from crawling on us. In 2018, we slept on white sheets in a first-class, air-conditioned hotel room. Our 1969 breakfast was pound cake or crumbled crackers with peanut butter and jelly, a can of fruit eaten with a plastic spoon, and hot cocoa "in season." In 2018, our day started with a made-to-order omelet, fresh fruit, cold fruit juice, and freshly made danish pastry or doughnuts. Back then, we humped (walked) everywhere with a 40-lb. pack. Today we rode in an air-conditioned van and left our daypacks inside as we walked around. Instead of drinking lukewarm, bitter-tasting water out of a plastic canteen (in 1969), flavored with presweetened Kool-Aid (or unsweetened Kool-Aid for the strongest among us), we had iced bottled spring water from a cooler in the van, supplemented with cold, fresh fruit. In 1969, we wore the same sweat-absorbing, cotton jungle fatigues for weeks at a time, steel helmets, and jungle boots. This time we had clean clothes every day—quick-dry, lightweight pants and shirts, hiking shoes, and ventilated hats. Some of us even wore underwear. On the last day, I sat with Glyn's son David and celebrated the trip's end with a cold beer. In 1969, we drank our soda and beer in the morning or evening because that's when it was coolest. It was never cold.

While serving in Vietnam, I never imagined going back. I am glad I did. I needed to see those places again. In 1969, I mostly followed the guy in front of me and did what they told me. In 2018 I wanted to see if the places I went to, that we fought over, made more strategic sense now than they did then. They don't. Driving from Da Nang to Quang Ngai each day gave me more perspective about how big the country is—the vastness of the mountains and the flatlands. There was no way 540,000 soldiers (only about 1/3 serving in combat) could control that country. We were, as we later found out, just doing our part in a war of attrition. We were bait to draw the NVA/VC into the open so that the full might of the U.S. military—artillery, bombs, rockets—could rain down on them. Choosing our battles wisely was the way to high NVA/VC casualties and crushing defeats for them was the way to a U.S. victory.

Each day of our Vietnam trip, we got more used to the heat. Old ways came back. Our big meals were in the morning and the evening. In the afternoon heat, we drank more water and ate lighter—crackers and fruit. Each day we got more used to being there and seeing the Vietnamese people. I started to enjoy walking around: walking across fields, the banks of rice paddies, following trails, streams, and narrow walking bridges. Kind of like 1969 but with a significant difference—no threat of being killed! The truth is that, in 1969, once I got used to the heat I didn't mind the humping. It was like backpacking and camping with regular resupply. Rice paddies or mountains, it didn't matter.

I didn't get to talk to the Vietnamese as much as I wanted. Our driver wasn't an interpreter. We didn't speak much Vietnamese other than to give directions. In hindsight, I wish I had taken the time to learn more of the language. The people working in the fields were busy. They still plant rice and harvest as they did then. The fields are much bigger due to the irrigation. I saw mostly old people, people around my age—older and younger—working. I didn't see any teens or other young people. I think most of them have scooters and go to the city to work. I seldom saw infants and young children in the countryside. Young people who work in the hotels spoke a little English. The least conversational of them had three basic questions they asked each time they saw us. "When did you arrive? How long are you staying? Are you enjoying your stay?" Oddly, they asked us what Vietnam was like 49 years ago.

Most people were friendly; some even joked with us—the guy who wanted me to pose with an American dollar as if he had to pay me to take a picture, the woman who noticed Glyn dragging as we walked along the street who wanted to give him some free gas to get him going. Some Vietnamese were indifferent, but no one was angry. Even an old woman who vociferously let Glyn know that she did not want to have her picture taken smiled at me when I clasped my hands in front of me and bowed to apologize.

Vietnam is a Communist country, but capitalism has taken hold. It welcomes and caters to tourists. There are a great number of hotels—independents and all the major chains like Sheraton and Marriott. The downtown of Da Nang is lit up like Las Vegas—wide streets and neon lights, huge expansion bridges, new "skyscrapers" downtown, and plenty of people on scooters. There are shops along each street and the side street selling name-brand clothes, shoes, backpacks, and electronics, just like those sold in the U.S. Check your labels for "Made in Vietnam" stickers. There was even a shop with a large selection of porcelain toilets. Progress has, indeed, come to Vietnam.

The road from Tam Ky to Quang Ngai was almost all open-air shops and large manufacturing plants. We saw few police or soldiers. Glyn, David, and I could travel the countryside and walk wherever we wanted. People smiled, waved, and gave us a "thumbs up," and some flashed a peace sign, the "V" we used to exchange with other soldiers back in 1969. Vietnam will remain Communist, but it is not a threat to us.

Although I am sure there are some, we did not see any monuments or plaques celebrating Communist victories over the Americans. There was a park in Da Nang with a tank, an airplane, a helicopter, and weapons left behind by the Americans, or more likely the ARVN—the Army of the Republic of Vietnam—the Saigon regime. What we saw elsewhere were rows of coffins commemorating the war dead—the Vietnamese who fought the Americans. In 1969, we wondered if the

Vietnamese villagers cared what government controlled Vietnam or if they just wanted to work their fields. I don't know what they think today. The American soldiers and most of the Vietnamese soldiers are now gone. I saw plenty of closed military posts. The villagers remain, working their fields.

I admit the trip was mostly selfish, but our friends and former soldiers were in Glyn's and my thoughts each day of the trip. I hope the trip, revisiting sites where we soldiered together, is seen as a small tribute to them—to their service.

VIETNAM TRIP WRITTEN BY DAVID HAYNIE
The Notification

I will begin by sharing how this trip came about for me. My father, sometime around 2016, when he started organizing a reunion for his platoon members he'd served with in Vietnam and writing his first book, *When I Turned Nineteen*, stated he would like to go back to Vietnam and visit the locations he served in. He spoke to several of his platoon members but could not get a commitment from anyone to go with him. I told him that, when he was ready to go, I would go with him. He had started to plan a trip for August of 2017, but for various reasons decided not to go. At one point, I told my wife, Tarie, I didn't think the trip would ever happen. Sometime around February 2018, my father called me and said the trip was on and that Mike and he were going in July of 2018. Although I thought when this trip happened, I would receive about a year's notice for planning purposes, I immediately responded that I would go.

The Planning and Prep Phase

My father is a planner. When he decides to do something, he's all in. I think Mike and I received a draft itinerary within a couple of days of being notified of the trip. After that, we received almost weekly updates of the planning progress. The weekly updates included grid coordinates of locations, maps, current crime rates, packing list, including recommended items, passport, and travel visa coordination, flight itineraries, hotel reservations, driver and transport coordination, and just about anything else that might be relevant for the trip. I don't believe a stone was left unturned as it related to planning and coordination. I think Mike and I both fell into the role of just doing what my father said. I should add that, on my behalf, Tarie made sure the coordination needed from my end got completed.

Once I received the packing list and recommended items, the shopping started. I was online checking out the things my father had purchased for the trip and comparing those to similar items I might buy. I'm one of those people who like to have all the gadgets and build kits for a given activity. The problem is I don't want to take from another kit to create a kit for a new event. Therefore, I have a lot of redundant equipment. About 90% of what I purchased was for the trip to Vietnam. At one point, Tarie commented on how my packing list was costing more than the cost of the trip. Of course, that was an exaggeration, since I had to fit everything I needed for a week into one small carryon, a backpack. Deciding not to check bags, we kept our items to a minimum. Almost every article of clothing I brought was wick-away or quick-dry material, and I had no cotton except for sleeping clothes.

I was excited about the trip and considered it a privilege to join my father and Mike. I wasn't sure how things would play regarding our ability to traverse the countryside or how my father and Mike would hold up with all the walking, hot weather, and, of course, the potential emotional stress from being back in Vietnam and from visiting the sites that contained painful memories. One of the early rules I stipulated was that there would be no excessive drinking. Having participated in a few reunions, I saw how quickly some of these old vets returned to their 18- or 19-year-old personas, once they got a little alcohol in their system. A local jail was the last place I wanted to visit while in Vietnam because one of them had a few too many and started something I might have to finish. Needless to say, this was never a problem.

Travel to Austin, Texas, June 13, 2018

Work was hectic right up to the time I would leave for the Vietnam trip. The week before the trip, I was in Las Vegas on a business trip, and while there a friend and I decided we would hike up Mount Charleston. I debated on doing the hike because I didn't want to injure myself before the Vietnam trip, but I decided it was worth the risk. Initially, we were going to hike up on Friday, June 8, and camp for the night, and return on Saturday, June 9, and fly home on Sunday, June 10th. As usual, work took precedence, and we couldn't start the hike until Saturday. We decided to make it a day hike, so we hiked more than 5,000 feet of elevation to about 12,000 feet in 8½ hours, for a total of 17.3 miles. It was a rewarding hike, and the first hike I'd done with this kind of elevation. I flew back home on Sunday, June 10, and arrived home that evening.

Having two days left, I made sure I had everything together that was needed before flying to Austin on June 13 to meet up with my father and Mike. I checked, double-checked, and triple-checked to make sure I had everything I needed and packed for the trip. One item was the peace-symbol necklace my father wore while in Vietnam. He wanted to wear the necklace during our visit to Vietnam. At my father's request, I had my Uncle, Russell Woodward, add some metal to the loop that the chain went through to provide additional strength where the metal had worn thin. My father wanted it repaired but wanted to keep the integrity of the medal, not wanting to make it look new or modify it any more than necessary. Russell had attempted the repair at my house but was unable to fix it, so he took it to his home in Georgia to complete the repair. He told me he would mail it to me, and I told him "Absolutely not." I would drive to Georgia and pick it up personally. During one of my business trips to Atlanta, I swung by his house, about an hour away, to retrieve the medal before heading back to North Carolina. Russell did an outstanding job on the medal, and my father was delighted with the results.

On the 13th, Tarie dropped me off at the airport, beginning my trip. Arriving in Austin, my father, Sherrie, and Mike greeted me.

Since I had no checked bags, we departed for home. I don't recall the conversation in the car or at the restaurant we stopped at for dinner, but I'm sure the discussion was about our expectations for the trip. My father had a packet prepared for each of us that contained all the information needed for the trip. We spent the evening going over the itinerary and rechecking our bags to make sure we had everything needed. Usually, my motto is "If I don't have it, I can buy it there." In this case, I wasn't sure that would work, so I rechecked my bag several more times. Mike got the spare bedroom, so I slept in the office. I was confident we'd done everything we could to prepare for the trip, so I fell asleep without any worries.

Travel to Vietnam June 14, 2018

Rising early, I cleaned up and had breakfast with everyone. Sherrie had purchased an assortment of snacks for us to choose from to take on the trip, and some of these snacks would become somewhat of a joke for the rest of the trip. My father turned into our personal snack pusher. Every time you turned around, he was asking you if you wanted one of his waffle snacks.

Arriving at the airport with no problems, we checked in for our flight. The first leg of the trip was from Austin to Dallas and would take only an hour. Once in Dallas, we found our gate and had a short wait to get on our flight to South Korea. This flight was a 14-and-a-half-hour flight. One of the things we were all dreading was the travel time to and from Vietnam. Before getting on the plane, Mike decided he wanted to get something to eat. We all ordered, and by the time it got to the table, we had to scarf it down so we could get to the gate on time to board the flight.

After boarding, we found our seats and took our agreed-upon positions—me at the window, my father in the center, and Mike in the aisle. We were on a Korean Air flight and happy with the accommodations. There was ample leg room, a monitor in the seat in front of us with a selection of entertainment to view, and a bag on the seat containing a toothbrush, toothpaste, slippers, sleeping mask, blanket, and pillow. Once settled into our individual spaces, we positioned our snacks, drinks, and anything else we wanted accessible for the trip. We even took our shoes off and put on the slippers.

Did I mention that Mike decided we should eat at the airport? No more than an hour after we took off, a flight attendant served a meal. I don't recall what it was, but it was the first of several meals and snacks we would receive on the flight. We did not eat anything before getting on the return flight. We talked during the flight, but most of the time, we were alone in our thoughts for the next 14 hours. I watched several movies—not sure how many—but enough that I remembered hoping there would be different movies for the return flight, so I would have something to watch when we came back. My father and Mike took a couple of opportunities to stretch their legs by walking laps around the airplane. You would think that, with 14 hours of time, there would be some stories to tell. But, really all I did was eat, watch movies, and sleep, and then repeated the whole process over again several times during the flight.

Arrive in Vietnam on June 15, 2018

On June 15, at about 4:30 PM we landed in Seoul, South Korea, with a 2-hour layover until we boarded the flight to Vietnam. I remember thinking it was odd that it had been daytime when we got on the plane in Austin and had remained daytime all the way to Korea. All of us took time to do several laps around the airport to stretch our legs. My father used the opportunity to post our progress to his Facebook page. The two hours went by quickly, and we were boarding the plane for the last leg of the trip. Four hours and forty-five minutes to go.

We landed in Vietnam around 9:30 PM. Following the crowd, we made our way to the line for customs. While in line, my father wanted to take some pictures, but he wasn't sure if it was allowed. I took several pictures with my phone while trying to conceal what I was doing. The customs officials were extremely business-like. No "Welcome," "Thank you," or any comments that I recall. He looked at my passport, travel visa, and their computer system and handed everything back without speaking a word.

Our driver, Binh, was waiting for us outside. I believe he had a sign with "Haynie" written on it. We thought we were going to have an SUV, but a sizeable three-row van was waiting for us. Binh did not speak much English and apparently had not been given all the information provided to the agency. My father told him the hotel name, and off we went. It was late at night, so you could not see much.

The airport we flew into was next to a large modern city, but we soon left Da Nang for a more rural area. It took us about an hour to reach the hotel. At one point, Binh turned down a narrow alley, and you could tell we all got concerned for a minute. He then stopped at a hotel, and it wasn't the hotel we were supposed to be staying at. We finally got it figured out, and Binh got us to our hotel.

My father had told us the hotel had air conditioning. Considering how warm it was outside at this time of night, I could only imagine the humidity during the daytime hours. When we walked into the lobby, it was hot. I asked the individual behind the counter if the rooms had AC. I understood they did. I don't recall if I said it out loud, but I most definitely thought to myself, *I hope the air conditioning in the room works better than the one in the lobby.*

We got checked in without a problem and received help from the front desk to coordinate the time that Binh should arrive in the morning. We walked out of the lobby, past the pool, up two flights of stairs, and down an open breezeway to our rooms. When I opened the door, I quickly realized the temperature in the room was not much different from the heat outside. I found the thermostat and turned it down to 65. We had an early departure in the morning, and it had been a long trip. I unpacked my bag, got cleaned up, and went to bed. Sometime, early in the morning, I woke and found that I was cold. While falling asleep, I'd left the AC unit blowing directly on me. I moved to the other side of the bed and went back to sleep.

POSTSCRIPT: MY BEST FRIEND AND MY OLDEST SON

June 16, 2018–June 18, 2018

Waking on time, I was ready for the day. The first obstacle of the morning was the shower. I'm not sure who the usual clientele was for the hotel, but I almost needed a step stool to get in and out of the tub. I was a little concerned about my father and Mike safely maneuvering through this obstacle each morning. In addition to the odd height of the shower, they built it in a manner that, without creating a dam, you would soak your entire floor. Other than this, the room had all the required amenities and served me well during the trip. I even had a few sodas and candies from the fridge. At an additional cost, of course.

I met my father and Mike at the hotel restaurant, as planned. There was an assortment of choices at the buffet as well as made-to-order omelets. The hosts and waitresses would use this opportunity to practice their English. Regardless of who spoke to you, it always seemed to be the same questions. "Where are you from?" and "Where are you going?" There were a few other questions that they asked, but I don't recall them. Everybody at the hotel was friendly and willing to assist. After breakfast, we gathered the items we would need for the day from our rooms and met at the lobby to wait for Binh. This would become our normal routine for the rest of the trip.

Binh was on time and ready to travel. My assigned position was the front passenger seat while operating as the navigator/translator. This is probably a good time to mention that I don't speak Vietnamese. Although Binh spoke more English than I did Vietnamese, it wasn't by much. We got through the day using my father's Google Maps and finger pointing to the points we wanted to visit. My father had defined grid coordinates we were trying to get to, so that added a bit more complexity to the process.

One of the other routines that started on the first day was our morning stop at a local vendor where Binh would purchase a few items like water, crackers, fruit, and ice for the day. Every morning we would get out, stretch our legs, and take a few pictures while Binh made the purchases and filled the cooler with ice and the goodies for the day. Typically, he would offer us something to eat while we waited. Although Mike and I would accept the offers, and eat what he gave us, my father rarely did. One time he handed us something that we could not identify. It had a brown skin that looked somewhat like an acorn that you had to peel off to expose a whitish fruit that was sweet and had a texture somewhat like grapes. I'm here to tell you about it, so I guess it was edible.

FSB Hill 4-11 was the first destination for the day. We followed the GPS and continued until we ran out of paved surface. As we got close to the area, my father and Mike were trying to identify terrain features. We got out of the vehicle and started walking toward the hill. From my father's description and pictures that I had seen of the hill during the time he and Mike were there, it was almost barren of any substantial vegetation, but that was more than 40 years ago. Today the hill is almost entirely covered with a thick growth of trees and underbrush, which made it difficult to identify specific terrain features that would help orient them to where they were on the hill. In addition to the vegetation, it was apparent that there had been some substantial digging and modifications to the area. There were individuals with backhoes and heavy machinery working in the area while we were there.

Once we'd established that we weren't going to be able to get up the hill from where we were, we headed back to the vehicle. On the way back, there were two women in traditional Vietnamese attire, working in the fields. My father and Mike stopped to talk to them and ask if there was another way up the hill, but there was a communication barrier. At one point, my father asked if he could take their picture, and they indicated it was OK.

We continued toward the vehicle. Once we got back to the van, my father noticed another pathway that seemed to make its way up the hill. He signaled for us to follow him, and we did. We made it up the hill and past several Vietnamese graves. Graveyards at these sites would become the norm for the rest of the trip. These graves/cemeteries were typically not graves of people who'd died during the war but more recently.

POSTSCRIPT: MY BEST FRIEND AND MY OLDEST SON

For me, it was a sobering moment to be standing in an area where my father, Mike, and numerous other soldiers had fought and bled; some had made the ultimate sacrifice. Like most of the trip, I would hang in the background and observe my father and Mike as they walked through the area and tried identifying key locations or discuss events that had occurred there. Often, these locations were where individuals were wounded or died.

After taking pictures and determining we could not get any further on the hill from this path, we headed back to the vehicle. Did I mention it was hot? We were all drenched by the time we got to the van. I was the only one who'd thought to bring a towel or washcloth from the room, and I wasn't going to share, at least not until I finished using it, but by that time nobody else wanted it.

We decided to drive to the other side of the hill to see if there was a pathway we could use to climb to the top. The driver drove as far as he could, and the three of us found ourselves walking down a single-track driveway between rice paddies toward the backside of the hill. We stopped to take pictures of a water buffalo and its calf trying to stay cool in the rice paddies. After about a quarter mile, we walked into a vast cemetery. We made our way through the graveyard and up the hill.

There were signs that there had been a fire on this side of the hill, and the vegetation hadn't grown back. The area was clear and allowed us to get a good view of the landscape once we got to the top. My father and Mike had stated that a different platoon had occupied this side of the hill. Unbeknown to my father, I picked up a couple of rocks on our way down and would give him one before we left to return home.

We spent the next couple of days visiting locations of significant events and firebases where my father and Mike had spent time. We walked along dikes in rice paddies, through fields, banana tree groves, cemeteries, and dirt roads to get to these locations. As stated before, I typically stayed in the back, observing and listening to these two soldiers point out places where brothers were wounded or killed. On several occasions, unbeknown to them, I would record their conversations.

One of the stops was at a firebase where my father and Mike remembered seeing the South China Sea from the top of the Hill. We climbed as far as we could but could not see the sea. Time had changed the terrain, and memories were not as good as they once were. I climbed a little further and entered the forest on a small path. I found signs of rubber trees harvested for their sap. The further I went, the thicker the trees got. I turned around and rejoined my father and Mike as we descended the hilltop, where we found Binh waiting for us.

We made our way to an area called the Rice Bowl. A dam had been built that turned half of the Rice Bowl area into a lake. Vietnamese teenagers were hanging out on the dam and waving and giggling at us. This was especially true when my father accidentally stepped backward into a large pile of water-buffalo dung. All he could do was laugh with them. We looked off into the distance, and my father pointed out a location that Mike had to help retrieve soldiers Killed In Action (KIA) from a vehicle.

We made our way to the area where the forest fire was that my father's platoon had been dropped into the middle of one afternoon. My father and Mike believed that the highway, back then, was further down the mountain. From where we stood, it did not look nearly as high or steep as they remembered. As with all the sites we visited, it was always exhilarating to stand in the same location that these two men had many years before and listen to them talking about what was going on and who was there and where they stood.

One day we stopped in an area where my father and Mike had operated. We had to find a pathway under the railroad bridge to get to the road. Once we got there, my father started talking about one of his memories—hearing chimes from a nearby temple. As I looked around, I noticed a structure peeking out of the tree line that looked like it could be the temple. I pointed it out to my father, and he agreed. I got up on the railroad tracks and tried to get a better view. Not seeing much more than I could initially see from the ground, we walked back the way we came and turned right along the road toward where we saw the structure. Sure enough, it was an old temple. Based on my father's story and the location and age of this temple, it was most likely the same temple he'd heard the sounds coming from more than 40 years ago. He never saw it back then, but now his memory had been validated by finding the location.

June 19, 2018

From the beginning, Binh kept asking if we wanted to go to My Lai. On June 19, we loaded the van and told Binh to take us to My Lai. While visiting, it was evident that the view from the Vietnamese standpoint was that this incident was a government-directed attack on Vietnamese civilians as opposed to a group of soldiers who took it upon themselves to act in a way that was not authorized or condoned. I believe all countries have their version of history. That is not to say that their version is incorrect, but instead, it's from their viewpoint.

While walking around, there were times I felt a little uneasy, as though, as an American, I was being compared to the soldiers who had participated in these actions several decades ago. At one point, while Mike was reading a document, a Vietnamese woman stood uncomfortably close off to one side of him and just stared at him. My father was approached by a young Vietnamese woman who, while crying, asked him how he felt about what had occurred here. Although, at times, it felt as though I were walking in an area where I wasn't welcome, I'm thankful we took the opportunity to visit the site and see the perspective from the other side.

Next, we made our way to the South China Sea beach, to where my father and Uncle Wayne had initially reported together, and where my father had first met Mike. It was the last location my father and Mike were together after they got rear jobs toward the end of their time in Vietnam. I'm not sure how to explain it except to say that it was an incredible opportunity to stand at the location and have my father point out where he and my uncle had lived and slept as well as where he'd sat with Mike, talking while looking out into the sea.

Mike and my father spoke about how they used to swim in these waters, and for a moment, I thought they were going to do so again for one last time. We got back in the vehicle and made our way back down the beach to a monument we had passed earlier. I don't recall what the memorial was, but I did remember that it had nothing to do with the War. Binh pulled a couple of Tiger beers out of the cooler and offered us one. My father declined the offer, but Mike and I accepted. We sat, drinking our beer at what would be the last site we would visit that had any direct significance for my father or Mike.

On our way back to the hotel, Mike let me know that he had to go to the restroom, and one of my duties was being the interpreter. I had been using the evenings to learn a few Vietnamese words, and lucky for us, "bathroom" was one of them. I told Binh *"Phong Tam."* Binh looked at me and said, "Hotel." I asked him how long, and he told me 15 minutes. I asked Mike if he could wait 15 minutes, and he said "Yes, but not much longer." A couple of minutes later Binh picked up his phone and called someone. After a short conversation, he handed me the phone. The individual on the other end asked me where I wanted to go. I told him one of the guys in our group needed to go to the bathroom. The response was *Where did you need to go?* Something was not translating as anticipated, so I told the individual I would figure it out.

I started watching the side of the road for a good place to stop and noticed a tree line with no buildings. Telling Binh *"dung o day,"* which means "Stop here." He pulled over, and I told Mike to go to the trees. Binh saw what Mike was doing, looked at me, laughing, and said, "toilet." I was still not sure, but my guess is *Phong Tam* would translate more into where you bathe. It was a good thing we'd stopped because the 15 minutes was more like an hour.

Once we got to the hotel, my father told Binh to come back to the hotel the next day at 6:30 PM. We planned on spending the day at the hotel area until we left for the airport to catch our flight back to the States.

POSTSCRIPT: MY BEST FRIEND AND MY OLDEST SON

June 20, 2018

Our last day in Vietnam started the same way as our previous days. We all met at the hotel restaurant for breakfast. After breakfast, we decided we would walk around town. When we went to the lobby, the person at the front desk told us Binh had just left and that he had been there for more than an hour waiting for us. Once again, there was something lost in translation from the previous night. Binh had left his number with the front desk, so my father asked them to call him and explain that we were going to stay in the hotel area for the day, and that we needed him to pick us up later that evening to go to the airport.

We then left the hotel and took a left onto the busy street. We walked for about a mile and a half, observing the sights. As always, there were a million mopeds on the roads, carrying all sorts of items, from entire families of 4 or 5 people, to chickens, produce, and about anything else they could strap to them. One of the interesting things we came across that we all took a picture of was a round wicker boat sitting in the water. My father and Mike both commented on seeing similar boats during their time in Vietnam.

As we made our way back to the hotel, we stopped at a store and purchased soda and a snack. We also stopped at another store that sold North Face bags. I bought two sling bags and a backpack. The sling bag became the travel bag that I kept at my seat with snacks and other items for the trip home.

We returned to the hotel. Mike and I checked out of our rooms, and we all consolidated into my father's room. We would spend the next few hours getting cleaned up, napping, and getting ready for our flight later that evening. As always, Binh was on time, and we loaded up and started making our way to the airport. We arrived at the airport about three hours early. We wanted to ensure that there were no surprises, and since we were unable to check in electronically, we tried to allow plenty of time.

We arrived at the airport, thanked Binh, and give him one last tip. Once we entered the airport, there were people everywhere, and we could not figure out where we needed to go. Finally, a guard told my father which line we needed to wait in. We were the first ones in the line, and because there were no signs to inform us that it was the right line, we still were not sure we were in the right place. Later, a few other people got in line behind us, but they ended up getting into a different line, which again, had us doubting if we were in the correct place. We decided to stay where we were, and, after some time, the sign over the counter displayed our flight. We got checked in, received our boarding passes, and headed to our gate.

The first leg of the trip was uneventful. We landed in Seoul, South Korea, where we had a five-hour layover. After the regular restroom runs, laps around the airport, and some sleep, we finally boarded the plane for our trip back to the States. Unfortunately, this flight was not on Korean Air. We quickly realized that fact when we sat down and had little to no legroom. We settled in uncomfortably for a 13-hour flight back to the States. As before, the rhythm was a movie, eat, sleep, and repeat. We landed in Detroit, where we said our goodbyes to Mike, and then my father and I headed to our last flight of the day. We landed in Austin at 5:30 PM on June 21, where we met Sherrie and drove to the house. The next morning, I caught an early flight from Austin to Raleigh, where my wife, Tarie, picked me up, and we headed home.

Retrospect

I felt extremely privileged and honored that I was offered and took the opportunity to join my father and Mike on this trip. It was both emotionally rewarding and educational. Although I suspect the country of Vietnam looks a lot different from what it did more than 40 years ago, there are still some key aspects of that culture that are still intact today.

As we drove around the countryside, you could still see Vietnamese people in traditional attire tending the rice paddies and various other activities. I rarely saw any machinery in the fields. It appeared they accomplished most of the work as they had for generations. There were no chain stores to be found. Families lived in the backside of their stores or eating establishments. Traffic signs and lanes seemed to be only suggestions. It was amazing that there weren't more accidents than there were. Every day on the roadways, it looked like a moped parade. Overall, the people were friendly and accommodated us. I always felt at ease and never felt as though I might be in danger.

I believe this was a unique opportunity that few sons got to experience with their fathers. I will always cherish this experience and look back on it fondly. I'm proud of the family tradition of military service to this country and honored to be a part of that legacy. I've always striven to live up to the standards and accomplishments of my ancestry. I especially have always tried to emulate the example that my father repeatedly provided. Military service has forever been commonplace in my family, and I suspect it will continue for many generations after me.

APPENDIX A

DAILY JOURNAL ABBREVIATIONS EXPLAINED

The terms listed below are used in the Division Daily Journal and explain each abbreviation as it appears in the logs.[5]

(-) = the unit referenced is operating without one of its sub-units. (Example: A company may be working without one of its platoons.).
11th Bde = 11th Infantry Brigade. Parent unit for the 3/1st Inf. Bn.
1/20 = 1/20th Inf Bn. Sister battalion of the 3/1st Inf. Bn.
4/21 = 4/21st Inf. Bn. Sister battalion of the 3/1st Inf. Bn.
4/3 = 4/3rd Inf. Bn. Sister battalion of the 3/1st Inf. Bn.
411 = LZ 411, the main firebase for the 3/1 Inf. Bn. (A.K.A. Hill 4-11)
60mm = mortar.
81mm = U.S. mortar size.
82mm = enemy mortar size.
105 = related to the 105mm howitzer.
106 = related to 106 Recoilless Rifle.
155 = related to the 155mm howitzer.

---

[5] FSB Hill 4-11. Accessed September 30, 2018. http://www.hill4-11.org/index-frames-1.html.

175 = related to the 175mm howitzer.
4.2 = U.S. mortar.
acft = aircraft.
ACR = Armored Cavalry Regiment.
Aeroscout = airborne infantry from Warlords (B/123 Avn Bn); or Blue Ghosts (F/8 Cav); or D Trp 1/1 av.
AK-47 = Standard enemy automatic assault rifle, of Russian design.
AO = Area of Operations.
Arty = Artillery fire.
ARVN = Army of the Republic of (South) Vietnam.
AS = Air Strike by Air Force or Marine jet fighter-bombers. Usually F4 Phantoms (Marines or Air Force) or A4 Skyhawks (Marines).
Aslt = Assault.
AW = Automatic Weapons fire.
AT = Anti Tank.
B40 = Enemy hand-held rocket used against bunkers and armor.
Basketball = Air Force plane that provided illumination by a flare at night.
BC = Body Count.
BDA = Bomb Damage Assessment.
BDE = Brigade.
BH = Bee Hive.
Blade time = Time in the air for a helicopter.
Bn = battalion.
BT = Booby Trap.
(C) = Confirmed by body count (as opposed to probable).
CA = Combat Assault.
Cav = Armored cavalry or Air cavalry.
cbt = combat.
C&C = Command and Control by a commanding officer.
CHICOM = Chinese Communist manufacture item.
Chieu Hoi = In Vietnamese, this means "Open Arms." Named for a program to encourage Viet Cong to return to the "Open Arms" of their South Vietnamese government.

APPENDIX A

CIA'd = Captured in action.
CLDC = Chu Lai Defense Command.
closed = Military term based on "closing with your enemy."
CO = Commanding Officer.
Co = company.
Commo = Communications.
cont = continued.
coord = grid coordinates.
CP = Command Post.
CS/CSW = Crew served or Crew served weapon.
dest = destroyed.
doc = documents.
Dolphins = Huey slick helicopters from 174 AHC.
dustoff = helicopter medical evacuation.
E Trp 1/1st Cav. = armored cavalry troop assigned to the 11th Inf. Bde.
en = enemy.
el = element (Also ele).
eng = engaged.
Eng = Engineer unit (like U.S. 19th Engineer Bn).
fd = found (also fnd).
fr = from.
FRD = friendly.
frnd = friendly.
FSB = Fire Support Base.
GSW = Gunshot wound.
GVN = Government of (South) Vietnam.
HE = High Explosive.
Helix = Call sign for Air Force Forward Air Controller (small planes).
HG = Hand Grenade.
HI = Harassment and Interdiction.
Hoi Chanh = Former enemy who had changed to the South Vietnamese side.
HQ = Headquarters A.K.A HQS.

Inf = infantry.
KBA = Killed by Artillery.
KHA = Killed due to hostile action.
KIA = Killed in action.
LNO = Liaison officer.
loc = location.
LOH = Light Observation Helicopter.
LP = listening post.
Lt = light (Lt Bde = Light Infantry Brigade).
LZ = Landing Zone.
M-1 = M-1 U.S. Carbine.
MAF = Marine Amphibious Force (HQ for I Corps in Da Nang).
MAF = Military age female.
MAM = Military age male.
MEDCAP = Medical Assistance Program.
MFW = Multiple Fragment Wounds.
msn = mission.
Napalm = Flammable jellied gasoline used in bombs.
NBK = Non-Battle Killed.
NBW = Non-Battle Wounded.
NC = No Change.
NE = North East.
neg = negative.
NLP = Night Laager position.
off station = Aircraft have left the area.
on station = Aircraft are in a location to perform their mission.
OP = Outpost.
opn = operation.
(P) = Probable, when referring to KIA.
PF = Popular Forces (South Vietnamese allies).
pj = pajamas (to describe the silky black garb worn by most Vietnamese).
plt = platoon (or plat).
PRC 25 = Backpack radio for communications from the field.

APPENDIX A

PRU = Provisional Reconnaissance Units (South Vietnamese).
psn = position or POS or POSN.
PSYOPS = Psychological Operations.
ptl = patrol.
PW = prisoner of war.
PZ = Pickup zone.
rcn = recon company (Reconnaissance Company).
rd = round fired/captured.
rec = received or recvd or rec'd.
Res = result.
RF = Regional Forces (South Vietnamese allies).
rocket pocket = area to be defended around a large base that was within the range of powerful 122mm or 140mm Russian-designed rockets.
RPG = Rocket-propelled grenade. Anti-Tank or anti-bunker weapon.
SA = Small Arms fire. Also S/A.
San Juan Hill = 11th Bde base located at BS634380 (five miles northwest of Duc Pho).
S&D = Search and Destroy mission.
scty = security.
Shadow = Large powerful U.S. Air Force gunships (C-130s decked out with lots of guns and firepower.
Shark = Gunships from 174 AHC (direct helicopter support for units of the 11 Inf. Bde).
SITREP = Situation Report.
Sky Spot = Air Force method of directing bomb runs at night or low visibility through a computerized ground-based radar guidance system.
Smoke Ship = Helicopter with special equipment that allowed it to lay smoke between the enemy locations and the friendly locations.
Sniffer = Usually refers to helicopter set up with a special nitrogen detector. It would detect higher concentrations of nitrogen, which, usually in hostile areas, meant a concentration of enemy soldiers.

Spooky = Air Force gunships built from the venerable C-47 (military variant of the twin-engined Douglas DC-3. Armed with mini-guns and lots of firepower).

Starlight = Refers to a special low-light telescope.

sweep = Search and clear an area.

TF = Task Force.

Tgt = target.

trip flare = small flare set up with trip line.

TSN = Tanh Son Nhut RVN (large base in southern South Vietnam).

UNSEF = Unknown size enemy force.

US = American soldier.

Utility = Utility helicopter used to fly resupply and etc.

VC = Viet Cong (Enemy).

VCS = Viet Cong Suspect.

VN = Vietnamese.

VR = Visual Reconnaissance.

WHA = Wounded due to hostile action.

WIA = Wounded in action.

wpn = weapon.

Warlord = B/123rd Avn Bn. This could refer to either the helicopter gunships or the scout teams.

WP = White phosphorous explosive round or grenade.

APPENDIX B

FIRE SUPPORT BASE HILL 4-11

This article was transcribed by me as written in the *Southern Cross* newspaper dated July 30, 1969, written by SP4 Tony Swindell. The event occurred on July 8, 1969.

New Firebase for 11th, ARVNs

A mid-morning combat assault by A Co., 3rd Bn., 1st Inf. swept across a scorching coastal plain to secure a new battalion firebase named LZ 4-11 atop a hill seven miles west of Quang Ngai City.

The hill, holding a commanding view of the surrounding area, sits on the edge of the battalion's new area of operation and will be the staging point for intensive pressure against local-force Viet Cong.

As the 11th Bde soldiers struggled up the rocky, brush-covered slope, they encountered numerous mines and booby traps along the crest of the hill. Employing a minesweeping device commonly used by combat engineers to clear roads, the soldiers found booby-trapped grenades, 2.75-inch rockets, and a canister full of napalm with a firing device planted in the ground.

"My men had to watch every step they made," said 2LT John F. Baxter (Gainesville, Fla.), First Platoon leader. "It seemed as if there was a booby trap under every other bush."

Assigned to the preliminary work of securing and clearing the new LZ, A Co. began digging in and prepared a temporary helicopter pad for the first loads of supplies and equipment. The sound of bulldozers and road graders from C Co., 26th Engr. Bn. could be heard in the distance as they cleared a supply road from Quang Ngai City to the new firebase.

The landing zone's name was chosen to represent the cooperation between the 4th ARVN Regt. and the 11th Bde. The 3rd Bn., 4th ARVN Regt., and the 4th ARVN Tank Bn. have been working closely with the Americal units in that area to provide security for the engineers and also secure the terrain around the site of the new LZ. (11th IO)

This article was transcribed by me as written in the *Southern Cross* newspaper dated July 30, 1969, written by SP4 Tony Swindell. The event occurred on July 11, 1969.

VC Serenade Wasted on Infantry

LZ-4-11—It was a clear, peaceful night for the 11th Bde's A Co., 3rd Bn., 1st Inf. on their new firebase until the Viet Cong decided to hold an impromptu concert for the Americal Division soldiers.

"It was about 9 or 10 pm when I began hearing the song 'Where Have All the Flowers Gone?'" explained 1LT Lewis D. Adams Jr. (West Point, Ga.), artillery forward observer for A Co. "Then this voice came on, asking us why we were fighting in Vietnam. It was really strange because the voice was very clear and spoke in excellent English."

SP4 James Shelton (Raytown, Mo.), radio telephone operator for the company commander, continued the story. "The first song was 'Where Have All the Flowers Gone?' followed by 'Oh, Susannah' and 'North to Alaska.' As far as I could tell, the songs were the original American versions.

"Then this guy started telling us to come over to his side and help get rid of the 'trouble-makers' in Vietnam. He added that this was a special broadcast for all soldiers, officers, and ARVN's. They must have thought we had interpreters up on the hill, because part of the time they spoke in Vietnamese."

While the company listened in wonderment to the music and broadcast, 1LT Adams called for artillery to silence the talkative Communist PSYOP team which he estimated to be 800 to 900 meters northwest of the firebase.

"I must have directed over 100 rounds into the area," commented 1LT Adams, "and I was sure that we must have either gotten them or at least scared them away. But as soon as the noise subsided and the smoke cleared away, they were broadcasting again, chiding us for our poor marksmanship. They said if we didn't leave Vietnam, we would be wiped out like we were in Korea. It was really something."

SP4 Shelton, who was listening closely to the broadcast and relaying what he heard to the battalion tactical operations center at LZ Bronco, added: "Whatever broadcasting system they were using was big to cover that distance so clearly. We think it was a portable PA outfit with a remote microphone so the VC could broadcast in a bunker or under cover safe from the artillery."

After about 15 minutes, the Vietnam-style disc jockey and propagandist ended his message apparently unharmed, but he would have been disappointed at the reaction from the amused soldiers. Several commented that the broadcast was "better than a show." (11th IO)

This article was transcribed by me as written in the *Southern Cross* newspaper dated December 19, 1969, written by PFC Mark Geiser.

INFANTRYMEN AID THE CONSTRUCTION OF THE TU MY RESETTLEMENT AREA

FSB 4-11—A flurry of activity has entered east of here as a joint Division-GVN operation begins to take hold. The result is Tu My Resettlement Village. Located five miles west of Quang Ngai City, the village has a present population of 4,289 people. The number is expected to push close to the 5,000 mark before the end of the year. The operation had its beginning in early July when the 3rd Bn., 1st Inf., 11th Inf. Bde., working with the 4th ARVN Regiment, was moved into the Quang Ngai Valley to set up a fire support base.

Apparent to the People

It soon became apparent to the people that this was their chance to move from VC-controlled areas. According to District Senior Advisor Ken Gould, "There were three reasons why the people decided to come under government control."

"The VC had taken all their young people from them and had enlisted them as soldiers or as porters, and they knew that the presence of the U.S. forces would provide security for the movement."

The first group of people to pack up their belongings and move were 300 Montagnards who came to the outskirts of Quang Ngai. They were closely followed by another 500 lowland Vietnamese.

1969 Pacification Program

Because the new village was not part of the 1969 pacification program, special permission had to be granted by the Saigon and Provincial governments for the construction of the village.

Rather than having the people set up permanent homes near Quang Ngai, it was decided to make special plans for the village to be relocated near the new firebase. Special allocations provided food and other supplies. Shelters were built for the people until they were to move again.

In late July the District Chief, MAJ Hoa, conferred with the then battalion commander, LTC George V. Ellis (Kent, Ohio), as to when the people would be moved to the new village. Due to the amount of enemy activity during this time, it was decided to wait until the area was secure for the big move.

By the middle of September, the move was fully coordinated; 800 people began their trek to their new homes. Construction started immediately upon arrival.

People Increasing Daily

With the number of people increasing daily, buildings were erected to allow for expansion. Tin for roofing and food supplies were sent in to fulfill the needs of the people. Cement was brought in to reinforce the sides of the wells. Rice-gathering parties were sent out to gather the crops of rice in the area.

In the early stages of settlement, two MEDCAP teams a week were sent from FSB 4-11 to administer medical aid to the people. Since that time the need has diminished to a point where one team is needed a week. Vietnamese nurses have helped to decrease the need for U.S. assistance.

The village has been a significant rallying point for Hoi Chanhs. In the last two months, 136 have "chieu hoied" at Tu My. One of these recently led C Co. of the 3rd Bn., 1st Inf., to a large cache of 36 weapons.

As the District Senior Advisor stated, "The reason for the high number is attributed to the Revolutionary Development cadre in the area who are getting the word out to the people in the village and they, in turn, are contracting those not under GVN control."

Evidence of Freedom

Evidence of the freedom that the people have acquired is exemplified by the free election that will be held before the end of the year to select village leaders.

Defense and security of the village are provided jointly by U.S. personnel and ARVN forces. PF platoons are also working in the area. The People's Self Defense Force personnel are being trained by the U.S. and ARVN forces in defense of the village.

Explaining the role of the 3rd Bn., 1st Inf., Battalion Commander LTC Leslie J. Stottle (Clarksville, Tenn.), stated, "We have a twofold mission: providing security and defense for the village and working with the village cadre in meeting their needs."

Greater Chance for Survival

The colonel added, "The people are now under the control of the Vietnamese government. Security has been reestablished in the area, and thereby a complete turnover has taken place."

District Senior Advisor Gould explained, "The people now live much better than they did before. They have a much greater chance for survival, for the village has given them 'new hope.'" (11th IO)

DIVISION DAILY JOURNAL ENTRIES AMERICAL DIVISION TACTICAL OPERATION CENTER CHU LAI, RVN

July 10, 1969—Typhoon Tess

Line item—27 2220 (C) Severe Weather warning: Typhoon Tess expected to hit at 110100 on SE Asia land with winds up to 70 knots. Typhoon condition in effect with expectation of flying debris and flooding of lowlands. (See appendix A)

July 11, 1969—Hill 4-11 NVA PSYOPS

Line item—68 2100 (U) 11th Bde, SGT McCaig, A/3/1 Inf, BS528741 at 2040 Hours, loudspeaker broadcasting US Chieu Hoi (surrender) messages, "Where Have all the Flowers Gone?" "North to Alaska," and "Oh, Susannah" were played.

JULY 14, 1969—
Juan Ramos and Eldon Reynolds killed and Tim "Dusty" Rhoades wounded.

Line item—110 2250 (U) 11th Bde, SGT McKeaque, A/3/1, FSB 411, BS539732 at 2120 Hours, received 60mm mortar & Chicom Hand Grenades & Small Arms Fire from 4 sides, results: 2 US KIA & 1 WIA (E), Dustoff complete at 2215 Hours. Notified III MAF SGT Cardon. (See appendix A)

August 13, 1969—
Ambush Robert Swindle, Richard "Rebel" Wellman, and Jerry Ofstedahl killed and Frank Brown wounded.

Line item—61 1153 (C) 11th Bde, MSG Henderson, A/3/1, B/1/1 Cav, and Gunships, BS562742 at 1148H, made contact with Unknown Size Enemy Force.

1. Gunships received Automatic Weapons Fire & Small Arms Fire w/negative hits. Air Force Forward Air Controller on station at this time, artillery is being adjusted.
2. 1210 Hours, BS562743, received Small Arms Fire, engaged Unknown Size Enemy Force, results: 1 NVA KIA, 1 AK-47 CIA.
3. 1225 Hours, BS564743, CC/3/1 & Air Force Forward Air Controller observed approximately 50 NVA.
4. 1235 Hours, BS562743, engage 2 NVA with weapons, results: 2 NVA KIA, 2 AK-47s CIA, 1 US WIA (M).
5. 1215 Hours, BS562743, B/1/1 Cav has 3 US WIA (E) (1 shell shock), Dustoff complete at 1230 Hours. 1515 Hours, BS546755, totals: 7 NVA KIA, 5 AK-47 CIA, 3 RPG-2 CIA, 5 US KIA, 5 US WIA (E), 2 APC minor damage. 1730 Hours, breakdown of US losses: B/1/1 Cav: 2 US KIA, 2 US WIA (E). A/3/1: 3 US KIA, 3 US WIA (E). 1805 Hours, 3 IWC, 1x.50 cal

Machinegun CIA. A/3/1, 1830 Hours, BS564755, engaged & killed 1 NVA. 1910 Hours, BS564755, 1 US WIA (E). Contact broken at 1830 Hours, results: 5 US KIA, 6 US WIA (E), 10 NVA KIA, 8 IWC, and 4 CSWC. Notified C/S PFC Galvan, G-3 SP Baucum, G-2 CPT Young, III MAF SSG Hoffmeyer, USARV MAJ Wills, and MAJ Fitzgerald. (See appendix A)

August 15, 1969—
Command Detonated Bomb Paul Ponce, Joe Mitchell, James Anderson and Danny Carey killed and Mike Dankert, Ray "Alabama" Hamilton, Bill Davenport, Tommy Thompson, Ryan Okino, Charlie Deppen, and Glyn Haynie were wounded.

Line item—94 2100 (C) 11th Bde, LT Hotary, B/1/1 Cav, A-C/3/1, BS549750 at 1645 Hours, reference Daily Journal Form entry #70, a command detonated mine consisting of 2x250 lb bombs was blown, results: 3 US KIA from A/3/1, 9 US WIA (E) from A/3/1, 3 US WIA (E) from B/1/1 Cav, 1 US WIA (E) from C/3/1. Passed to SGT Fish III MAF. (See appendix A)

August 19, 1969—Tank Hits Mine

Line item—72 1620 (C) 11th Bde, MSG Henderson, B/1/1 Cav, BS578747 at 1600 Hours.

1. Tank detonated mine (believed to be 1x500 lb bomb), results: 4 US WIA (E) from B/1/1 Cav, 1 US WIA (E) from A/3/1, Dustoff complete at 1635 Hours.
2. B/1/1 Cav, 1655 Hours, track detonated 1x.50cal round lying on the ground, results: 1 US WIA (E), Dustoff complete at 1720 Hours. (See appendix A)

APPENDIX B

JANUARY 14, 1970—
Ambush Gary Morris and Roger Kidwell killed, and Bill Davenport and Pete Zink were wounded.

Line item—89 1250 11 Bde, Sp Robinson, A/3-1 Inf, BS507710 at 1250 Hours, in contact with Unknown Size Enemy Force. Results: 2xUS KIA, 3xUS WIA(E). Dustoff complete 1500 Hours. At 1610 Hours 1xUS WIA(E), Dustoff complete 1640 Hours. At 1721 Hours, BS512708 received more Small Arms Fire. Results: 3xUS WIA(E), Dustoff ship on station received Small Arms Fire. Dustoff 1xUS completed 1800 Hours. Ship is down at 411. Will be hooked to Chu Lai 15 Jan. Element moved to secure bodies of 2xKIA received Automatic Weapons Fire & Hand Grenade close to bodies, only able to retrieve weapons. Bodies Missing in Action until tomorrow when they will be recovered. Results: 2xMIA, 7xWIA (E). Shadow on station at 1945 Hours, out of contact at 2100 Hours. Will sweep at first light. Notify: Sgt Stabbs, III MAF at 142230H. (See appendix A)

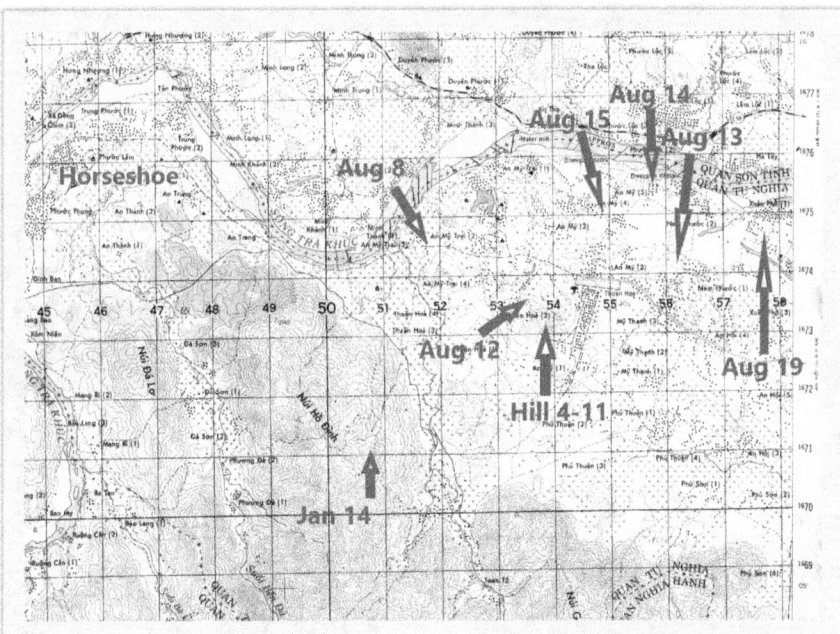

Figure A–1 The military map is indicating Hill 4-11 and specific locations and dates that are important to us. *Map furnished by Leslie Hines.*

March 15, 1970—Willie Matson Killed

Line item—59 1900 11th Bde, Sp Clough, A/3-1 Inf, (en) BS433412 at 1855 Hours, received heavy Small Arms Fire & Chicom Hand grenade from an estimated NVA platoon. Engaged area with Small Arms, Automatic Weapons & artillery fire & Ground Support. Results: 1xUS KIA. Negative enemy assessment. Will sweep at first light. (See appendix A)

APPENDIX C

THE FIRE
Division Daily Journal Entries Americal Division Tactical Operation Center Chu Lai, RVN

May 24, 1969—The Fire

Line Number—86 2400 A/3-1 Combat Assault (CA) from a Pickup Zone vicinity BS841228 to a cold Landing Zone vicinity BS805185 completed at 1240 Hours. (See appendix A)

Note: I believe the Landing Zone coordinates is a typo and should be BS905185, not BS805185. Company night defensive position on May 25 was BS917170.

Note: The log had no mention of the fire.

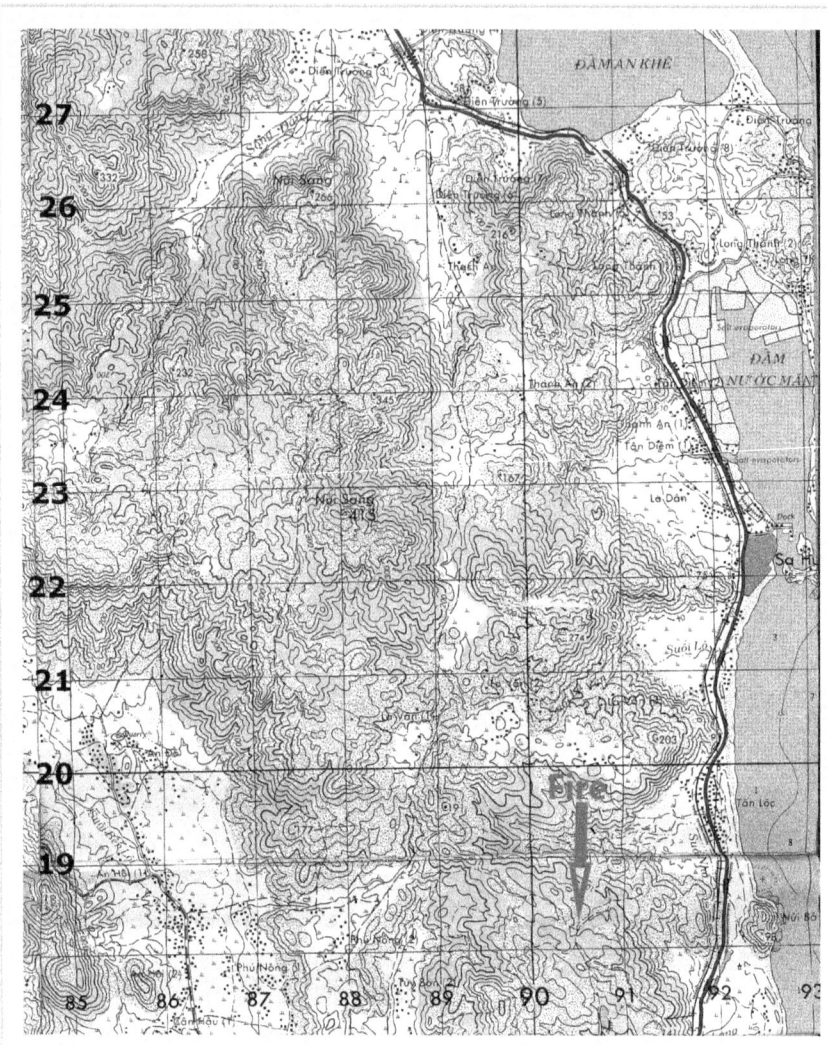

Figure A-2 The military map is indicating the location of the fire on May 24, 1969. *Map furnished by Alan Brinton.*

APPENDIX D

FIRE SUPPORT BASE CHARLIE BROWN AND BRIDGE

This article, without a title, was transcribed by me as written in the Bronco Tribute Vol II No 18 dated Friday, May 30, 1969.

Alpha Company moved off Charlie Brown as Co C moved on. Two nights before, they had caught a sapper squad trying to sneak through the perimeter wire. At least three of the VC bit the dust in the blast of a Claymore and hand grenades.

Since Wed, 21 May, Alpha has been patrolling and sweeping "ambush alley" and the territory north and west of Charlie Brown.

Best wishes from 1st Platoon and the rest of Co A to *SP4 Jerry W. Ofstedahl*. Next week he goes to Tokyo where he plans to meet his fiancée, marry her, and enjoy a brief honeymoon during his seven days of leave.

FINDING MY PLATOON BROTHERS

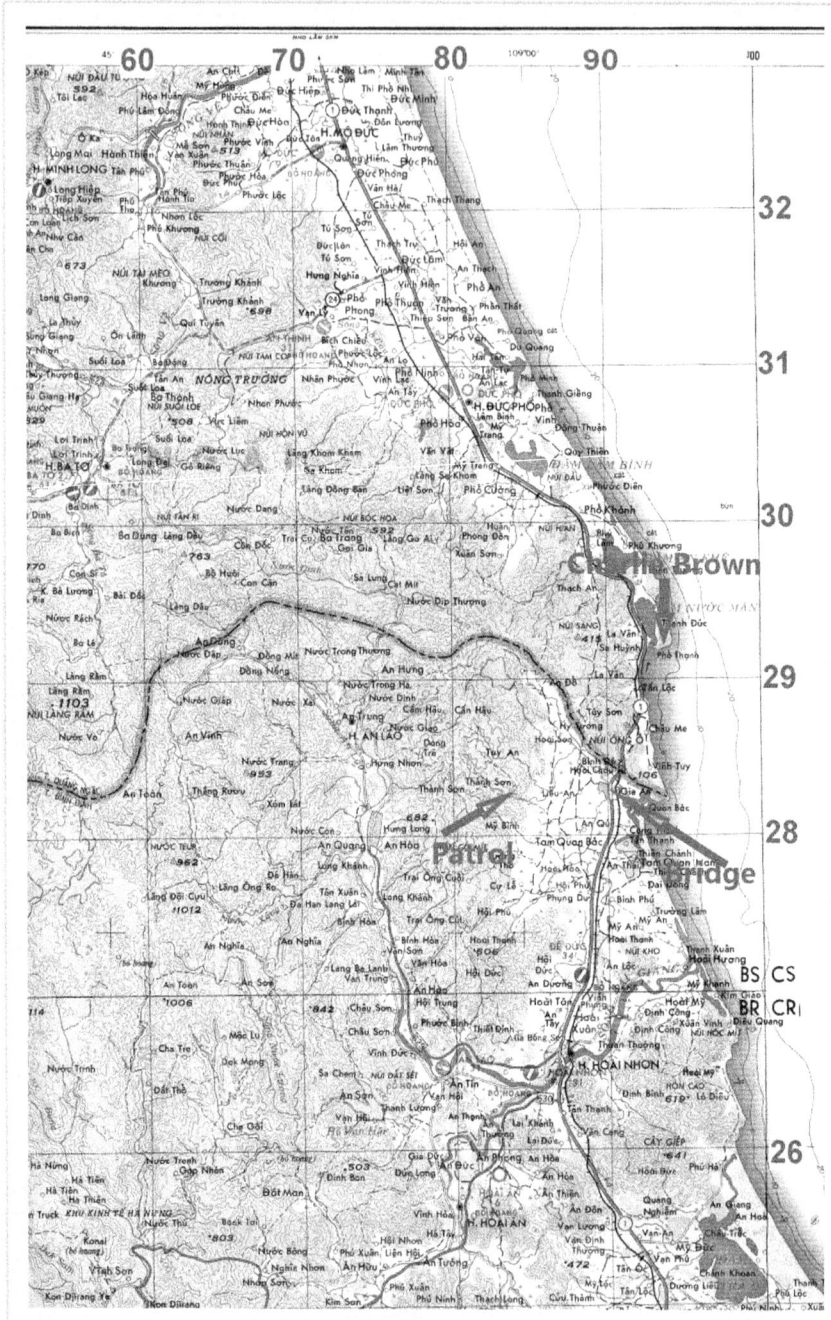

Figure A–3 The military map is indicating the location of FSB Charlie Brown, the Bridge, and Mike's first patrol location May 1969. *Map furnished by Alan Brinton.*

APPENDIX E

OUR FIRST LOSS, FIRE SUPPORT BASE DEBBIE, AND THE RICE BOWL

This article was transcribed by me as written in the *Southern Cross* newspaper dated July 23, 1969. The event occurred on July 2, 1969.

Ambush Squelched

LZ BRONCO—Enemy soldiers of the 2nd Regt., 3rd NVA Division are discovering ambushes directed against 11th Inf. Bde units come at a very high price. Twenty-two NVA died when their recent ambush against A Co., 3rd Bn., 1st Inf. and APCs from E Trp., 1st Cav. was crushed with combined firepower from air strikes, artillery, gunships, and heavy machinegun fire.

Hide in Stream

A Co. and the APCs were on a coordinated sweeping mission west of fire support base Debbie when they were hit by intense fire from a stream bed at the edge of a woodline.

The lead APC moving up a stream bed nearby hit a mine and then took three RPG hits, pinning down cavalrymen. Answering the call for help, four more APCs rushed to the scene while air strikes pounded the Communist fortifications.

"It was a well-prepared ambush," noted PFC Bill Mead (Oto, Iowa), "because we put 150 rounds of M-79 fire into the area before we entered. They didn't move a muscle or give themselves away at all."

In describing the initial contact, 1LT Terry Ehrich (Cherokee, Iowa), stated, "I don't know how many of them there were, but they had my 24 men and seven tracks pinned down. We had fire coming in from all directions."

Flush NVA

Following raids from Marine Phantom jets and gunships of the Army's 123rd Avn. Bn., the men of A Co. and the APCs pushed forward to root out the remaining enemy troops. As they advanced toward the woodline, the bodies of 14 enemy soldiers were found.

The enemy fire, not as intense or as concentrated as before, was crushed by continuing gunship and APC fire as the soldiers overran the enemy positions. Found among the enemy dead were three AK-47s and three RPG launchers with five rounds of ammo.

The infantrymen made another sweep of the same area the next morning and found the bodies of eight more enemy soldiers, five killed by airstrikes and three by small arms. (11th IO)

DIVISION DAILY JOURNAL ENTRIES AMERICAL DIVISION TACTICAL OPERATION CENTER CHU LAI, RVN

June 14, 1969—Bruce Tufts killed and Dennis Rowe, Nick VanDyke, and Mike Dankert were wounded.

0115 (C) 11th Bde, LT Hotary, A/3/1, BS893273 at 0007 Hours, received satchel charges and/or Chicom Hand Grenade, result: 1

US Killed In Action (KIA), 3 US Wounded In Action (WIA) (E), Dustoff complete at 0050 Hours. (See appendix A)

July 2, 1969—Rice Bowl Battle

Line item—52 1545 (C) 11th Bde, MSG Henderson, 1A/3/1 & E/1st Cav, BS842285 at 1510H.

1. Made contact with unidentified size enemy force, received small arms fire, automatic weapons fire, .50 cal & Rocket Propelled Grenade fire (RPG).
2. A (-)/3/1 with Combat Assault from Landing Zone Debbie to contact area. Results so far: 4 US Killed In Action (KIA), 9 US Wounded In Action (WIA) (E), 1 Armored Personnel Carrier (APC) combat loss.
3. Pickup Zone 1607 Hours, Landing Zone 1625 Hours, Combat Assault complete & hot, results: 3 NVA KIA, 1 RPG-7 Captured In Assault.
4. Air Force Forward Air Controller on station at 1645 Hours. 4 APCs were added to contact at 1615 Hours to reinforce unit.
5. 1755 Hours, 4 NVA KIA.
6. 1810 Hours, 3 NVA KIA, 1 RPG-7, 5 RPG rounds & 1 AK-47 captured.
7. Results so far: 3 US KIA from E/1st Cav, 3 US WIA (E) from E/1st Cav, 4 US WIA (E), 1 US WIA (M) from A/3/1, 1 US KIA from A/3/1.
8. 1900 Hours, still receiving Automatic Weapons Fire, Small Arms Fire, Rocket Propelled Grenade fire (RPG), & 60mm Mortar fire.
9. 2000 Hours, G/S & Command and Control extended until 2100 Hours.
10. 2050 Hours, COL Treadwell declared a tactical emergency and that 3/1 Command and Control be extended until 2200 Hours, from LT Hotary 11th Bde Duty Officer.
11. 2330 Hours, contact broken at 2030 Hours, troops returned to LZ Debbie.

12) Results: 4 US KIA, 7 US WIA (E), 1 US WIA (M), 15 NVA KIA, 3 IWC, 4 CSWC, captured: numerous documents and 40 lb satchel charge strapped to the body on NVA, A/3/1 destroyed satchel charge & body in place. Notified III MAF CPT Phillips at 2100 Hours, USARV MAJ Wilkerson at 2100 Hours, C/S, G-3, G-2. (See appendix A)

July 4, 1969—Track Hits Mine

Line item—51 1335 (C) 11th Bde, SFC Winkler, A/3/1, E/1st Cav, BS848293 at 1330 Hours, Armored Personnel Carrier (APC) hit large mine, result: 2 US KIA, 3 US WIA (E), track is on fire, Dustoff complete at 1328 Hours, track combat loss. Notified C/S SP Bailey, G-3 LTC Davis, G-2 MAJ Oglesby. (See appendix A)

APPENDIX E

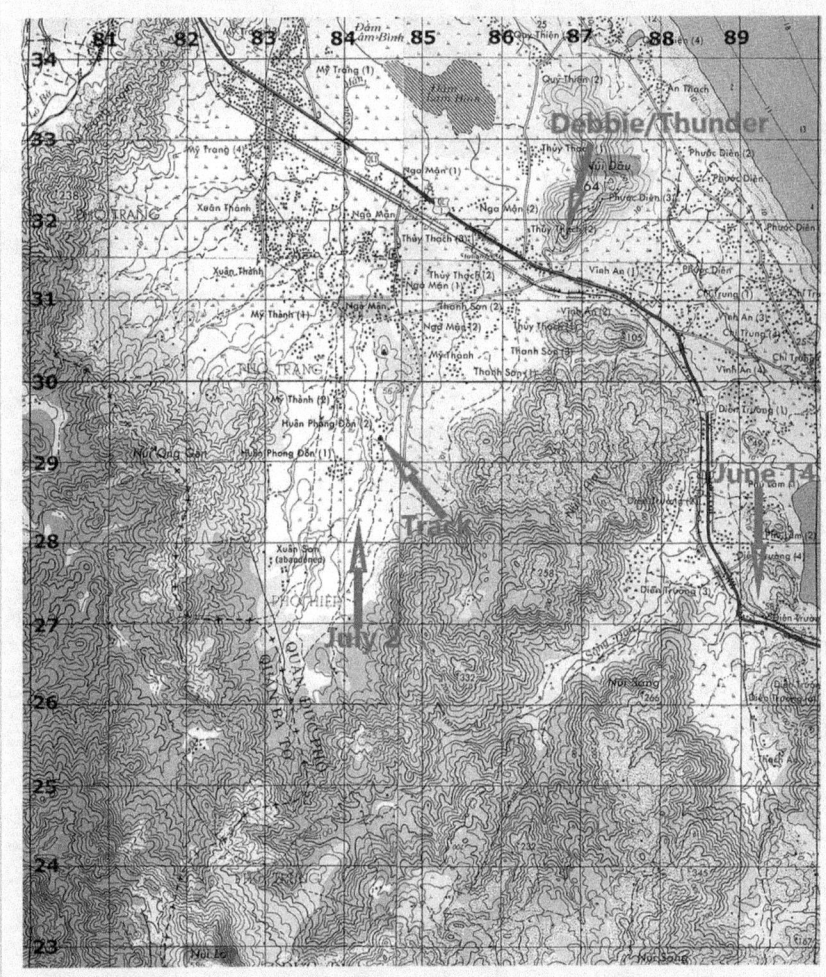

Figure A-4 The military map is indicating the location of FSB Debbie, the action of June 14 and July 2, 1969, locations. *Map furnished by Alan Brinton.*

APPENDIX F

FIRE SUPPORT BASE BRONCO

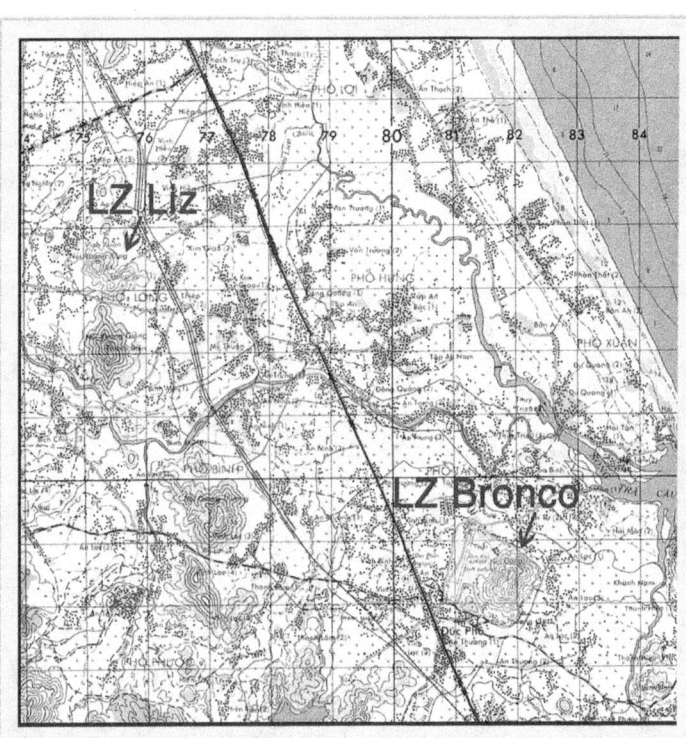

Figure A–5 The military map is indicating the location of FSB Bronco, the 11th Brigade Headquarters, and Landing Zone Liz. *Map furnished by Leslie Hines.*

APPENDIX G

COMBAT CENTER

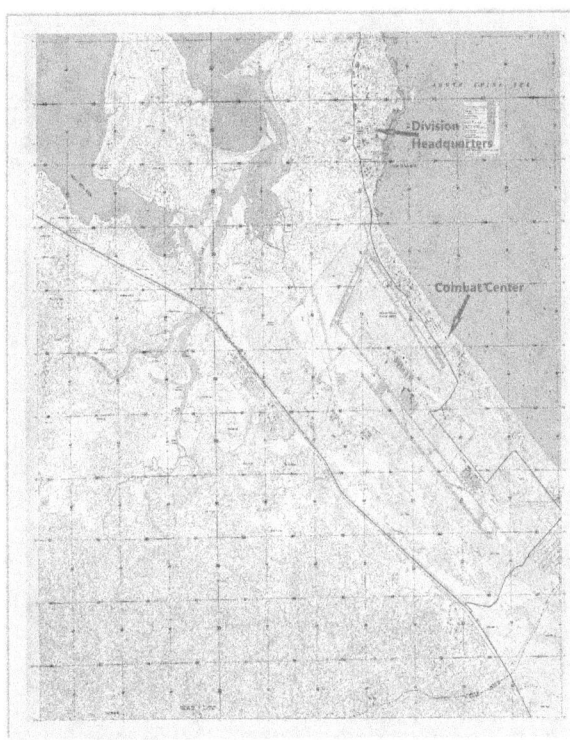

Figure A-6 The military map is indicating the location of the Americal Division Headquarters and the Combat Center. *Map furnished by Leslie Hines.*

ABOUT THE AUTHOR

After retiring from the Army, Haynie earned an AAS degree in Management, a BS degree in Computer Information Systems, and an MA degree in Computer Resources and Information Systems. He worked as a software engineer/project manager for eight years before teaching at Park University as a full-time instructor. Haynie continued as an adjunct instructor for thirteen more years. He also worked as an adjunct instructor for the Graduate program at Saint Edwards University for one year.

Figure 29 Glyn Haynie. Photograph by Shannon Prothro Photography.

Glyn Haynie and his wife of 32 years, Sherrie, currently reside in Texas. They have five children, fourteen grandchildren, and four great-grandchildren. Three of their sons have served combat tours in either Iraq or Afghanistan. This is a family in which service to their country is a family tradition.

Author's Website http://www.glynhaynie.net
Author's e-mail glyn@glynhaynie.com

I hope you enjoyed this book. Would you do me a favor?

Like all authors, I rely on online reviews, and your opinion is invaluable. Would you take a few moments now to share your assessment of my book on Amazon or any other book-review website you prefer? Your opinion will help the book marketplace to become more transparent and useful to all.

Thank you very much!

www.ingramcontent.com/pod-product-compliance
Lightning Source LLC
Chambersburg PA
CBHW070730020526
44118CB00035B/1121